A YEAR

OF

POETRY TEA TIME

The Essential Guide to Everything Poetry and Tea

Also by Christine Owens
Relaxed Homeschooling

A YEAR

OF

POETRY TEA TIME

The Essential Guide to Everything Poetry and Tea

Written and Edited by

Christine Owens

Illustrated by Quentin Owens

Cover art painted by Ashley Hawkes

For more poetry tea time ideas

Visit www.AYearofPoetryTeaTime.com

A Year of Poetry Tea Time: The essential Guide to Everything Poetry and Tea

First Printing, 2020

Illustrations by Quentin Owens
Cover Art by Ashley Hawkes

Owens, Christine
A Year of Poetry Tea Time: The Essential Guide to Everything Poetry and Tea
ISBN: 978-1-954270-*00*-8
ISBN: 978-1-954270-01-5 (electronic)

This book is dedicated to

My wonderful Grandmother
Trudy Faulkner

Acknowledgments

This book has been quite the undertaking and I would like to thank those that helped make it a reality. Thank you to Ashley Hawkes for creating the beautiful cover art that makes this book look so inviting. Thank you to my brother Robert Faulkner for all the hours he spent editing and formatting so the pages were nice to look at. Thank you to Abby Bowman for her very thorough additional edits.
Thank you to Jake Smith from the UK and Vanessa Koutsoukos from Australia for being my Brit and Aussie lesions. And I can't forget to thank my husband for his support. And last but not least, a BIG thank you to my Launch team who made this book a success. You know who you are.

Thank you to the following people and their businesses for judging and promoting the 2020 International Homeschool Poetry contest

Kent and Amy Bowler
www.**revolutionaryheroes.com**
Freedom based classes for teens and parent mentoring

Sarah Janisse Brown
www.funschooling.com/
Owner and creator of Fun Schooling, Thinking Tree Books and Dyslexia Games

Forest Lybrand
www.**forrestlybrand.com**
Author and Artist of whimsical chapter books

Kathy Mellor
www.**unleashingyourvoice.com**
Speech, Debate, and Writing coach for teens

Niccole Flowers Perrine
www.**nperrine.com**
Author of the Tansy Joy & Too Many Tangles book series

Sarah Watson
www.**beyondelementary.com**
Encouraging homeschooling moms

Table of Contents

Forward

"Let us see! Let us see Mrs. Stacy!" (I realize my last name isn't Stacy, but this keeps me feeling young).

My class is on the other side of a double curtain waiting for me to open the curtains, while I put the last finishing touches on our four-course meal for our poetry tea time. I've hired two homeschooled young men about the age of twelve, paying them ten dollars each and whatever food they want at the end, to help serve us our four-course meal. I quickly give them a crash course in serving etiquette. Now it's time.

I part the curtains and my students enter. You would have thought the student's eyes were opening for Christmas morning. Their eyes lit up like fireflies as they came in two by two to find their place setting around the table set for eleven. One classmate helped the other find their place setting first, just like at a fancy ball, and then they would find their own. All of them remembered to stay standing behind their chair until the host, I, sat down first.

The table was set with my finest dishes in the fanciest place setting with multiple spoons, forks, and four cups! We had been working on dining etiquette for weeks so they knew what each cup was for and what utensil went with which part of the meal.

During our poetry tea time each student is able to present up to three of their favorite poems, never repeating one they've shared before. From the beginning I showed them correct presenting skills, i.e. no slurring words, making eye contact with your audience periodically, stating the name of the poem and the author or anonymous if they don't know, etc. I shared with them a few iconic movie clips of poems being presented, like Anne Shirley from *Anne of Green Gables* presenting "The Highwayman." And they speak into a microphone, which is sometimes a large spoon, at a proper music stand.

When I first presented this idea to my class of boys and girls from ages eight to thirteen, it was my boys who gave me the biggest grief. (The youngest age I have presented poetry tea time to is seven, and the oldest has been thirteen). They were not convinced it would be much fun, they said. In that first discussion about it, I showed them right then what the place setting looked like, after rummaging through all my cupboards and kitchen drawers to find everything. Their eyes grew to the size of saucers as they were convinced that, yes, this is something they would like, and no it wouldn't be *that* painful to eat fancy for one meal. The least that could happen is they would get delicious food.

Now it is the boys who are clamouring for our four-course meal in a few month's time for our poetry tea time. I host these four-course meals for our poetry tea time about four times a year. Around the big holidays and special occasions.

I'm convinced children would not care if you hosted your poetry tea times with paper plates and plastic utensils. Presenting this new idea to them helps them to see there are new and fun ways to incorporate the finer things in life. I have not once had a child say to me that this was boring. On the contrary, every child has repeatedly asked when the next one was going to be!

A Year of Poetry Tea Time has made tea time so accessible to everyone who wishes to incorporate it. The simplicity is inspiring, the poetry imaginative; it takes the frustration away and leaves peace in its path. It is a resource I wish I would have had from the beginning. Utilize it! Treasure it. It is invaluable.

It is one of my hopes that children around the world will have these poetry tea times presented to them in a way that ignites excitement in their eyes and minds. When their tastes are presented with finer things than french fries and hot dogs, their minds will rise to higher ideals. They will start to hold themselves to higher standards as their confidence in themselves soars. It's funny how much impact a little tea cup and a few lines of poetry can have, don't you think?

— Stacy Riggs, Arizona, USA

Stacy Riggs is a poetry lover, home educator and mother who strives to provide the best for her children. She strives to create memories and educational experiences for children in her community.

Introduction

A Year of Poetry Tea Time is designed to make poetry a fun and enjoyable experience. It's the poetry book that should be on every home or classroom bookshelf. It will provide for you three hundred, age-appropriate poems in diverse styles and themes. This first volume is designed to help introduce you and your listeners to poetry of many styles. With all the poems tucked into one book, you won't have to search through volumes and volumes of poetry collections. Not only will it become your go-to book for poetry tea time, but also bedtime, mom school, classroom, homeschool, and more. You will learn how to hold an intimate to large poetry tea time, how to identify different styles of poetry, the history of tea, short bios on every poet included in the book, and more. You will also find great tea time recipes with which to adorn your table or picnic blanket.

I promise you that if you use this book for your poetry tea time you will have fresh new poetry all year long and everything you need to make your tea time a success. Not only will it save you a lot of time, but it will make it a breeze to put poetry team time together. Your guests (your children, class, or friends) will have a meaningful experience, boys and girls alike. Yep! Boys love poetry tea time too. You can be ready for a quick, impromptu poetry tea time by the time the water boils.

Not only does the book provide poetry and recipes for tasty treats, it is stuffed with so much more.
Features that are included in this book:
—You can find the definition of challenging words right under the poem for quick reference
—300+ poems; enough to read one poem every weekday of the year
—A glossary of over 270+ terms and the poems they are found in
—130 mini poet bios stuffed full of facts
—56 quotes by famous poets to evoke creativity and inspiration
—60+ activity suggestions
—Poems can be looked up by poet, theme, and country
—Chapters are organized by monthly themes for quick relevant poetry
—A section for you to write your own poetry
—The history of tea
—Learn about different kinds of tea
—Learn about herbal tea and how to make your own
—Learn correct tea etiquette
—25+ Recipes for simple and elegant, child-friendly, tea-time treats
—Explanation of poetry styles and terms
—Field trip suggestions
—Learn how to host a poetry tea time
And More

This collection will give you everything you need, neatly nestled between the covers of a single book.

After over twenty years of collecting poetry and reading it to children, in schools and at home, I have found that children of all ages enjoy poetry whether silly or thought provoking. With the right exposure, children from ages two to seventeen can learn to appreciate the poetry of A. A. Milne, as well as enjoy Longfellow and Shakespeare. Not only do children start to understand literary concepts, like imagery and rhyme, they also expand their minds with a rich vocabulary and learn the complexity of emotions.

Thousands of families around the world are already enjoying the magic that comes from sharing poetry. Gathering around the table, sharing glances while sipping on tea, and pondering the poetry that is being read or recited. Laughter, discussion, and smells fill the air as participants share their thoughts on a passage. This scene can be yours.

Don't put off poetry until your children are older. Now is the time to heat up the water and pull out your tea. Establish a love for poetry now. Don't deprive your children of this mind changing experience. It's especially great for those who may be reluctant to listen to books. It's time to read poetry and watch the wheels turn in the little heads that you're reading to. Build bonds and build minds starting today.

How to Use the book

I created this book to take the stress out of exploring poetry and having a poetry tea time. Spending the time to find relevant and age-appropriate poetry can be very time consuming, especially if your children are young or poetry is new to you. There is nothing more frustrating than reading a poem aloud and feeling underwhelmed because you have no clue what the meaning of it was. I am confident that *A Year of Poetry Tea Time* will prevent this problem from happening to you. So, let's learn how to use this book.

Original punctuation, spelling, and emphasis have been maintained from the original poetic works. Additionally, unique, poem formatting was kept to the original format where possible.

TEA HISTORY
Here you will find history and fun facts related to tea. Where did it originate? How did it become such a popular drink in England? Is tea only made in China? When did tea arrive in Australia? Use this section to answer dozens of questions your children may ask.
TIP: *Share a fun tea fact each month or have a fun day exploring tea history.*

POETRY STYLES & TERMS
This section will help you learn about different poetry styles and terms. This will help you better educate the children in your life. Some poets are associated with a certain style of poetry. Just flip to this section to find a concise explanation and broaden everyone's understanding.
TIP: *Throw a sticky note in as a bookmark for lightning speed reference.*

THE POETRY CHAPTERS
This book was created with the idea that people would be using it as an educational resource hand in hand with tea time. For this reason, I have organized the chapters by month. Each month contains poetry that will line up with seasons, holidays, and related themes. Each chapter contains twenty-five or more poems. This gives you at least one poem per weekday. Or you could hold a poetry tea time once a week and read five or more poems as your listeners sip their cuppa (English slang for cup of tea) and nibble on a cookie.
TIP: *Poems could be assigned for memorization, recitation, or copy work.*

THE POETS CORNER
Here I have provided for you some blank pages for you to either write our own poetry or to give you a spot to add some of your own favorite poetry.

RECIPES
This section is to help you get started on creating tasty treats for your poetry tea time. I have included a broad array of fare from simple to elegant, sweet to savory, that is guaranteed to please the palate of even the pickiest eater. There are many recipes that are naturally gluten free and gluten free adjustments are included for every recipe. Some

recipes are included because they are mentioned in a poem. All recipes are made from scratch so you can learn and apply cooking skills. Cooking from scratch is a valuable life skill and increases self-confidence.

TIP: *Use these recipes to teach cooking skills to your children.*

KINDS OF TEA
I included this section to help you understand the differences between teas. I had no clue what made each one special and thought you would appreciate the same knowledge. There is also a part about herbal teas.

TIP: *Try to create your own special, family tea blend.*

TEA ETIQUETTE
Do you pour the tea or the milk first? How do you stir your tea? Who pours the tea? For those interested in teaching a little refinement, make sure to read about proper English tea etiquette. You will learn the basics of serving, eating, and drinking tea at your next poetry tea time.

TIP: *Use this as an opportunity to teach correct table etiquette and hold your own etiquette tea or dinner. Your children or class gets to dress up and try out their new dining skills.*

THE GRACIOUS HOST: PLANNING YOUR POETRY TEA TIME
This section will walk you through how to host a poetry tea time, casual or elegant. Selecting a theme, party size, menu, poetry to be read, how to invite guests, and more.

TIP: *Print out the planner at www.ayearofpoetryteatime.com*

BRINGING POETRY TO LIFE
Poetry doesn't have to only be experienced at home. In this section you will learn of other creative ways to explore and share the magic of poetry.

TIP: *Pick at least four ways you are going to bring poetry to life this year.*

POETRY RABBIT TRAILS
Hop off the path and blaze your own trail as you engage in learning activities inspired by the poetry in this book. With 65+ activities to choose from you will get to explore science, art, geography, cooking, music, writing and more.

TIP: *Be prepared by reading through the activities ahead of time..*

POETRY FIELD TRIPS
This is a list of museums, childhood homes and other significant poetry sites you can visit.

TIP: *Pick a location nearest you and plan to learn about and take a trip to learn about a poet in depth.*

POETS QUOTES
There are a total of fifty-six famous poet quotes included in this book. Twelve of them are located at the beginning of each chapter. The rest can be found under "Quotes by Famous Poets." I tried to include quotes that promoted poetry, learning, education and would inspire one to do his or her best.

TIP: *These quotes can be used to start your week off with a great message, used on a fun letter board, or even used as copy work or memorization. You can even use them to learn about additional poets.*

MINI POET BIOS

I have included a mini bio for every single poet featured in this collection. You will find the years they were born and died along with the country they were born in or most popular in. For instance, some poets who became very popular in Australia were actually born in England. When this happens, it is mentioned in their bio where they were actually born. When able, I included what inspired the poet to write poetry and how they received their education. If any poet had a life challenge as a child, I included it so children could see others overcoming obstacles. I included the ages they were first published, especially if they were published as a child. Often you will find the names of their first publication or their most popular works. When the word "collection" is used, it is referring to a book containing a collection of poetry. A term to keep an eye out for is *posthumous,* which means after the poet's death; some poets had poetry published after they had passed away. Another term used often is *pseudonym* which is another term for pen name.

TIP: *Create a poetry timeline and add a poet when you read one of their poems.*

VOCABULARY (GLOSSARY)

Poetry has stood the test of time exposing us to words that are no longer used, rarely used, or spelt differently. Some words may be familiar, but struggle to actually define them when asked by inquiring minds. To help you out, I have included vocabulary definitions for any words that are not commonly used every day. You will find this information in two places. First, they are included right below the poem for quick reference. Second, they are located in the glossary. In the glossary, not only will you find the word and definition, but also any other poems that contain that particular word. Why did I bother doing this? So, you could read another poem and experience the word in multiple contexts. I tried to include all relevant definitions so you can deduce which one it is.

TIP: *Use the vocabulary words to create a fun spelling bee, picking words that would be age appropriate for your children or class.*

A Tea Cup Sized History of Tea

The First Sip
- Tea is the second most popular drink in the world. Second only to water, it is enjoyed all over the world. Fun fact, tea was not originally used as a drink. That's right, for thousands of years, India's state of Assam and the Chinese provinces of Sichuan and Yunnan would use tea leaves for chewing, like bubble gum without the bubble. It isn't known exactly when tea turned into a drink, but there is a legend dating back to 2500 BCE. It is said that Shennong (Divine Farmer), a mythical emperor of prehistoric China, was boiling some water when some tea leaves fell into the water. He tasted the boiled tea water and he loved it. He taught others to grow, make, and drink tea.

A Sip on the Road
- Buddhist monks and merchants from Sichuan and Yunnan provinces packed their bags and horses and spread tea North along the Silk Road. Monks enjoyed how tea kept them awake during meditation. Tea was used as medicine and tasted bitter but during the Tang dynasty the flavour of tea was improved. This drinkable tea was called "matcha" and tea houses and gardens were becoming popular; so popular that the emperor wanted everyone to pay their tributes (taxes) in tea, forcing everyone to plant and grow tea. This made the emperor rich in tea and he started to trade with other parts of Asia, along the Tea-Horse Road.

A Few Sips Later
- In 1610 the Dutch East India Company took the first load of tea to Amsterdam.
- In 1645 tea had reached England, but they were a country of coffee drinkers and the tea was only used for medical issues.
- In 1650 tea was introduced to America by Peter Stuyvesant. A Dutch settlement in New Amsterdam, later named New York, was known for drinking tea.
- By 1670 tea had spread to Boston, but it still was not a public, social experience.

Everyone Wants a Sip
- In 1662 Catherine of Braganza (from Portugal) married King Charles II and one of the many things she took to England were some crates labelled *Transporte de Ervas Aromaticas*. These were crates filled with loose tea. Some believe that this is how we ended up with the word "TEA." Her drinking tea and having "tea drinking experiences" made the popularity of drinking tea explode. The use of pretty porcelain tea cups and mugs were also popularized by Queen Catherine. The aristocrats (upper class) were soon all enjoying tea and eventually it spread to all classes.

-

A Sip in America
- In 1689 the Honourable East Indian Company started to import tea from China.
- The early 1700s produced millions of British tea drinkers.
- By the 1720s tea was a staple in both colonial, American and British women loved their tea.
- Unfortunately, King George III decided to create lots of taxes on the people of the American colonies. This included a tea tax.
- This led to the Boston Tea Party in 1772, when angry colonists dumped 342 chests of tea into the Boston Harbor in protest against the taxation. This event was one of the steps toward the American Revolutionary War. The Boston Tea Party caused a major shift in tea drinking in America. Tea was considered to be very unpatriotic and people switched to coffee.

A Sip of War
- Back in China the Emperor was only interested in selling tea for silver; the limits on silver in England led to trading tea for opium.
- In 1757 the East India Company colonized Bengal after successfully winning the Battle of Plassey. This made it possible for them to take control of a large amount of the surrounding areas.
- Within fifteen years the country was turned into a giant opium factory. Sadly, the country was poorly managed and ten million people starved.
- The trading of tea for opium made England rich, but led to a widespread drug addiction in China. One in every three people were addicted to opium.
- In 1839 the emperor realized that something drastic had to be done. He sent an official to the trade ports in Canton and he dumped 1.2 million kilos of opium into the sea. This led to two different opium wars from 1839–1860. Unfortunately, China did not fare well during the first war. It ended in a peace treaty forcing China to pay for the war, wasted opium, and handing Hong Kong over to British rule.

A Sip Down Under
- Tea, as the Brits knew it, was not in Australia until 1794, by way of Governor Arthur Phillip.
- It's believed that people learned to use sweet sarsaparilla as a tea from local Aboriginal people.
- Not until 1819 was it added to the rations of the convicts who were transported to Australia.

A Sip with a Duchess
- Back in England, in the early 1840s, Anna, the seventh Duchess of Bedford found that she was often hungry around four o'clock in the afternoon and hated waiting for the late evening meal.
- She would ask for tea, bread, butter, and cakes or sweets to be brought to her room.
- Eventually she invited others to join her and this led to the afternoon tea we know today.
- She also popularized the use of pretty porcelain tea cups and mugs.

A Sip of Deception
- Meanwhile, the East India Company decided that they needed to find a way to grow their own tea, but China did not allow any of their plants to leave the country.
- So the East Indian Company sent a Scottish botanist, Robert Fortune, to China in 1848 to learn how to grow, process, and manufacture the tea that the British loved so much. He managed to smuggle out plants (Camellia Sinensis), equipment, and a few tea masters so the East India
- Companies could start their own tea plantations in India. Conditions on these tea plantations were no better than those found in the opium fields.

A Little More to Sip On
- Australia's first official tea plantation was started in the 1890s
- In 1901 Mary Molaren and Roberta C. Lawson put in for a patent on a "tea leaf holder"
- In 1908 an American, Thomas Sullivan, sold tea samples in tiny silk bags, accidentally used as a tea bag.
- During WWII, tea delivery from the Dutch East Indies was interrupted due to the conflict. Australians lived with a tea ration from 1942 to 1950.
- In 1953 Tea bags became popular in England
- Tea is pronounced both "tea" (tea transported by the Dutch merchants) and "Cha." (tea transported via the Silk Road).
- Today China, India, and Kenya are the leading producers of tea.
- Organizations like Fair Trade and Ethical Tea Partnership have been working to improve the work conditions and pay for those working to produce tea for the entire world.

Discussing Poetry with Children

You are about to enter a fun new realm of imagination and intrigue. A world that will have your children laughing, pondering, and looking forward to what they will hear next. Children are capable of having deep conversations and developing critical thinking skills that will shape their future. But remember, all children are different. To some, critical thinking will come naturally, where others need a little help to develop such skills.

Below you will find an array of questions you can ask your children about any poem. Refer to the Poetry Styles & Terms section if you are unfamiliar with any of the poetry vocabulary. The questions are in basic categories to make it easier to find questions that are relevant.
–Make sure to encourage your child to explain their answer. Giving yes or no answers does not show understanding of concepts.
–If your children are at a loss for words, after giving them some silent time to think, then share your thoughts with them and ask if they have any other ideas.
–Don't belittle your child if they don't see or understand a poem, even if it seems obvious to you.
–If you're not sure what a poem means, then give your kids a chance to figure it out. Poetry is unique as it can mean something to one person and something completely different to another. Remind your children of this concept and embrace their different ideas.

Questions related to poetry terms and style
–Do you think the meaning of this poem is obvious or does it have hidden meanings?
–Does this poem take place in a person's mind (lyric poetry) or at a physical location?
–Does this poem use imagery?
–Does this poem use rhyming words?
–Is this poem a narrative poem, which tells a story?
–Does this poem use satire?
–Did you notice a rhyme scheme in this poem?
–Was this poem meant to be romantic?
–What symbolism was used?

Questions related to feelings
–How did this poem make you feel?
–Do you like how this poem made you feel?
–Have you ever felt this way about something?
–What do you think caused the person to write this poem?
–How do you think the poet felt when he/she wrote the poem?
–Have you ever been in the same situation as the poet?

Questions about content
–Did you hear any new words?
–Do you think the poet was writing about something real or imaginary?
–What was the coolest part of the poem?
–Did you notice a specific style of poetry?
–What was the overall theme of the poem?
–Do you like this style of poetry?
–Would you have ended the poem the same?

Questions about values/morals
–What is this poem trying to teach us?
–Do you agree with the poet's point of view?
–Does this poem align with your family's values?
–How can this poem influence your decisions?

Questions that will work for any poem
–Why do you like or dislike this poem?
–What does this poem make you think of?
–Did you hear any words that were new to you?

Poetry Styles & Terms

Alliteration—using a letter sounds repetitively to create intrigue within a written work. Tongue twisters are a good example. Check out a Dr. Seuss book and look at all of the alliteration he uses.

Abecedarius poem— an acrostic, where the first word, strophe or verse appears in the order of the alphabet.

Acrostic—a word puzzle, poem or an composition where the letter at the beginning of each line spells a word or words.

Anaphora—using the same word or phrase over and over at the beginning or end of each line.

Blank Verse—poetry that is written with a meter, but without rhyming lines. It is almost always in Iambic Pentameter. John Milton's *Paradise Lost* is an entire epic poem that was written in blank verse.

Caesura—a pause that is made purposely. Usually, you know there is this pause because of punctuation. Things like dashes, slashes, and common punctuation. These usually appear in the middle of a line. Emily Dickinson loved to use caesura.

Couplet—a short, two-line verse. A couplet on its own creates a stanza.

Enjambment—there is no punctuation at the end of lines telling the reader not to stop. Instead, they are to read continuously without pause.

Free Verse—there are no rules to bind you when writing in free verse. There is no meter or rhyming unless the poet has chosen to do so. And even if they do they do not need to stick to it. It can be as long or as short as you would like. The poet is free to use alliteration, personification, and rhyme. "Fog" by Carl Sandburg is an example of free verse.

Foot—the name given to a unit or measurement in poetry. For example, a foot can represent two or three syllables. An iamb is the most common foot where it has two syllables and has a pattern of unstressed and stressed syllables.

Georgian Poets—there was a series of poem anthologies that were published by Harold Monro during the time of King George V. The poetry included in these anthologies are referred to as Georgian poets. There were five volumes published between 1912 and 1922. The style at the time was primarily romanticism, hedonism, and sentimentality.

Haiku—a Japanese form of poetry originally written about nature. A haiku has only three lines and follows a specific syllable pattern. The first line must have five syllables, the second line must have seven syllables and the third line has another five syllables. The lines do not rhyme.

Iamb—a two syllable part of a complete meter. The first syllable being unstressed and the second being stressed. Another term for this is "a foot." The rhythm can be compared to a heartbeat.

Iambic Pentameter—a specific meter (rhythm) found in poetry. William Shakespeare is famous for his use of Iambic Pentameter. Each line has ten syllables which switch back and forth between stressed and unstressed syllables. There are five iambs in each line of the Iambic Pentameter. For those of you who are math minded: 2 syllables per iamb X 5 iambs per line = a 10-syllable line.

Internal Rhyme—where the rhyme happens in the center of a line.

Imagery—when a poet, or writer, uses words to create an image in the reader's mind. This includes metaphorical and figurative language.

Limerick—typically limericks are comical. They always have five lines. They follow a special rhyming pattern. The first, second and fifth line must rhyme and the third and fourth line have their own rhyme.

Lyric Poetry—Poetry that focuses on the feeling and thoughts of a single speaker. For instance, a poem expressing one's feelings of love or despair.

Meter—the pattern of beats (rhythm) within a line of poetry. Sometimes people will refer to the meter as a foot, or feet. It correlates with the number of feet in a line.
–Manometer has one foot
–Dimeter has two feet
–Trimeter has three feet

Monorhyme—when the ending rhyme sound of each line is the same.

Narrative Poetry—a poem that tells a story. They contain characters and have a beginning, middle, and end like a story. An example is Edgar Allen Poe's "The Raven."

Quatrain Poetry—a four-line poem or a four-lined stanza within a poem. They can use different rhyme scheme patterns.

Satire—the use of sarcasm, humor, mockery and exaggeration to make fun of people and/or society. It is a comical way to point out flaws and provoke a person or society to act and make a change. Techniques like exaggeration and irony are used to accomplish this. A caricature is a great visual example of satire.

Renku—a poem that is collaborated on with two or more poets. So much so that they even alternate who reads each alternating line. Each stanza must be self-standing. Each stanza may seem random, but there is supposed to be an association of some sort from one stanza to the next. There needs to be contrast from stanza to stanza. This style has many additional criteria that take practice to master.

Rhyme Schemes—it identifies the set pattern of rhyming for a particular poem. Rhyme schemes are represented by a set of capital letters. These letters can be used to identify which lines have matching rhymes. Rhyme Schemes that are often used are:
AAAA: each line ends with the same rhyme like Cat, Bat, Rat, Sat
ABAB: lines one and three rhyme and line two and four rhyme like play, phone, clay, stone
AABB: the first two lines rhyme and the second two lines rhyme like book, took, hair, care
ABCB: here only the second-and fourth-lines rhyme like flower, rain, daisy, pain

Romantic Poetry—scholars looking back in time to government, poetry, and art that they considered to be a virtuous time. A time of true nobility, poets tried to bring the style and grace of the Roman Era. So the term "Romantic" has to do with the Romans not love.

Shi fu— Shi means poetry in Chinese. Fu was a popular form of poetry during the Han dynasty. Fu means "rhapsody." Fu are parts of a poem that go into extreme extensive detail about a single place, person or detail. It also goes out of its way to use rare words. These poems were chanted, not sung. This style has been around since about 3 BCE.

Sonnet—a poem with fourteen lines and uses Iambic Pentameter. William Shakespeare is well known for his sonnets. The rhyme scheme typically used was ABAB CDCD EFEF GG.

Stanza—a grouping of lines.

Strophe—divisions within a poems structure containing stanzas with lines of varying length. This occurs often in free verse poetry and odes.

Syllable—this is a part of a word that only has a single beat or sound to it.

Tercet—a three lined poem or stanza.

Trochee—a foot opposite of the Iamb. Its syllables are stressed and then unstressed. An example of this is in the first line of William Bakes "The Tyger."

January

"The Fool doth think he is wise, but the wise man knows himself to be a fool."
—William Shakespeare

New Year Greeting
By Emily Mary Barton

CAST thy cloudy mantle round thee,
Weep to leave us, good old Year!
Kind and hopeful we have found thee,
Shall we part without a tear?
While that tear yet glitters o'er us,
New Year! may thy dawning bright,
Gild th' uncertain path before us,
With the rainbow hues of light!

The Year
By Caroline W. Leakey

EACH season, bringing beauty, yields back praise
To its kind God,—the God of all the year!
Nature ne'er flags, but brings fair vernal gear
To deck her sweetest child—young Spring-time days,
And Summer's brilliant garb and golden tress,
Entwined with flowery gems and jewels of dew,
And rich Autumnal robe of blended hue;
Then chastened Winter's frost-bespangled-dress,—
Each in succession beautiful! and each,
To those who learn, this silent lesson teach,
That we, in our estate from youth to age,
Are still beneath the care of Nature's Lord,
And through our life His love will still afford
Pleasures befitting to each different stage.

Never Give All Your Heart
By W. B. Yeats

Never give all the heart, for love
Will hardly seem worth thinking of
To passionate women if it seem
Certain, and they never dream
That it fades out from kiss to kiss;
For everything that's lovely is
But a brief, dreamy, kind delight.
O never give the heart outright,
For they, for all smooth lips can say,
Have given their hearts up to the play.
And who could play it well enough
If deaf and dumb and blind with love?
He that made this knows all the cost,
For he gave all his heart and lost.

A Scrawl
By James Whitcomb Riley

I want to sing something - but this is all -
I try and I try, but the rhymes are dull
As though they were damp, and the echoes fall
Limp and unlovable.

Words will not say what I yearn to say -
They will not walk as I want them to,
But they stumble and fall in the path of the way
Of my telling my love for you.

Simply take what the scrawl is worth -
Knowing I love you as sun the sod
On the ripening side of the great round earth
That swings in the smile of God.

A Caution
By Robert Herrick

That love last long, let it thy first care be
To find a wife that is most fit for thee.
Be she too wealthy or too poor, be sure
Love in extremes can never long endure.

I Broke the Spell that Held Me Long
By William Cullen Bryant

I broke the spell that held me long,
The dear, dear witchery of song.
I said, the poet's idle lore
Shall waste my prime of years no more,
For Poetry, though heavenly born,
Consorts with poverty and scorn.

I broke the spell–nor deemed its power
Could fetter me another hour.
Ah, thoughtless! how could I forget
Its causes were around me yet?
For wheresoe'er I looked, the while,
Was Nature's everlasting smile.

Still came and lingered on my sight
Of flowers and streams the bloom and light,
And glory of the stars and sun; –
And these and poetry are one.
They, ere the world had held me long,
Recalled me to the love of song.

---

fetter—*anything that restrains or prevents something from moving; like chains around a person's hands or feet or ropes tied around an animal's limbs*

Marsh Hymn – Thou and I
By Sidney Lanier

So one in heart and thought, I trow,
That thou might'st press the strings and I might draw the bow
And both would meet in music sweet,
Thou and I, I trow.

---

trow—*to think or ponder on something; if a person is to suppose, believe or trust something*

A Minuet of Mozart
By Sara Teasdale

Across the dimly lighted room
The violin drew wefts of sound,
Airily they wove and wound
And glimmered gold against the gloom.

I watched the music turn to light,
But at the pausing of the bow,
The web was broken and the glow
Was drowned within the wave of night.

A Little Bird I Am
By Louisa May Alcott

"A little bird I am,
Shut from the fields of air,
And in my cage I sit and sing
To Him who placed me there:
Well pleased a prisoner to be,
Because, my God, it pleases Thee!

"Naught have I else to do;
I sing the whole day long;
And He whom most I love to please
Doth listen to my song,
He caught and bound my wandering wing,
But still He bends to hear me sing."

The Captive Dove
By Anne Brontë

Poor restless dove, I pity thee;
And when I hear thy plaintive moan,
I mourn for thy captivity,
And in thy woes forget mine own.
To see thee stand prepared to fly,
And flap those useless wings of thine,
And gaze into the distant sky,
Would melt a harder heart than mine.

In vain—in vain! Thou canst not rise
Thy prison roof confines thee there;
Its slender wires delude thine eyes,
And quench thy longings with despair.

Oh, thou wert made to wander free
In sunny mead and shady grove,
And far beyond the rolling sea,
In distant climes, at will to rove!

Yet, hadst thou but one gentle mate
Thy little drooping heart to cheer,
And share with thee thy captive state,
Thou couldst be happy even there.

Yes, even there, if, listening by,
One faithful dear companion stood,
While gazing on her full bright eye,
Thou might'st forget thy native wood.

But thou, poor solitary dove,
Must make, unheard, thy joyless moan;
The heart that Nature formed to love
Must pine, neglected, and alone.

---

delude—*to trick, deceive or beguile someone*
plaintive—*one who complains, expresses sorrow or sadness*
mead—*in Latin it means "to be wet;" it is also an alcoholic drink made from honey and water; in England there is also a geographical area north of Oxford, England called Sunnymead*
solitary—*to live alone or to be removed from all company*

What is Pink?
By Christina Rossetti

What is pink? A rose is pink
By the fountain's brink.
What is red? A poppy's red
In its barley bed.
What is blue? The sky is blue
Where the clouds float through.
What is white? A swan is white
Sailing in the light.
What is yellow? Pears are yellow,
Rich and ripe and mellow.
What is green? The grass is green,
With small flowers between.
What is violet? Clouds are violet
In the summer twilight.
What is orange? Why, an orange,
Just an orange!

On the Vowels
By Jonathan Swift

We are little airy creatures,
All of different voice and features;
One of us in glass is set,
One of us you'll find in jet.
T'other you may see in tin,
And the fourth a box within.
If the fifth you should pursue,
It can never fly from you.

Letters
By Ralph Waldo Emerson

Every day brings a ship,
Every ship brings a word;
Well for those who have no fear,
Looking seaward well assured
That the word the vessel brings
Is the word they wish to hear.

The Australian Flag
By Francis William Lauderdale Adams

   Pure blue flag of heaven
With your silver stars,
   Not beside those crosses'
Blood-stained torture-bars:

   Not beside the token
The foul sea-harlot gave,
   Pure blue flag of heaven,
Must you ever wave!

   No, but young exultant,
Free from care and crime,
   The soulless selfish England
Of this later time:

   No, but, faithful, noble,
Rising from her grave,
   Flag of light and liberty,
For ever must you wave!

---

exultant—*to feel or proclaim triumph*

Good King Arthur
Anonymous (English rhyme)

When good king Arthur ruled this land,
    He was a goodly king;
He stole three pecks of barley-meal,
    To make a bag-pudding.

A bag-pudding the king did make,
    And stuffed it well with plums:
And in it put great lumps of fat,
    As big as my two thumbs.

**Bag pudding recipe on page 281

Fashion
By Ada Cambridge

See those resplendent creatures, as they glide
O'er scarlet carpet, between footmen tall,
From sumptuous carriage to effulgent hall -
A dazzling vision in their pomp and pride!
See that choice supper - needless - cast aside -
Though worth a thousand fortunes, counting all,
To them for whom no crumb of it will fall -
The starved and homeless in the street outside.
Some day the little great god will decree
That overmuch connotes the underbred,
That pampered body means an empty head,
And wealth displayed the last vulgarity.
When selfish greed becomes a social sin
The world's regeneration may begin.

---

resplendent—*when something is highly appealing because it is very shiny, bright and/or rich in color*
effulgent—*to emit a bright and shining flood of light like the sun*
pomp—*a parade or procession of grand splendor; like the entrance of a king into a room or a graduation ceremony*

Epitaph
By Johann Wolfgang von Goethe

As a boy, reserved and naughty;
As a youth, a coxcomb and haughty;
As a man, for action inclined;
As a greybeard, fickle in mind.
Upon thy grave will people read:
This was a very man, indeed!

---

coxcomb—*a person who is cocky and vein; a person who exaggerates his/her accomplishments*
fickle—*to be wishy washy, unable to make up one's mind*

The Genteel Family
By Kate Greenaway

Some children are so naughty,
And some are very good;
But the Genteel Family
Did always what it should.

They put on gloves when they went out,
And ran not in the street;
And on wet days not one of them
Had ever muddy feet.

Then they were always so polite,
And always thanked you so;
And never threw their toys about,
As naughty children do.

They always learnt their lessons
When it was time they should;
And liked to eat up all their crusts
They were so very good.

And then their frocks were never torn,
Their tuckers always clean;
And their hair so very tidy
Always quite fit to be seen.

Then they made calls with their mamma
And were so very neat;
And learnt to bow becomingly
When they met you in the street.

And really they were everything
That children ought to be;
And well may be examples now
For little you and me.

Barter
By Sara Teasdale

Life has loveliness to sell,
      All beautiful and splendid things,
Blue waves whitened on a cliff,
      Soaring fire that sways and sings,
And children's faces looking up
      Holding wonder in a cup.

Life has loveliness to sell,
      Music like a curve of gold,
Scent of pine trees in the rain,
      Eyes that love you, arms that hold,
And for your spirit's still delight,
      Holy thoughts that star the night.

Spend all you have for loveliness,
      Buy it and never count the cost;
For one white singing hour of peace
      Count many a year of strife well lost,
And for a breath of ecstacy
      Give all you have been, or could be.

I Remember, I Remember
By Thomas Hood

I remember, I remember,
The house where I was born,
The little window where the sun
Came peeping in at morn;
He never came a wink too soon,
Nor brought too long a day,
But now, I often wish the night
Had borne my breath away!

I remember, I remember,
The roses, red and white,
The vi'lets, and the lily-cups,
Those flowers made of light!
The lilacs where the robin built,
And where my brother set
The laburnum on his birthday,—
The tree is living yet!

I remember, I remember,
Where I was used to swing,
And thought the air must rush as fresh
To swallows on the wing;
My spirit flew in feathers then,
That is so heavy now,
And summer pools could hardly cool
The fever on my brow!

I remember, I remember,
The fir trees dark and high;
I used to think their slender tops
Were close against the sky:
It was a childish ignorance,
But now 'tis little joy
To know I'm farther off from heav'n
Than when I was a boy.

Block City
By Robert Louis Stevenson

What are you able to build with your blocks?
Castles and palaces, temples and docks.
Rain may keep raining, and others go roam,
But I can be happy and building at home.

Let the sofa be mountains, the carpet be sea,
There I'll establish a city for me:
A kirk and a mill and a palace beside,
And a harbour as well where my vessels may ride.

Great is the palace with pillar and wall,
A sort of a tower on the top of it all,
And steps coming down in an orderly way
To where my toy vessels lie safe in the bay.

This one is sailing and that one is moored:
Hark to the song of the sailors aboard!
And see, on the steps of my palace, the kings
Coming and going with presents and things!

Now I have done with it, down let it go!
All in a moment the town is laid low.
Block upon block lying scattered and free,
What is there left of my town by the sea?

Yet as I saw it, I see it again,
The kirk and the palace, the ships and the men,
And as long as I live and where'er I may be,
I'll always remember my town by the sea.

---

kirk—*Scottish word for church*

Winter Time
By Robert Louis Stevenson

Late lies the wintry sun a-bed,
A frosty, fiery sleepy-head;
Blinks but an hour or two; and then,
A blood-red orange, sets again.

Before the stars have left the skies,
At morning in the dark I rise;
And shivering in my nakedness,
By the cold candle, bathe and dress.

Close by the jolly fire I sit
To warm my frozen bones a bit;
Or with a reindeer-sled, explore
The colder countries round the door.

When to go out, my nurse doth wrap
Me in my comforter and cap;
The cold wind burns my face, and blows
Its frosty pepper up my nose.

Black are my steps on silver sod;
Thick blows my frosty breath abroad;
And tree and house, and hill and lake,
Are frosted like a wedding cake.

The Snow-Blossom
By Clark Ashton Smith

But yestereve the winter trees
Reared leafless, blackly bare,
Their twigs and branches poignant-marked
Upon the sunset-flare.

White-petaled, opens now the dawn,
And in its pallid glow,
Revealed, each leaf-lorn, barren tree
Stands white with flowers of snow.

---

poignant—*pointed, sharp, can be referring to taste, smell, or feelings such as regret or sadness*
pallid—*to be pale, lacking color*

Winter's Wait
By Melissa Crowther

Out in the woods the wind sings a song,
Through the window it calms me when weary.

The winter is cold, unrelenting and long.
My eyes begin to be bleary.

Through the dull, bleak drab and darkness of days,
I'll sit with my cup of tea.

There's a smile on my lips as I soften my gaze.
A cocoon of cotton and me.

In a Chair
By Sir John Collings Squire

The room is full of the peace of night,
The small flames murmur and flicker and sway,
Within me is neither shadow, nor light,
 Nor night, nor twilight, nor dawn, nor day.

For the brain strives not to the goal of thought,
And the limbs lie wearied, and all desire
Sleeps for a while, and I am naught
But a pair of eyes that gaze at a fire.

Good Book
By Edgar Guest

Good books are friendly things to own.
If you are busy they will wait.
They will not call you on the phone
Or wake you if the hour is late.
They stand together row by row,
Upon the low shelf or the high.
But if you're lonesome this you know:
You have a friend or two nearby.

The fellowship of books is real.
They're never noisy when you're still.
They won't disturb you at your meal.
They'll comfort you when you are ill.
The lonesome hours they'll always share.
When slighted they will not complain.
And though for them you've ceased to care
Your constant friends they'll still remain.

Good books your faults will never see
Or tell about them round the town.
If you would have their company
You merely have to take them down.
They'll help you pass the time away,
They'll counsel give if that you need.
He has true friends for night and day
Who has a few good books to read.

February

"I've learned that people will forget what you said, people will forget what you did, but people will never forget how you made them feel."
—Maya Angelou

Woods in Winter
By Henry Wadsworth Longfellow

When winter winds are piercing chill,
And through the hawthorn blows the gale,
With solemn feet I tread the hill,
That overbrows the lonely vale.
O'er the bare upland, and away
Through the long reach of desert woods,
The embracing sunbeams chastely play,
And gladden these deep solitudes.
Where, twisted round the barren oak,
The summer vine in beauty clung,
And summer winds the stillness broke,
The crystal icicle is hung.
Where, from their frozen urns, mute springs
Pour out the river's gradual tide,
Shrilly the skater's iron rings,
And voices fill the woodland side.
Alas! how changed from the fair scene,
When birds sang out their mellow lay,
And winds were soft, and woods were green,
And the song ceased not with the day!
But still wild music is abroad,
Pale, desert woods! within your crowd;
And gathering winds, in hoarse accord,
Amid the vocal reeds pipe loud.
Chill airs and wintry winds! my ear
Has grown familiar with your song;
I hear it in the opening year,
I listen, and it cheers me long.

The Respectable Folks
By Henry David Thoreau

The respectable folks,—
Where dwell they?
They whisper in the oaks,
And they sigh in the hay;
Summer and winter, night and day,
Out on the meadow, there dwell they.
They never die,
Nor snivel, nor cry,
Nor ask our pity
With a wet eye.
A sound estate they ever mend,
To every asker readily lend;
To the ocean wealth,
To the meadow health,
To Time his length,
To the rocks strength,
To the stars light,
To the weary night,
To the busy day,
To the idle play;
And so their good cheer never ends,
For all are their debtors, and all their friends.

February Twilight
By Sara Teasdale

I stood beside a hill
Smooth with new-laid snow,
A single star looked out
From the cold evening glow.

There was no other creature
That saw what I could see --
I stood and watched the evening star
As long as it watched me.

Bond and Free
By Robert Frost

Love has earth to which she clings
With hills and circling arms about—
Wall within wall to shut fear out.
But Thought has need of no such things,
For Thought has a pair of dauntless wings.

On snow and sand and turf, I see
Where Love has left a printed trace
With straining in the world's embrace.
And such is Love and glad to be.
But Thought has shaken his ankles free.

Thought cleaves the interstellar gloom
And sits in Sirius' disc all night,
Till day makes him retrace his flight,
With smell of burning on every plume,
Back past the sun to an earthly room.

His gains in heaven are what they are.
Yet some say Love by being thrall
And simply staying possesses all
In several beauty that Thought fares far
To find fused in another star.

---

dauntless—*to have no fear, nothing holds you back, unstoppable.*
thrall—*a slave*

On Being Brought from Africa to America
By Phillis Wheatley

'Twas mercy brought me from my Pagan land,
Taught my benighted soul to understand
That there's a God, that there's a Saviour too:
Once I redemption neither sought nor knew.
Some view our sable race with scornful eye,
"Their colour is a diabolic die."
Remember, *Christians, Negros,* black as *Cain,*
May be refin'd, and join th' angelic train.

---

benight—*to shroud in darkness*

39

Topsy Turvey World
By William Brightly Rands

If the butterfly courted the bee,
And the owl the porcupine;
If the churches were built in the sea,
And three times one was nine;
If the pony rode his master,
If the buttercups ate the cows,
If the cat had the dire disaster
To be worried, sir, by the mouse;
If mamma, sir, sold the baby
To a gypsy for half-a-crown;
If a gentleman, sir, was a lady-
The world would be Upside Down!
If any or all of these wonders
Should ever come about,
I should not consider them blunders,
For I should be Inside Out!

Lover's Philosophy
By Percy Bysshe Shelley

The fountains mingle with the river
And the rivers with the ocean,
The winds of heaven mix forever
With a sweet emotion;
Nothing in the world is single,
All things by a law divine
In one another's being mingle—
Why not I with thine?

See the mountains kiss high heaven,
And the waves clasp one another;
No sister-flower would be forgiven
If it disdain'd its brother;
And the sunlight clasps the earth,
And the moonbeams kiss the sea—
What is all this sweet work worth
If thou kiss not me?

Of Love
BY Robert Herrick

How Love came in, I do not know,
Whether by th' eye, or eare, or no:
Or whether with the soule it came
(At first) infused with the same:
Whether in part 'tis here or there,
Or, like the soule, whole every where:
This troubles me: but as I well
As any other, this can tell;
That when from hence she does depart,
The out-let then is from the heart.

Ae Fond Kiss
By Robert Burns

Ae fond kiss, and then we sever;
Ae fareweel, and then forever!
Deep in heart-wrung tears I'll pledge thee,
Warring sighs and groans I'll wage thee.
Who shall say that Fortune grieves him,
While the star of hope she leaves him?
Me, nae cheerfu' twinkle lights me;
Dark despair around benights me.

I'll ne'er blame my partial fancy,
Naething could resist my Nancy;
But to see her was to love her;
Love but her, and love forever.
Had we never lov'd sae kindly,
Had we never lov'd sae blindly,
Never met—or never parted—
We had ne'er been broken-hearted.

Fare thee weel, thou first and fairest!
Fare thee weel, thou best and dearest!
Thine be ilka joy and treasure,
Peace. enjoyment, love, and pleasure!
Ae fond kiss, and then we sever;
Ae fareweel, alas, forever!
Deep in heart-wrung tears I'll pledge thee,
Warring sighs and groans I'll wage thee!

---

benight—*to shroud in darkness*

41

Frederick Douglass
By Paul Laurence Dunbar

A hush is over all the teeming lists,
And there is pause, a breath-space in the strife;
A spirit brave has passed beyond the mists
And vapors that obscure the sun of life.
And Ethiopia, with bosom torn,
Laments the passing of her noblest born.

She weeps for him a mother's burning tears—
She loved him with a mother's deepest love.
He was her champion thro' direful years,
And held her weal all other ends above.
When Bondage held her bleeding in the dust,
He raised her up and whispered, "Hope and Trust."

For her his voice, a fearless clarion, rung
That broke in warning on the ears of men;
For her the strong bow of his power he strung,
And sent his arrows to the very den
Where grim Oppression held his bloody place
And gloated o'er the mis'ries of a race.

And he was no soft-tongued apologist;
He spoke straightforward, fearlessly uncowed;
The sunlight of his truth dispelled the mist,
And set in bold relief each dark hued cloud;
To sin and crime he gave their proper hue,
And hurled at evil what was evil's due.

Through good and ill report he cleaved his way.
Right onward, with his face set toward the heights,
Nor feared to face the foeman's dread array,—
The lash of scorn, the sting of petty spites.
He dared the lightning in the lightning's track,
And answered thunder with his thunder back.

When men maligned him, and their torrent wrath
In furious imprecations o'er him broke,
He kept his counsel as he kept his path; '
Twas for his race, not for himself he spoke.
He knew the import of his Master's call,
And felt himself too mighty to be small.

No miser in the good he held was he,—
His kindness followed his horizon's rim.
His heart, his talents, and his hands were free

To all who truly needed aught of him.
Where poverty and ignorance were rife,
He gave his bounty as he gave his life.

The place and cause that first aroused his might
Still proved its power until his latest day.
In Freedom's lists and for the aid of
Right Still in the foremost rank he waged the fray;
Wrong lived; his occupation was not gone.
He died in action with his armor on!

We weep for him, but we have touched his hand,
And felt the magic of his presence nigh,
The current that he sent throughout the land,
The kindling spirit of his battle-cry.
O'er all that holds us we shall triumph yet,
And place our banner where his hopes were set!

Oh, Douglass, thou hast passed beyond the shore,
But still thy voice is ringing o'er the gale!
Thou'st taught thy race how high her hopes may soar,
And bade her seek the heights, nor faint, nor fail.
She will not fail, she heeds thy stirring cry,
She knows thy guardian spirit will be nigh,
And, rising from beneath the chast'ning rod,
She stretches out her bleeding hands to God!

---

weal—*in Latin it means "to be strong;" republic or state; happiness or prosperity*

Desire
By Samuel Taylor Coleridge

Where true Love burns Desire is Love's pure flame;
It is the reflex of our earthly frame,
That takes its meaning from the nobler part,
And but translates the language of the heart.

How Do I Love Thee?
By Elizabeth Barret Browning

How do I love thee? Let me count the ways.
I love thee to the depth and breadth and height
My soul can reach, when feeling out of sight
For the ends of being and ideal grace.
I love thee to the level of every day's
Most quiet need, by sun and candle-light.
I love thee freely, as men strive for right.
I love thee purely, as they turn from praise.
I love thee with the passion put to use
In my old griefs, and with my childhood's faith.
I love thee with a love I seemed to lose
With my lost saints. I love thee with the breath,
Smiles, tears, of all my life; and, if God choose,
I shall but love thee better after death.

A Hymn to Love
By Robert Herrick

I will confess
With cheerfulness,
Love is a thing so likes me,
That, let her lay
On me all day,
I'll kiss the hand that strikes me.

I will not, I,
Now blubb'ring cry,
It, ah! too late repents me
That I did fall
To love at all,
Since love so much contents me.

No, no, I'll be
In fetters free;
While others they sit wringing
Their hands for pain,
I'll entertain
The wounds of love with singing.

With flowers and wine,
And cakes divine,
To strike me I will tempt thee;
Which done, no more
I'll come before
Thee and thine altars empty.

---

fetter—*anything that restrains or prevents something from moving; like chains around a person's hands or feet or ropes tied around an animal's limbs*

When You and I Grow Up
By Kate Greenaway

When you and I
Grow up Polly
I mean that you and me,
Shall go sailing in a big ship
Right over all the sea.
We'll wait till we are older,
For if we went to-day,
You know that we might lose ourselves,
And never find the way.

To Helen
By Edgar Allen Poe

Helen, thy beauty is to me
   Like those Nicean barks of yore,
That gently, o'er a perfumed sea,
   The weary, way-worn wanderer bore
   To his own native shore.

On desperate seas long wont to roam,
   Thy hyacinth hair, thy classic face,
Thy Naiad airs have brought me home
   To the glory that was Greece.
   And the grandeur that was Rome.

Lo! in yon brilliant window-niche
   How statue-like I see thee stand!
The agate lamp within thy hand,
   Ah, Psyche from the regions which
   Are Holy Land!

The Land of Counterpane
By Robert Louis Stevenson

When I was sick and lay a-bed,
I had two pillows at my head,
And all my toys beside me lay,
To keep me happy all the day.

And sometimes for an hour or so
I watched my leaden soldiers go,
With different uniforms and drills,
Among the bed-clothes, through the hills;

And sometimes sent my ships in fleets
All up and down among the sheets;
Or brought my trees and houses out,
And planted cities all about.

I was the giant great and still
That sits upon the pillow-hill,
And sees before him, dale and plain,
The pleasant land of counterpane.

_____

leaden—*heavy and unable to move, made of lead*

Retrospect
By Sir Arthur Conan Doyle

There is a better thing, dear heart,
Than youthful flush or girlish grace.
There is the faith that never fails,
The courage in the danger place,
The duty seen, and duty done,
The heart that yearns for all in need,
The lady soul which could not stoop
To selfish thought or lowly deed.
All that we ever dreamed, dear wife,
Seems drab and common by the truth,
The sweet sad mellow things of life
Are more than golden dreams of youth.

Faults

By Sara Teasdale

They came to tell your faults to me,
They named them over one by one;
I laughed aloud when they were done,
I knew them all so well before,—
Oh, they were blind, too blind to see
Your faults had made me love you more.

Faith

By Reagan Dregge

My stride
has stretched
and lengthened
–loosened–
reaching wide.
Faith, though little,
makes fruitful, not futile.
Winter is a bank of seeds
stored in the cool dark cellar;
slumber, the quiet of a snow-stilled field.

---

futile—*when something is useless, pointless, unable to produce anything*

Vivien's Song
By Alfred Lord Tennyson

'In Love, if Love be Love, if Love be ours,
Faith and unfaith can ne'er be equal powers:
Unfaith in aught is want of faith in all.
'It is the little rift within the lute,
That by and by will make the music mute,
And ever widening slowly silence all.
'The little rift within the lover's lute
Or little pitted speck in garnered fruit,
That rotting inward slowly moulders all.
'It is not worth the keeping: let it go:
But shall it? answer, darling, answer, no.
And trust me not at all or all in all'

---

rift—*when something is torn or split apart, a split in something*

Camilla
By Victor James Daley

Camilla calls me heartless: hence you see
Logic in love has little part.
How can I otherwise than heartless be
Seeing Camilla has my heart?

Cupid
By Ben Jonson

Beauties, have ye seen this toy,
Called love, a little boy
Almost naked, wanton, blind,
Cruel now, and then as kind?
If he be amongst ye, say!
He is Venus' runaway.

He hath of marks about him plenty;
Ye shall know him among twenty;
All his body is a fire,
And his breath a flame entire,
That, being shot like lightning in,
Wounds the heart, but not the skin.

He doth bear a golden bow,
And a quiver, hanging low,
Full of arrows, that outbrave
Dian's shafts, where, if he have
Any head more sharp than other,
With that first he strikes his mother.

Trust him not: his words, though sweet,
Seldom with his heart do meet;
All his practice is deceit,
Every gift is but a bait;
Not a kiss but poison bears,
And most treason in his tears.

If by these ye please to know him,
Beauties, be not nice, but show him,
Though ye had a will to hide him.
Now, we hope, ye'll not abide him,
Since ye hear his falser play,
And that he's Venus' runaway.

The Lady Who Offers Her Looking-Glass to Venus
By Mathew Prior

Venus, take my votive glass:
Since I am not what I was,
What from this day I shall be,
Venus, let me never see.

---

votive—*an item that is given to represent a vow fulfilled; this could be a medal, glass, or other object*

Sweethearts Wait on Every Shore
By Henry Lawson

She sits beside the tinted tide,
That's reddened by the tortured sand;
And through the East, to ocean wide,
A vessel sails from sight of land.

But she will wait and watch in vain,
For it is said in Cupid's lore,
That he who loved will love again,
And sweethearts wait on every shore.

The Answer
By John Frederick Freeman

O, my feet have worn a track
Deep and old in going back.
Thought released turns to its home
As bees through tangling thickets come.
One way of thought leads to the vast
Desert of the mind, and there is lost,
But backward leads to a dancing light
And myself there, stiff with delight.
O, well my thought has trodden a way
From this brief day to that long day

March

"Hope is the thing with feathers that perches in the soul And sings the tune
without the words And never stops at all."
—Emily Dickinson

Goosey, Goosey, Gander
By Anonymous
(English rhyme, original 1784 text)

Goose-a goose-a gander,
Where shall I wander?
Up stairs and down stairs,
In my lady's chamber;
There you'll find a cup of sack
And a race of ginger

Song of the Bell
By William Henry Giles Kingston
(translated from German)

Bell! thou soundest merrily,
When the bridal party
    To the church doth hie!
Bell! thou soundest solemnly,
When, on Sabbath morning,
    Fields deserted lie!

Bell! thou soundest merrily;
Tellest thou at evening,
    Bed-time draweth nigh!
Bell! thou soundest mournfully;
Tellest thou the bitter
    Parting hath gone by!

Say! how canst thou mourn?
How canst thou rejoice?
    Thou art but metal dull!
And yet all our sorrowings,
And all our rejoicings,
    Thou dost feed them all!

God hath wonders many,
Which we cannot fathom,
    Placed within thy form!
When the heart is sinking,
Thou alone canst raise it,
    Trembling in the storm!

Rosy, My Dear
By Louisa May Alcott

"Rosy, my dear,
Don't cry,--I'm here
To help you all I can.
I'm only a fly,
But you'll see that I
Will keep my word like a man."

A GOOD HUSBAND
By Robert Herrick

A Master of a house, as I have read,
Must be the first man up, and last in bed.
With the sun rising he must walk his grounds;
See this, view that, and all the other bounds:
Shut every gate; mend every hedge that's torn,
Either with old, or plant therein new thorn;
Tread o'er his glebe, but with such care, that where
He sets his foot, he leaves rich compost there.

_____

glebe—*land, soil, or earth*

Baby Mine
By Kate Greenaway

Baby mine, over the trees;
Baby mine, over the flowers;
Baby mine, over the sunshine;
Baby mine, over the showers.

Baby mine, over the land;
Baby mine, over the water.
Oh, when had a mother before
Such a sweet such a sweet, little daughter!

A Good Boy
By Robert Louis Stevenson

I woke before the morning, I was happy all the day,
I never said an ugly word, but smiled and stuck to play.

And now at last the sun is going down behind the wood,
And I am very happy, for I know that I've been good.

My bed is waiting cool and fresh, with linen smooth and fair,
And I must be off to sleepsin-by, and not forget my prayer.

I know that, till to-morrow I shall see the sun arise,
No ugly dream shall fright my mind, no ugly sight my eyes.

But slumber hold me tightly till I waken in the dawn,
And hear the thrushes singing in the lilacs round the lawn.

A Minor Bird
By Robert Frost

I have wished a bird would fly away,
And not sing by my house all day;

Have clapped my hands at him from the door
When it seemed as if I could bear no more.

The fault must partly have been in me.
The bird was not to blame for his key.

And of course there must be something wrong
In wanting to silence any song.

The Belated Swallow
By Mary Hannay Foott

The Belated Swallow.
"And the birds of the air have nests."
Belated swallow, whither flying?
The day is dead, the light is dying,
The night draws near:
Where is thy nest, slow put together,
Soft-lined with moss and downy feather,
For shelter-place in stress of weather
And darkness drear?
Past, past, above the lighted city,
Unknowing of my wondering pity,
Seaward she flies.
Alas, poor bird! what rude awaking
Has driven thee forth, when storms are breaking,
And frightened gulls the waves forsaking
With warning cries?
Alas, my soul! while leaves are greenest
Thy heedless head thou fondly screenest
Beneath thy wing.
How bravely thou thy plumage wearest,—
How lightly thou life's burthen bearest,—
How happily thy home preparest,—
In careless spring!
Yet Destiny the hour may bring thee
When none of all that sing can sing thee
To joy or rest!
When all the winds that blow shall blow thee;
And, ere the floods shall overflow thee,
The sunlight linger but to show thee
Thy shattered nest!

The Martyr Tree
By Henry Parkes

RIGHT through its heart the fire's red teeth
Had gnaw'd and torn their cinderous way;
The sap still mounted from beneath,
Its tortured ribs to bind and stay.
And there the grand old tree remains,
In garniture of glistening leaves,
Rejoicing in the winds and rains;
But o'er the past it never grieves.
And still it rears its martyr form,
And still it wears its crown of green,
And still it braves the thunder-storm,
Though through its heart the fire has been.

---

cinderous—*another word used to refer to a hot coal or cinder*
garniture—*a set or collection embellishment or decorations on something*

Quarantine
By Lily Martinez

After all this time
Years spent in solitude
My youth spent wishing
To be a part of life
At last I'm ready
To freely join the world
Live life with others
Thrive under the bright sun
Savor new freedom
But now we're all alone
Held captive by fear
All know my suffering
All now share my pain
How I have endured life
Up until this point
With an intimate grasp
Of being alone

The Lion and the Unicorn
Anonymous (English rhyme)

The lion and the unicorn
Were fighting for the crown
The lion beat the unicorn
All around the town.
Some gave them white bread,
And some gave them brown;
Some gave them plum cake
and drummed them out of town.
And when he had beat him out,
He beat him in again;
He beat him three times over,
His power to maintain.

Speak of the North! A Lonely Moor
By Charlotte Brontë

Speak of the North! A lonely moor
Silent and dark and tractless swells,
The waves of some wild streamlet pour
Hurriedly through its ferny dells.

Profoundly still the twilight air,
Lifeless the landscape; so we deem
Till like a phantom gliding near
A stag bends down to drink the stream.

And far away a mountain zone,
A cold, white waste of snow-drifts lies,
And one star, large and soft and lone,
Silently lights the unclouded skies.

A Day
By Emily Dickinson

I'll tell you how the sun rose, —
A ribbon at a time.
The steeples swam in amethyst,
The news like squirrels ran.

The hills untied their bonnets,
The bobolinks begun.
Then I said softly to myself,
"That must have been the sun!"

But how he set, I know not.
There seemed a purple stile
Which little yellow boys and girls
Were climbing all the while

Till when they reached the other side,
A dominie in gray
Put gently up the evening bars,
And led the flock away.

_____

bobolink—*a small black and white bird with half of its head being yellow, also referred to as the "rice bird" and is found in North and Central America*
stile—*alternate spelling of the word style or can be referring to a set of stairs or steps*
dominie—*in Scotland it means schoolmaster and in the USA it means clergyman*

The Wound
By Thomas Hardy

I climbed to the crest,
    And, fog-festooned,
The sun lay west
    Like a crimson wound:

Like that wound of mine
    Of which none knew,
For I'd given no sign
    That it pierced me through.

---

festoon—*a garland or decoration that is hung with a sagging center, sometimes with its ends hanging down loose; it can also be a carved decoration representing a wreath that could include fruits, flowers, and leaves*

Nessie
By Reagan Dregge

The Loch Ness Monster's
shape was born
In shadow-shrouded chasms
Long thought to haunt the
misty deeps
Of cold and lightless fathoms
Some say she is a
fairy beast
A figment spun from tales
While others claim a
dinosaur
Or remnant kin of whales
Myths multiply and
theories mount
But just the other day
I watched her swallow
up the sun
Then wink and float away!

---

fathom—*a measurement of depth, deep thought*

What Are Heavy?
By Christina Rossetti

What are heavy? Sea-sand and sorrow;
What are brief? Today and tomorrow;
What are frail? Spring blossoms and youth;
What are deep? The ocean and truth.

The Lake Isle of Innisfree
By W. B. Yeats

I will arise and go now, and go to Innisfree,
And a small cabin build there, of clay and wattles made:
Nine bean-rows will I have there, a hive for the honey-bee;
And live alone in the bee-loud glade.
And I shall have some peace there, for peace comes dropping slow,
Dropping from the veils of the morning to where the cricket sings;
There midnight's all a glimmer, and noon a purple glow,
And evening full of the linnet's wings.
I will arise and go now, for always night and day
I hear lake water lapping with low sounds by the shore;
While I stand on the roadway, or on the pavements grey,
I hear it in the deep heart's core.

---

wattle—*in Latin it means shoot; it is a flexible stick or twig, a collection of sticks that are woven among each other; a stick used for supporting a thatched roof; to use twigs to bind something*
linnet—*a small bird from the finch family; found all over Europe and many bordering countries and continents; it is brown and grey with a red forehead and chest*

Our Australian Land
By J. Sheridan Moore

YOUNG and fresh, and wondrous rich,
Our Land before us lies;
A glorious gift of Providence
To prize, as freemen prize:
Oh, while the sun's auspicious rays
In our blue heavens shine,
With hearts as warm we'll thank thee, God,
For this great boon of Thine!
A bulwark wall around our coast,
Which seas have not effaced—
To guard us from all outward foes,
Thy sovran hand hath placed.
And there are strongholds, too, within—
And there are ramparts good—
The union of stout-hearted men—
The rights of nationhood.
Our Land is fair—her skies are bright—
Her heart is made of gold;
And all the wonders of her wealth
Time only can unfold.
And, therefore, 'tis our duty clear
To work right manfully,
That brighter, purer, ampler far
Her moral realm may be.
Then, like the native tree that sheds
Its rugged bark, we'll try
To cast each year some fault away—
Some harsh deformity.
And, like the faithful evergreens
That fringe our golden plains,
Perennial let our virtues live,
Whatever season reigns.
O Star of Peace, around us shed
Thy tender, placid light:
Inspire our hearts—illume our minds—
And keep them sound and bright!
O Sun of Freedom, 'mid our gloom,
In holiest glory rise,
To purify Australian hearts—
To light Australian skies!

auspicious—*to be favorable, having promise, prosperous, signs of success.*

boon—*can mean a gift or present, a prayer, or can also mean kind*

bulwark—an earthen wall, rampart, or fortification that is able to withstand cannon fire or stand up to enemy attack

efface—to remove a mark from the surface of something, to be worn out.

A Red, Red Rose
By Robert Burns

O my Luve's like a red, red rose,
That's newly sprung in June;
O my Luve's like the melodie
That's sweetly play'd in tune.
As fair are thou, my bonie lass,
So deep in luve am I;
And I will luve thee still, my Dear,
Till a' the seas gang dry.
Till a' the seas gang dry, my Dear,
And the rocks melt wi' the sun:
I will luve thee still, my dear,
While the sands o' life shall run.
And fare thee weel, my only Luve!
And fare thee weel, a while!
And I will come again, my Luve,
Tho' it were ten thousand mile!

Break, Break, Break
By Alfred Lord Tennyson

Break, break, break,
On thy cold gray stones, O sea!
And I would that my tongue could utter
The thoughts that arise in me.
O, well for the fisherman's boy,
That he shouts with his sister at play!
O, well for the sailor lad,
That he sings in his boat on the bay!
And the stately ships go on
To their haven under the hill;
But O for the touch of a vanished hand,
And the sound of a voice that is still!
Break, break, break,
At the foot of thy crags, O sea!
But the tender grace of a day that is dead
Will never come back to me.

I Travelled among Unknown Men
By William Wordsworth

I travelled among unknown men,
In lands beyond the sea;
Nor, England! did I know till then
What love I bore to thee.

'Tis past, that melancholy dream!
Nor will I quit thy shore
A second time; for still I seem
To love thee more and more.

Among thy mountains did I feel
The joy of my desire;
And she I cherished turned her wheel
Beside an English fire.

Thy mornings showed, thy nights concealed,
The bowers where Lucy played;
And thine too is the last green field
That Lucy's eyes surveyed.

Italia
By Oscar Wilde

Italia! thou art fallen, though with sheen
Of battle-spears thy clamorous armies stride
From the north Alps to the Sicilian tide!
Ay! fallen, though the nations hail thee Queen
Because rich gold in every town is seen,
And on thy sapphire-lake in tossing pride
Of wind-filled vans thy myriad galleys ride
Beneath one flag of red and white and green.
O Fair and Strong! O Strong and Fair in vain!
Look southward where Rome's desecrated town
Lies mourning for her God-anointed King!
Look heaven-ward! shall God allow this thing?
Nay! but some flame-girt Raphael shall come down,
And smite the Spoiler with the sword of pain.

In a Library
By Emily Dickinson

A precious, mouldering pleasure 't is
To meet an antique book,
In just the dress his century wore;
A privilege, I think,
His venerable hand to take,
And warming in our own,
A passage back, or two, to make
To times when he was young.
His quaint opinions to inspect,
His knowledge to unfold
On what concerns our mutual mind,
The literature of old;
What interested scholars most,
What competitions ran
When Plato was a certainty,
And Sophocles a man;
When Sappho was a living girl,
And Beatrice wore
The gown that Dante deified.
Facts, centuries before,
He traverses familiar,
As one should come to town
And tell you all your dreams were true:
He lived where dreams were sown.
His presence is enchantment,
You beg him not to go;
Old volumes shake their vellum heads
And tantalize, just so.

A World Beyond
By Bowditch, Nathaniel Ingersoll

SCIENCE long watched the realms of space,
A planet's devious path to trace:
Convinced of heaven's harmonious law,
"A World beyond" Leverrier saw.

Thus when he views earth's sins and woes,
With a like faith the Christian knows
There is a world beyond, to prove
God's perfect wisdom, power, and love.

Vignette

By J. Sheridan Moore

IN the shining day—
In the shadowy night—
On his quiet way—
'Mid the world's fierce strife—
Where the flowers bloom—
Where the forests fade—
When his soul's in gloom—
When in light arrayed—
The Poet, to his instinct true,
Sings:— 'TIS THE WORK HE IS CALLED TO DO.

My Kingdom
By Louisa May Alcott

A little kingdom I possess
where thoughts and feelings dwell,
And very hard I find the task
of governing it well;
For passion tempts and troubles me,
A wayward will misleads,
And selfishness its shadow casts
On all my words and deeds.

How can I learn to rule myself,
To be the child I should,
Honest and brave, nor ever tire
Of trying to be good?
How can I keep a sunny soul
To shine along life's way?
How can I tune my little heart
To sweetly sing all day?

Dear Father, help me with the love
That casteth out my fear;
Teach me to lean on thee,
and feel That thou art very near,
That no temptation is unseen
No childish grief too small,
Since thou, with patience infinite,
Doth soothe and comfort all.

I do not ask for any crown
But that which all may win
Nor seek to conquer any world
Except the one within.
Be thou my guide until I find,
Led by a tender hand,
Thy happy kingdom in myself
And dare to take command.

April

"Clouds come floating into my life, no longer to carry rain or
usher storm, but to add color to my sunset sky."
—Rabindranath Tagore

April
By Sara Teasdale

The roofs are shining from the rain,
The sparrows twitter as they fly,
And with a windy April grace
The little clouds go by.

Yet the back-yards are bare and brown
With only one unchanging tree
I could not be so sure of spring
Save that it sings in me.

In April
By Rainer Maria Rilke
Translated By Jessie Lemont

Again the woods are odorous, the lark
Lifts on upsoaring wings the heaven gray
That hung above the tree-tops, veiled and dark,
Where branches bare disclosed the empty day.

After long rainy afternoons an hour
Comes with its shafts of golden light and flings
Them at the windows in a radiant shower,
And rain drops beat the panes like timorous wings.

Then all is still. The stones are crooned to sleep
By the soft sound of rain that slowly dies;
And cradled in the branches, hidden deep
In each bright bud, a slumbering silence lies.

---

odorous—*when something has a sweet fragrant scent*
timorous—*void of courage, scared of danger, nervousness*
croon—*to sing, say or hum something in a low soft voice*

Spring
By Gerard Manley Hopkins

Nothing is so beautiful as spring—
When weeds, in wheels, shoot long and lovely and lush;
Thrush's eggs look little low heavens, and thrush
Through the echoing timber does so rinse and wring
The ear, it strikes like lightnings to hear him sing;
The glassy peartree leaves and blooms, they brush
The descending blue; that blue is all in a rush
With richness; the racing lambs too have fair their fling.
What is all this juice and all this joy?
A strain of the earth's sweet being in the beginning
In Eden garden.—Have, get, before it cloy,
Before it cloud, Christ, lord, and sour with sinning,
Innocent mind and Mayday in girl and boy,
Most, O maid's child, thy choice and worthy the winning.

Nothing Gold Can Stay
By Robert Frost

Nature's first green is gold,
Her hardest hue to hold.
Her early leaf's a flower;
But only so an hour.
Then leaf subsides to leaf.
So Eden sank to grief,
So dawn goes down to day.
Nothing gold can stay.

Earth
By Joseph B. Soldano

How beautiful the Earth, water, and sky.
Where birds and clouds roam so high.
The sun beams down with rays so sweet.
On mounds of rye, clover, and wheat.
The moon at night casts it's glow.
The tides run silent, but swiftly flow.
Life is delicate, and who knows best,
Planet earth, our mother's nest.

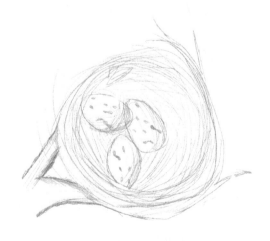

The Caterpillar
By Robert Graves

Under this loop of honeysuckle,
A creeping, coloured caterpillar,
I gnaw the fresh green hawthorn spray,
I nibble it leaf by leaf away.

Down beneath grow dandelions,
Daisies, old-man's-looking-glasses;
Rooks flap croaking across the lane.
I eat and swallow and eat again.

Here come raindrops helter-skelter;
I munch and nibble unregarding:
Hawthorn leaves are juicy and firm.
I'll mind my business: I'm a good worm.

When I'm old, tired, melancholy,
I'll build a leaf-green mausoleum
Close by, here on this lovely spray,
And die and dream the ages away.

Some say worms win resurrection,
With white wings beating flitter-flutter,
But wings or a sound sleep, why should I care?
Either way I'll miss my share.

Under this loop of honeysuckle,
A hungry, hairy caterpillar,
I crawl on my high and swinging seat,
And eat, eat, eat—as one ought to eat.

----

spray—*a small shoot extending from a branch; small particles of water that leaves a wave and floats around in the air*

The Yellow Violet
By William Cullen Bryant

When beechen buds begin to swell,
And woods the blue-bird's warble know,
The yellow violet's modest bell
Peeps from the last year's leaves below.

Ere russet fields their green resume,
Sweet flower, I love, in forest bare,
To meet thee, when thy faint perfume
Alone is in the virgin air.

Of all her train, the hands of Spring
First plant thee in the watery mould,
And I have seen thee blossoming
Beside the snow-bank's edges cold.

Thy parent sun, who bade thee view
Pale skies, and chilling moisture sip,
Has bathed thee in his own bright hue,
And streaked with jet thy glowing lip.

Yet slight thy form, and low thy seat,
And earthward bent thy gentle eye,
Unapt the passing view to meet
When loftier flowers are flaunting nigh.

Oft, in the sunless April day,
Thy early smile has stayed my walk;
But midst the gorgeous blooms of May,
I passed thee on thy humble stalk.

So they, who climb to wealth, forget
The friends in darker fortunes tried.
I copied them—but I regret
That I should ape the ways of pride.

And when again the genial hour
Awakes the painted tribes of light,
I'll not o'erlook the modest flower
That made the woods of April bright.

---

beechen—*something belonging to the beech tree.* unapt—not ready or unprepared
mould—*another spelling of mold, but the term "water mould" refers to a specific organism
(Oomycetes) that looks like a fungi* nigh—something is near, happening soon
bade—*to ask or order someone, the past tense of bid.* ape—to mimic or imitate something

Flower Salute
By Johann Wolfgang von Goethe

This nosegay, 'twas I dress'd it,

Greets thee a thousand times!
Oft stoop'd I, and caress'd it,

Ah! full a thousand times,
And 'gainst my bosom press'd it

A hundred thousand times!

_____

Nosegay—*a small bundle of flowers*

Field Path
By John Clare

The beams in blossom with their spots of jet
Smelt sweet as gardens wheresoever met;
The level meadow grass was in the swath;
The hedge briar rose hung right across the path,
White over with its flowers--the grass that lay
Bleaching beneath the twittering heat to hay
Smelt so deliciously, the puzzled bee
Went wondering where the honey sweets could be;
And passer-bye along the level rows
Stoopt down and whipt a bit beneath his nose

_____

swath—*an area or row grass or grain cut by a scythe or lawn mower*

I Wandered Lonely as a Cloud
By William Wordsworth

I wandered lonely as a cloud
That floats on high o'er vales and hills,
When all at once I saw a crowd,
A host, of golden daffodils;
Beside the lake, beneath the trees,
Fluttering and dancing in the breeze.

Continuous as the stars that shine
And twinkle on the milky way,
They stretched in never-ending line
Along the margin of a bay:
Ten thousand saw I at a glance,
Tossing their heads in sprightly dance.

The waves beside them danced; but they
Out-did the sparkling waves in glee:
A poet could not but be gay,
In such a jocund company:
I gazed—and gazed—but little thought
What wealth the show to me had brought:

For oft, when on my couch I lie
In vacant or in pensive mood,
They flash upon that inward eye
Which is the bliss of solitude;
And then my heart with pleasure fills,
And dances with the daffodils.

Jocund—*lively, happy, airy, comes from the latin word jocus/jocundus meaning joke*

The Echoing Green
By William Blake

The sun does arise,
And make happy the skies.
The merry bells ring
To welcome the Spring.
The sky-lark and thrush,
The birds of the bush,
Sing louder around,
To the bells' cheerful sound.
While our sports shall be seen
On the Echoing Green.

Old John, with white hair
Does laugh away care,
Sitting under the oak,
Among the old folk,
They laugh at our play,
And soon they all say.
'Such, such were the joys.
When we all girls & boys,
In our youth-time were seen,
On the Echoing Green.'

Till the little ones weary
No more can be merry
The sun does descend,
And our sports have an end:
Round the laps of their mothers,
Many sisters and brothers,
Like birds in their nest,
Are ready for rest;
And sport no more seen,
On the darkening Green.

The Rainy Day
By Henry Wadsworth Longfellow

The day is cold, and dark, and dreary
It rains, and the wind is never weary;
The vine still clings to the mouldering wall,
But at every gust the dead leaves fall,
　　And the day is dark and dreary.

My life is cold, and dark, and dreary;
It rains, and the wind is never weary;
My thoughts still cling to the mouldering Past,
But the hopes of youth fall thick in the blast,
　　And the days are dark and dreary.

Be still, sad heart! and cease repining;
Behind the clouds is the sun still shining;
Thy fate is the common fate of all,
Into each life some rain must fall,
　　Some days must be dark and dreary.

---

mouldering—*when something is decaying, crumbling, or turning to dust*
repining—*not being content with oneself; complaining or fretting*

He Is Coming
By Kathryn Nielson

When the sky is dark,
And the thunder claps.
He is coming.

When the trees tremble,
And the earth quakes.
He is coming.

When the wind whirls,
And the rain falls.
He is coming.

When the rain stops falling,
And the earth stops quaking.
He has come.

Lines Written in Early Spring
By William Wordsworth

I heard a thousand blended notes,
While in a grove I sate reclined,
In that sweet mood when pleasant thoughts
Bring sad thoughts to the mind.

To her fair works did Nature link
The human soul that through me ran;
And much it grieved my heart to think
What man has made of man.

Through primrose tufts, in that green bower,
The periwinkle trailed its wreaths;
And 'tis my faith that every flower
Enjoys the air it breathes.

The birds around me hopped and played,
Their thoughts I cannot measure:—
But the least motion which they made
It seemed a thrill of pleasure.

The budding twigs spread out their fan,
To catch the breezy air;
And I must think, do all I can,
That there was pleasure there.

If this belief from heaven be sent,
If such be Nature's holy plan,
Have I not reason to lament
What man has made of man?

---

sate—*to be satisfied, to be full or stuffed*

A Musical Instrument
By Elizabeth Barrett Browning

WHAT was he doing, the great god Pan,
Down in the reeds by the river ?
Spreading ruin and scattering ban,
Splashing and paddling with hoofs of a goat,
And breaking the golden lilies afloat
With the dragon-fly on the river.

He tore out a reed, the great god Pan,
From the deep cool bed of the river :
The limpid water turbidly ran,
And the broken lilies a-dying lay,
And the dragon-fly had fled away,
Ere he brought it out of the river.

High on the shore sate the great god Pan,
While turbidly flowed the river ;
And hacked and hewed as a great god can,
With his hard bleak steel at the patient reed,
Till there was not a sign of a leaf indeed
To prove it fresh from the river.

He cut it short, did the great god Pan,
(How tall it stood in the river !)
Then drew the pith, like the heart of a man,
Steadily from the outside ring,
And notched the poor dry empty thing
In holes, as he sate by the river.

This is the way,' laughed the great god Pan,
Laughed while he sate by the river,)
The only way, since gods began
To make sweet music, they could succeed.'
Then, dropping his mouth to a hole in the reed,
He blew in power by the river.

Sweet, sweet, sweet, O Pan !
Piercing sweet by the river !
Blinding sweet, O great god Pan !
The sun on the hill forgot to die,
And the lilies revived, and the dragon-fly
Came back to dream on the river.

Yet half a beast is the great god Pan,
To laugh as he sits by the river,
Making a poet out of a man :

The true gods sigh for the cost and pain, —
For the reed which grows nevermore again
As a reed with the reeds in the river.

---

ban—*a curse or something that has been prohibited*
turbidly—*haughtily or proudly*
sate—*to be satisfied, to be full or stuffed*
hewed—*made smooth by cutting*
pith—*the soft inside of a plant or tree that is spongy*

An Ancient Pond!
By Matsuo Basho
Translated By William George Aston

An ancient pond!
With a sound from the water
Of the frog as it plunges in.

Alma Mater
By Niccole Perrine

Dewdrop pearls standing on a leaf,
Morning sunrise, brisk and brief.
Birdsong chorus greets the day,
Cows are lowing near the hay.

Sleepy moon blinks to see bright sun,
Cocks crow aloud: "This day's begun!"
Tulips open to cerulean sky,
Impudent squirrels streak nearby.

Brooks babble amid tall trees,
"Humm-drumm" buzz busy bees.
Mama kneads dough with a sigh,
Papa fastens a plow nearby.

The children dress and wash and comb,
Their chatter makes their house a home.
Their impish faces are filled with cheer,
As they tease and laugh for all to hear.

The day is new, the night is gone,
We sing a fresh, brand-new song.
Morning hasn't broken, she's freshly cast,
Nature's in session: Spring's first in her class.

---

cerulean—*A deep blue colored sky*
impudent—*acting boldly with little thought of others*
impish—*mischievous, doing naughty things for fun*

Cecily Parsley
By Beatrix Potter

Cecily Parsley
lived in a pen,
And brewed good ale
for gentlemen;

GENTLEMEN came
every day,
Till Cecily Parsley
ran away.

---

ale—*an alcoholic drink similar to beer*

Extremes
By James Whitcomb Riley

I

      A little boy once played so loud
      That the Thunder, up in a thunder-cloud,
      Said, "Since I can't be heard, why, then
      I'll never, never thunder again!"

II

      And a little girl once kept so still
      That she heard a fly on the window-sill
      Whisper and say to a lady-bird, -
      "She's the stilliest child I ever heard!"

My Sweet Little Sister
By Caden Gagnon

My sweet little sister,
As sweet as can be,
As sweet as honey,
Under a maple tree.

My sweet little sister,
Playing in the woods,
Singing and dancing,
With pretty red hoods.

Playing in the river,
Climbing lots of trees,
And sitting on a rock,
With a nice, warm breeze.

Every day and all day,
Singing,
Dancing,
Jumping,
Prancing,
The day and night away.

Every day and all day having great fun,
That's my sweet little sister everyone!

Willie Winkie
By William Miller

Wee Willie Winkie runs through the town,
Up stairs and down stairs in his night-gown,
Tapping at the window, crying at the lock,
Are the children in their bed, for it's past ten o'clock?

Hey, Willie Winkie, are you coming in?
The cat is singing purring sounds to the sleeping hen,
The dog's spread out on the floor, and doesn't give a cheep,
But here's a wakeful little boy who will not fall asleep!

Anything but sleep, you rogue! glowering like the moon,'
Rattling in an iron jug with an iron spoon,
Rumbling, tumbling round about, crowing like a cock,
Shrieking like I don't know what, waking sleeping folk.

Hey, Willie Winkie – the child's in a creel!
Wriggling from everyone's knee like an eel,
Tugging at the cat's ear, and confusing all her thrums
Hey, Willie Winkie – see, there he comes!"

Weary is the mother who has a dusty child,
A small short sturdy child, who can't run on his own,
Who always has a battle with sleep before he'll close an eye
But a kiss from his rosy lips gives strength anew to me

Creel—*a basket for holding fish*
thrum—*to strum an instrument, the end of a thread*
cock—*rooster*

Nonsenses – i
Edward Lear

There was an Old Man with a beard,
Who said, "It is just as I feared!-
Two owls and a hen,
Four larks and a wren,
Have all built their nests in my beard!"

First Arrivals
By Kate Greenaway

It is a Party, do you know,
And there they sit, all in a row,
Waiting till the others come,
To begin to have some fun.

Hark! the bell rings sharp and clear,
Other little friends appear;
And no longer all alone
They begin to feel at home.

To them a little hard is Fate,
Yet better early than too late;
Fancy getting there forlorn,
With the tea and cake all gone.

Wonder what they'll have for tea;
Hope the jam is strawberry.
Wonder what the dance and game;
Feel so very glad they came.

Very Happy may you be,
May you much enjoy your tea.

----

forlorn—*lonely or deprived*

The Weekly Mail
By Emily Mary Barton

A CHEERY note the horn is ringing,
Scarlet glimmers through the trees:
What may not the post be bringing
From our friends beyond the seas?
Yesterday the Orizona
Glided safely to the quay:
Did the bulky bags upon her
Hold a line for you or me?
You would like a foreign letter
In a neat Italian hand:
British stamps would please me better,
Tidings from the dear old land.
Mother's hopes that seldom fail her,
Stretch from Egypt to Japan,
For she knows her absent sailor
"Flies his kite" whene'er he can.
Father's wishes, sad and sober,
To a circular extend:
He wants to know if mines at Cobar
Mean to pay a dividend.
Shall we spike the wheel of fortune,
Shall we rush upon our fate?
Or with boding of misfortune
Meekly for our portion wait?
Now, from leathern wallet drawing,
Who shall make the lucky hit?
"Nay, my girls, no clapper-clawing,
Wait till I can empty it."
"There, that's all: there's not another."
Really now 'tis very hard:
Bills for father, stamps for mother,
And for me a Christmas card!!!

---

quay— *a wharf or structure onto which one secures a boat or ship*

The Dumb Soldier
By Robert Louis Stevenson

When the grass was closely mown,
Walking on the lawn alone,
In the turf a hole I found,
And hid a soldier underground.

Spring and daisies came apace;
Grasses hid my hiding place;
Grasses run like a green sea
O'er the lawn up to my knee.

Under grass alone he lies,
Looking up with leaden eyes,
Scarlet coat and pointed gun,
To the stars and to the sun.

When the grass is ripe like grain,
When the scythe is stoned again,
When the lawn is shaven clear,
Then my hole shall reappear.

I shall find him, never fear,
I shall find my grenadier;
But for all that's gone and come,
I shall find my soldier dumb.

He has lived, a little thing,
In the grassy woods of spring;
Done, if he could tell me true,
Just as I should like to do.

He has seen the starry hours
And the springing of the flowers;
And the fairy things that pass
In the forests of the grass.

In the silence he has heard
Talking bee and ladybird,
And the butterfly has flown
O'er him as he lay alone.

Not a word will he disclose,
Not a word of all he knows.
I must lay him on the shelf,
And make up the tale myself.

leaden—*heavy and unable to move, made of lead*
scythe—*a tool for cutting grass or grain*
grenadier—*a foot soldier*
dumb—*unable to speak*

May

"Rather than love, than money, than fame, give me truth."
—Henry David Thoreau

Daffodowndilly
By A. A. Milne

She wore her yellow sun-bonnet,
She wore her greenest gown;
She turned to the south wind
And curtsied up and down.
She turned to the sunlight
And shook her yellow head,
And whispered to her neighbour:
"Winter is dead."

The Fairies
By William Allingham

Up the airy mountain,
Down the rushy glen,
We darent go a-hunting
For fear of little men;
Wee folk, good folk,
Trooping all together;
Green jacket, red cap,
And white owls feather!

Down along the rocky shore
Some make their home,
They live on crispy pancakes
Of yellow tide-foam;
Some in the reeds
Of the black mountain lake,
With frogs for their watch-dogs,
All night awake

The First of May
By Caroline W Leakey

SCARCE had the dewy lips of morn
Breathed incense on sweet May new-born,
Than from a thousand fragrant bowers
Slily peeped forth the long-pent flowers,
And from a thousand trees along
Gushed out a stream of liquid song,
To welcome in the fairest day
Of joyous Nature's holiday;
And in the fields and lanes around,
A pleasant tramp and cheering sound
Of little feet and voices free,
Of children, in their hottest glee;
Of dark-eyed boy and tiny lass,
So early on the spangled grass,
And shouting, each one with his might.
WHY feeling such a strange delight,
If you should ask, not one could say,
Save, "Oh, it is the first of May!"

---

bowers—*shaded covering under a tree caused by branches*
spangle—*to glisten or shine, to be decorated in with small, shiny details*

We Have a Little Garden
By Beatrix Potter

We have a little garden,
A garden of our own,
And every day we water there
The seeds that we have sown.
We love our little garden,
And tend it with such care,
You will not find a faded leaf
Or blighted blossom there.

---

blighted—*disease happening to a plant, to stop growth, to frustrate, to be blasted*

Results
By Thelma Arlene DeGroff Field

The wind has blown,
At last twas spring
Tempted were the seeds to bring
Forth into the waiting seed
A shoot, a sprout, a bud begun.
With curious patience, loving care
I waited for a garden rare.
Tending to it's wants and needs
At last a harvest!
Alas just seeds.

A Seed I Sow
By Cayden Shepherd

A seed I sow,
I give it a shower.
A seed I grow,
Up comes a flower.
First autumn, then winter,
The flower dies.
But there in the center,
Another seed lies.

Late Spring
By Han Yu

The plants all know that spring will soon return,
All kinds of red and purple contend in beauty.
The poplar blossom and elm seeds are not beautiful,
They can only fill the sky with flight like snow

———————————————
contend—*to preserve or really try to gain something, to push against or oppose something*

Trees
By Sara Coldridge

The Oak is called the King of trees,
The Aspen quivers in the breeze,
The Poplar grows up straight and tall,
The Peach tree spreads along the wall,
The Sycamore gives pleasant shade,
The Willow droops in watery Glade,
The Fir tree useful timber gives,
The Beech amid the forest lives.

---

quiver—*shake*

The Hawthorn
By Victor James Daley

By the road, near her father's dwelling,
There groweth a hawthorn tree:
Its blossoms are fair and fragrant
As the love that I cast from me.

It is all a-bloom this morning
In the sunny silentness,
And grows by the roadside, radiant
As a bride in her bridal dress.

But ah me! at sight of its blossoms
No pleasant memories start:
I see but the thorns beneath them,
And the thorns they pierce my heart.

Apple Blossoms
By Horatio Algar Jr.

I sit in the shadow of apple-boughs,
In the fragrant orchard close,
And around me floats the scented air,
With its wave-like tidal flows.
I close my eyes in a dreamy bliss,
And call no king my peer;
For is not this the rare, sweet time,
The blossoming time of the year?

I lie on a couch of downy grass,
With delicate blossoms strewn,
And I feel the throb of Nature's heart
Responsive to my own.
Oh, the world is fair, and God is good,
That maketh life so dear;
For is not this the rare, sweet time,
The blossoming time of the year?

I can see, through the rifts of the apple-boughs,
The delicate blue of the sky,
And the changing clouds with their marvellous tints
That drift so lazily by.
And strange, sweet thoughts sing through my brain,
And Heaven, it seemeth near;
Oh, is it not a rare, sweet time,
The blossoming time of the year?

---

boughs—*branches of a tree (but not shoots of a tree)*
rift—*a split in something*

Nature
Henry David Thoreau

O Nature! I do not aspire
To be the highest in thy quire,—
To be a meteor in the sky,
Or comet that may range on high;
Only a zephyr that may blow
Among the reeds by the river low;
Give me thy most privy place
Where to run my airy race.
In some withdrawn, unpublic mead
Let me sigh upon a reed,
Or in the woods, with leafy din,
Whisper the still evening in:
Some still work give me to do,—
Only—be it near to you!
For I'd rather be thy child
And pupil, in the forest wild,
Than be the king of men elsewhere,
And most sovereign slave of care:
To have one moment of thy dawn,
Than share the city's year forlorn.

_____

quire—*another spelling of choir*
zephyr—*a breeze or light wind*
privy—*private*
mead—*in Latin it means "to be wet;" it is also an alcoholic drink made from honey and water; in England there is also a geographical area north of Oxford, England called Sunnymead*
din—*loud noise*
sovereign—*someone who is a ruler or most powerful*
forlorn—*sad and lonely, deprived*

To My Mother
By Edgar Allen Poe

Because I feel that, in the Heavens above,
The angels, whispering to one another,
Can find, among their burning terms of love,
None so devotional as that of "Mother,"
Therefore by that dear name I long have called you—
You who are more than mother unto me,
And fill my heart of hearts, where Death installed you
In setting my Virginia's spirit free.
My mother—my own mother, who died early,
Was but the mother of myself; but you
Are mother to the one I loved so dearly,
And thus are dearer than the mother I knew
By that infinity with which my wife
Was dearer to my soul than its soul-life.

Lines on a Sleeping Infant
By William Cowper

Sweet babe! whose image here express'd
Does thy peaceful slumbers show;
Guilt or fear, to break thy rest,
Never did thy spirit know.

Soothing slumbers! soft repose,
Such as mock the painter's skill,
Such as innocence bestows,
Harmless infant! lull thee still.

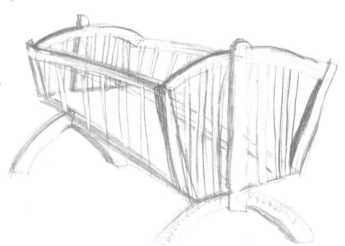

----

repose—*to lay down and rest*
lull—*to be still or calm*

Little Girls and Little Lambs
By Kate Greenaway

In the May-time flowers grow;
Little girls in meadows go;
Little lambs frisk with delight,
And in the green grass sleep at night.
Little birds sing all the day,
Oh, in such a happy way!
All the day the sun is bright,
Little stars shine all the night.
The Cowslip says to the Primrose,
"How soft the little Spring wind blows!"
The Daisy and the Buttercup
Sing every time that they look up.
For beneath the sweet blue sky
They see a pretty Butterfly;
The Butterfly, when he looks down,
Says, "What a pretty Flower Town!"

I Write about the Butterfly
By Louisa May Alcott

"I write about the butterfly,
It is a pretty thing;
And flies about like the birds,
But it does not sing.

"First it is a little grub,
And then it is a nice yellow cocoon,
And then the butterfly
Eats its way out soon.

"They live on dew and honey,
They do not have any hive,
They do not sting like wasps, and bees, and hornets,
And to be as good as they are we should strive.

Upon the Swallow
By Robert Herrick

This pretty bird, oh, how she flies and sings!
But could she do so if she had not wings?
Her wings bespeak my faith, her songs my peace;
When I believe and sing, my doubtings cease.

---

bespeak—*to speak of before; foretell*

Spring Night
By Sara Teasdale

The park is filled with night and fog,
The veils are drawn about the world,
The drowsy lights along the paths
Are dim and pearled.

Gold and gleaming the empty streets,
Gold and gleaming the misty lake,
The mirrored lights like sunken swords,
Glimmer and shake.

Oh, is it not enough to be
Here with this beauty over me?
My throat should ache with praise, and I
Should kneel in joy beneath the sky.
O, beauty, are you not enough?
Why am I crying after love,
With youth, a singing voice, and eyes
To take earth's wonder with surprise?

Why have I put off my pride,
Why am I unsatisfied,
I, for whom the pensive night
Binds her cloudy hair with light,
I, for whom all beauty burns
Like incense in a million urns?
O beauty, are you not enough?
Why am I crying after love?

---

pensive—*to be in deep thought*

At a Lunar Eclipse
By Thomas Hardy

Thy shadow, Earth, from Pole to Central Sea,
Now steals along upon the Moon's meek shine
In even monochrome and curving line
Of imperturbable serenity.
How shall I link such sun-cast symmetry
With the torn troubled form I know as thine,
That profile, placid as a brow divine,
With continents of moil and misery?

---

monochrome—*emitting light in a single color or a photo printed in a single color*
imperturbable—*unable to be disrupted or excited, calm*
placid—*tranquil, calm, little movement*
moil—*to be weary, work hard*

The Young Man's Song
By W. B. Yeats

I whispered, "I am too young,"
And then, "I am old enough";
Wherefore I threw a penny
To find out if I might love.
"Go and love, go and love, young man,
If the lady be young and fair,"
Ah, penny, brown penny, brown penny,
I am looped in the loops of her hair.

Oh, love is the crooked thing,
There is nobody wise enough
To find out all that is in it,
 For he would be thinking of love
Till the stars had run away,
And the shadows eaten the moon.
Ah, penny, brown penny, brown penny,
One cannot begin it too soon.

Age
By William Lisle Bowles

Age, thou the loss of health and friends shalt mourn!
But thou art passing to that night-still bourne,
Where labour sleeps. The linnet, chattering loud
To the May morn, shall sing; thou, in thy shroud,
Forgetful and forgotten, sink to rest;
And grass-green be the sod upon thy breast!

---

linnet—*a small bird from the finch family; found all over Europe and many bordering countries and continents; it is brown and grey with a red forehead and chest*

A Blown Rose
By Madison Julius Cawein

Lay but a finger on
        That pallid petal sweet,
It trembles gray and wan
        Beneath the passing feet.

But soft! blown rose, we know
        A merriment of bloom,
A life of sturdy glow, -
        But no such dear perfume.

As some good bard, whose page
        Of life with beauty's fraught,
Grays on to ripe old age
        Sweet-mellowed through with thought.

So when his hoary head
        Is wept into the tomb,
The mind, which is not dead,
        Sheds round it rare perfume.

---

pallid—*to be pale, lacking color*
wan—*a sickly pale hue*
bard—*ancient Celtic singer and storyteller of epic tales, poet*
fraught—*loaded with or heavy laden*
hoary—*hair that is white and grey*

The Village Blacksmith
By Henry Wadsworth Longfellow

Under a spreading chestnut-tree
    The village smithy stands;
The smith, a mighty man is he,
    With large and sinewy hands,
And the muscles of his brawny arms
    Are strong as iron bands.
His hair is crisp, and black, and long;
    His face is like the tan;
His brow is wet with honest sweat,
    He earns whate'er he can,
And looks the whole world in the face,
    For he owes not any man.
Week in, week out, from morn till night,
    You can hear his bellows blow;
You can hear him swing his heavy sledge,
    With measured beat and slow,
Like a sexton ringing the village bell,
    When the evening sun is low.
And children coming home from school
    Look in at the open door;
They love to see the flaming forge,
    And hear the bellows roar,
And catch the burning sparks that fly
    Like chaff from a threshing-floor.
He goes on Sunday to the church,
    And sits among his boys;
He hears the parson pray and preach,
    He hears his daughter's voice
Singing in the village choir,
    And it makes his heart rejoice.
It sounds to him like her mother's voice
    Singing in Paradise!
He needs must think of her once more,
    How in the grave she lies;
And with his hard, rough hand he wipes
    A tear out of his eyes.
Toiling,—rejoicing,—sorrowing,
    Onward through life he goes;
Each morning sees some task begin,
    Each evening sees it close;
Something attempted, something done,
    Has earned a night's repose.
Thanks, thanks to thee, my worthy friend,
    For the lesson thou hast taught!
Thus at the flaming forge of life

Our fortunes must be wrought;
Thus on its sounding anvil shaped
    Each burning deed and thought.

---

sinewy—*strong and firm*
brawny—*bulky, strong, and muscled*
bellow—*a tool for stoking a fire*
sledge—*a heavy headed hammer with a long handle*
sexton—*a lower officer of the church that takes care of remedial tasks*
chaff—*the husk left over after the corn is threshed*
thresh—*to beat grain from its shaft or corn from the cob*
parson—*a priest who is in charge of a perish (a territory)*

Opportunity
By Grace Kwok

Why sit? Why stay in such a world?
When far away are lands unfurled.
Why stand staring at a distant glow
When you could go and really know!

When you stare at ancient mystery,
When you look, what do you see?
People all have different eyes,
What I see may be to you, a surprise.

But many lack in bravery.
When danger comes, they scream and flee.
Peril sends through them a chill,
And the unknown is simply not a thrill.

But I wish, I want, to find and see
The lands of my own fantasy.
Lightning may flash, the winds may blow--
But I am going now, I want to know.

---

unfurled—*expanded or opened*

El Dorado
By Edgar Allen Poe

Gaily bedight,
   A gallant knight,
In sunshine and in shadow,
   Had journeyed long,
   Singing a song,
In search of Eldorado.

   But he grew old,
   This knight so bold,
And o'er his heart a shadow
   Fell as he found
   No spot of ground
That looked like Eldorado.

   And, as his strength
   Failed him at length,
He met a pilgrim shadow;
   "Shadow," said he,
   "Where can it be,
This land of Eldorado?"

   "Over the mountains
   Of the moon,
Down the valley of the shadow,
   Ride, boldly ride,"
   The shade replied,--
"If you seek for Eldorado!"

---

bedight—*adorned or decorated in dress*

The Owl and the Pussy Cat
Edward Lear

I.

The Owl and the Pussy-Cat went to sea
In a beautiful pea-green boat:
They took some honey, and plenty of money
Wrapped up in a five-pound note.
The Owl looked up to the stars above,
And sang to a small guitar,
"O lovely Pussy, O Pussy, my love,
What a beautiful Pussy you are,
You are,
You are!
What a beautiful Pussy you are!"

II.

Pussy said to the Owl, "You elegant fowl,
How charmingly sweet you sing!
Oh! let us be married; too long we have tarried:
But what shall we do for a ring?"
They sailed away, for a year and a day,
To the land where the bong-tree grows;
And there in a wood a Piggy-wig stood,
With a ring at the end of his nose,
His nose,
His nose,
With a ring at the end of his nose.

III.

"Dear Pig, are you willing to sell for one shilling
Your ring?" Said the Piggy, "I will."
So they took it away, and were married next day
By the Turkey who lives on the hill.
They dined on mince and slices of quince,
Which they ate with a runcible spoon;
And hand in hand, on the edge of the sand,
They danced by the light of the moon,
The moon,
The moon,
They danced by the light of the moon.

---

quince—*an yellow oblong fruit that grows abundantly in Cydonia, Crete*
runcible—*a spoon with a fork on its end, a spork*

A Parable
By Sir Arthur Conan Doyle

The cheese-mites asked how the cheese got there,
And warmly debated the matter;
The Orthodox said that it came from the air,
And the Heretics said from the platter.
They argued it long and they argued it strong,
And I hear they are arguing now;
But of all the choice spirits who lived in the cheese,
Not one of them thought of a cow.

---

cheese-mites—*mites (arachnids) that are used in the production of certain cheeses such as Mimolette*
orthodox—*those who follow a religious doctrine strictly*
heretics—*a person who teaches beliefs contrary to any particular religion*

June

"To be yourself in a world that is constantly trying to make you something else is the greatest accomplishment."
—Ralph Waldo Emerson

My Cathedral
By Henry Wadsworth Longfellow

Like two cathedral towers these stately pines
   Uplift their fretted summits tipped with cones;
   The arch beneath them is not built with stones,
   Not Art but Nature traced these lovely lines,
And carved this graceful arabesque of vines;
   No organ but the wind here sighs and moans,
   No sepulchre conceals a martyr's bones.
   No marble bishop on his tomb reclines.
Enter! the pavement, carpeted with leaves,
   Gives back a softened echo to thy tread!
   Listen! the choir is singing; all the birds,
In leafy galleries beneath the eaves,
   Are singing! listen, ere the sound be fled,
   And learn there may be worship without words.

---

stately—*majestic and dignified*
fretted—*its surface being made rough*
arabesque—*referring to Arabia*
sepulchre—*a stone monument where a dead body is put to rest*
martyr—*a person who dies for his beliefs*

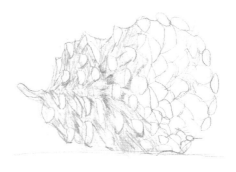

June
By Horatio Alger Jr.

Throw open wide your golden gates,
O poet-landed month of June,
And waft me, on your spicy breath,
The melody of birds in tune.

O fairest palace of the three,
Wherein Queen Summer holdeth sway,
I gaze upon your leafy courts
From out the vestibule of May.

I fain would tread your garden walks,
Or in your shady bowers recline;
Then open wide your golden gates,
And make them mine, and make them mine.

---

waft—*to be carried through water or air*
sway—*to influence and rule over through power*
vestibule—*a space or room one enters before entering the main building*
fain—*to do something gladly or pleased, because you must*
bowers—*shaded covering under a tree caused by branches*

Sonnet 18
By William Shakespeare

Shall I compare thee to a summer's day?
Thou art more lovely and more temperate:
Rough winds do shake the darling buds of May,
And summer's lease hath all too short a date:
Sometime too hot the eye of heaven shines,
And often is his gold complexion dimm'd;
And every fair from fair sometime declines,
By chance, or nature's changing course, untrimm'd;
But thy eternal summer shall not fade
Nor lose possession of that fair thou ow'st;
Nor shall Death brag thou wander'st in his shade,
When in eternal lines to time thou grow'st;
So long as men can breathe or eyes can see,
So long lives this, and this gives life to thee.

---

temperate—*calm, even, not overly passionate*

In the Heart of June
By James Whitcomb Riley

    In the heart of June, love,
You and I together,
    On from dawn till noon, love,
Laughing with the weather;
    Blending both our souls, love,
In the selfsame tune,
    Drinking all life holds, love,
In the heart of June.

    In the heart of June, love,
With its golden weather,
    Underneath the moon, love,
You and I together.
    Ah! how sweet to seem, love,
Drugged and half aswoon
    With this luscious dream, love,
In the heart of June.

---

aswoon—*to swoon, to sink into a faint*

Oh, Smiling Moon
By Juliette Hiller

Oh, smiling moon, why do you smile?
Please, tell to me your stories
Of goodness and the extra miles
Only you and God can see

Oh, smiling moon, high way up high
I see at me you smile
Are you your makers face when I
Forget myself for awhile?

Oh, smiling moon. Bright dark light
What see you that is funny?
The jokes you play upon the night
Will end when skies are sunny

A Skeeter Conversion
By Forrest Lybrand

It's too cold tonight for mosquitoes
And I thank God for that
In June they bred by the willows
And on my blood they grew fat

In the eves, out I'd sit, calm and idle
Thinking thoughts of goodwill to all kind
Then they bit, and I turned genocidal
I refuse to let bugs, on me, dine

Imagine a skeeter conversion
Them, songbirds—not vampire bats
A warbling insect dispersion
Till then I shall smash them all flat.

---

idle—*being inactive, doing nothing*
genocidal—*deliberately killing a large group*
conversion—*a change of disposition*
warbling—*singing*
disposition—*ones temperament*

In Possum Land
By Henry Lawson

In Possum Land the nights are fair,
the streams are fresh and clear;
no dust is in the moonlit air;
no traffic jars the ear.

With Possums gambolling overhead,
'neath western stars so grand,
Ah! would that we could make our bed
tonight in Possum Land

---

gambolling—*to playfully run and jump about*

At the Zoo
By A. A. Milne

There are lions and roaring tigers,
and enormous camels and things,
There are biffalo-buffalo-bisons,
and a great big bear with wings.
There's a sort of a tiny potamus,
and a tiny nosserus too -
But I gave buns to the elephant
when I went down to the Zoo!

There are badgers and bidgers and bodgers,
and a Super-in-tendent's House,
There are masses of goats, and a Polar,
and different kinds of mouse,
And I think there's a sort of a something
which is called a wallaboo -
But I gave buns to the elephant
when I went down to the Zoo!

If you try to talk to the bison,
he never quite understands;
You can't shake hands with a mingo -
he doesn't like shaking hands.
And lions and roaring tigers
hate saying, "How do you do?" -
But I give buns to the elephant
when I go down to the Zoo!

Our Crazy and Wonderful Zoo
By Nicholas C.A. Sparkman

High in the trees,
Monkeys swing in the breeze
Until one comes down,
And steals the zookeeper's keys!

Now hippos, giraffes, and two kangaroos,
Lions and tigers run free in the zoo!
Running and jumping, they play in the plaza,
Look in the café and you'll see a koala!

Otters and lemurs, with penguins and zebras,
Cheetahs and rhinos and even hyenas!
The zookeepers laugh and come along too,
But not before inviting the elephants and caribou!

Dancing and laughing, it was such a delight,
No one had ever quite seen such a sight!
Until the sun went down, they played the day through,
We love all the animals in our crazy and wonderful zoo!

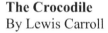

The Crocodile
By Lewis Carroll

How doth the little crocodile
    Improve his shining tail,
And pour the waters of the Nile
    On every golden scale!
How cheerfully he seems to grin,
    How neatly spreads his claws,
And welcomes little fishes in,
    With gently smiling jaws!

Song from Mardi
By Herman Melville

Like the fish of the bright and twittering fin,
Bright fish! diving deep as high soars the lark,
So, far, far, far, doth the maiden swim,
Wild song, wild light, in still ocean's dark.

A Jelly-Fish
By Marianne Morre

Visible, invisible,
A fluctuating charm,
An amber-colored amethyst
Inhabits it; your arm
Approaches, and
It opens and
It closes;
You have meant
To catch it,
And it shrivels;
You abandon
Your intent—
It opens, and it
Closes and you
Reach for it—
The blue
Surrounding it
Grows cloudy, and
It floats away
From you.

Seaside ABC's
By Cambry Glassett

Above the tow'ring cliffs and
Beneath the foamy spray,
Countless tiny animals
Do their work each day.
Everyone is wishin'
For food or fun or friend:
Ghost crabs out a searchin',
Herrings 'round the bend,
Impish little barnacles,
Jellyfish and more,
Kelp and washed-up seaweed,
Limpets by the shore.
Meet the tiny sandpiper—
Needle spindly legs.
Off she goes to her small home,
Picture-perfect eggs.
Quiet pink anemones,
Razor clams, oh my!
Seagulls set a-wheeling,
Turning in the sky.
Underneath the burning sun see
Vultures, whelks, and waves,
Whales and squid and seashells,
e**X**citing seashore caves.
Yay for all the creatures we've met today and now…
Zoo of the seashore, line up and take a bow!

––––––––––––––––––––
spray—*small particles of water that leaves a wave and floats around in the air*

Greece
By Oscar Wilde

The sea was sapphire coloured, and the sky
 Burned like a heated opal through the air;
 We hoisted sail; the wind was blowing fair
For the blue lands that to the eastward lie.
 From the steep prow I marked with quickening eye
 Zakynthos, every olive grove and creek,
 Ithaca's cliff, Lycaon's snowy peak,
 And all the flower-strewn hills of Arcady.
 The flapping of the sail against the mast,
 The ripple of the water on the side,
 The ripple of girls' laughter at the stern,
 The only sounds:- when 'gan the West to burn,
 And a red sun upon the seas to ride,
 I stood upon the soil of Greece at last.

---

sapphire—*a precious stone that comes in multiple colors, but most often thought of as blue*
prow—*the front pointed part of a ship, the bow*

On the Stork Tower
By Wang Zhihuan

The sun beyond the mountains glows;
The Yellow River seawards flows.
You can enjoy a grander sight,
By climbing to a greater height.

Haste Thee, Nymph
By John Milton

Haste thee, Nymph, and bring with thee
Jest, and youthful Jollity,
Quips and cranks and wanton wiles,
Nods and becks and wreathed smiles
Such as hang on Hebe's cheek,
And love to live in dimple sleek;
Sport that wrinkled Care derides,
And Laughter holding both his sides.
Come, and trip it, as you go,
On the light fantastic toe;
And in thy right hand lead with thee
The mountain-nymph, sweet Liberty;
And, if I give thee honour due,
Mirth, admit me of thy crew,
To live with her, and live with thee,
In unreproved pleasures free …

_____

nymph—*a magical spirit that dwells in nature like water and trees*
jest—*to joke*
jollity—*cheerful celebration*
quip—*to taunt or scoff*
wanton—*move or wander freely in a playful manner*
wiles—*manipulating and deceiving a person to convince them to do something*
Hebe—*daughter of Zeus and goddess of youth*
derides—*express contempt or ridiculing something or someone*
mirth—*social excitement, gayety, showing amusement with laughter and noise*
Unreproved—*uncensored, not to be blamed or criticized*

Regret for Peony Flowers
By Bai Juyi

I'm saddened by the peonies before the steps, so red,
As evening came I found that only two remained.
Once morning's winds have blown, they surely won't survive,
At night I gaze by lamplight, to cherish the fading red.

A Sunset Fantasy
By Victor James Daley

Spellbound by a sweet fantasy
At evenglow I stand
Beside an opaline strange sea
That rings a sunset land.

The rich lights fade out one by one,
And, like a peony
Drowning in wine, the crimson sun
Sinks down in that strange sea.

His wake across the ocean-floor
In a long glory lies,
Like a gold wave-way to the shore
Of some sea paradise.

My dream flies after him, and I
Am in another land;
The sun sets in another sky,
And we sit hand in hand.

Gray eyes look into mine; such eyes
I think the angel's are,
Soft as the soft light in the skies
When shines the morning star,

And tremulous as morn, when thin
Gold lights begin to glow,
Revealing the bright soul within
As dawn the sun below.

So, hand in hand, we watch the sun
Burn down the Western deeps,
Dreaming a charmed dream, as one
Who in enchantment sleeps;

A dream of how we twain some day,
Careless of map or chart,
Will both take ship and sail away
Into the sunset's heart.

Our ship shall be of sandal built,
Like ships in old-world tales,
Carven with cunning art, and gilt,
And winged with scented sails

Of silver silk, whereon the red
Great gladioli burn,
A rainbow-flag at her masthead,
A rose-flag at her stern;

And, perching on the point above
Wherefrom the pennon blows,
The figure of a flying dove,
And in her beak a rose.

And from the fading land the breeze
Shall bring us, blowing low,
Old odours and old memories,
And airs of long ago.

A melody that has no words
Of mortal speech a part,
Yet touching all the deepest chords
That tremble in the heart:

A scented song blown oversea,
As though from bowers of bloom
A wind-harp in a lilac-tree
Breathed music and perfume.

And we, no more with longings pale,
Will smile to hear it blow;
I in the shadow of the sail,
You in the sunset-glow.

For, with the fading land, our fond
Old fears shall all fade out,
Paled by the light from shores beyond
The dread of Death or Doubt.

And from a gloomy cloud above
When Death his shadow flings,
The Spirit of Immortal Love
Will shield us with his wings.

He is the lord of dreams divine,
And lures us with his smiles
Along the splendour opaline
Unto the Blessed Isles.

_____

opaline—*like a pearl*   gladioli—*the flower gladiolus*
tremulous—*trembling with fear* pennon—*a small banner or flag*
twain—*to be split in two*

Bounding O'er the Summer Sea
By Henry Parkes

BOUNDING o'er the summer sea,
Breezes blow, breezes blow!
Happy thoughts and fancies free,
Come and go, come and go!
Happy thoughts of Love's surprise,
Breezes blow, breezes blow!
Fancies of the loved one's eyes,
Beaming so, beaming so!
Bounding like a joyous spright,
Through the foam, through the foam!
Like a bird before the night,
Winging home, winging home!
Will they meet us, child and wife,
Bud and rose, bud and rose?
He who counts the sands of life,
Only knows, only knows!

Toiling Farmers
By Li Shen

Farmers weeding at noon,
Sweat down the field soon.
Who knows food on a tray
Thanks to their toiling day?

Work, Neighbor, Work
By Louisa May Alcott

"Work; neighbor, work!
Do not stop to play;
Wander far and wide,
Gather all you may.

We are never like
Idle butterflies,
But like the busy bees,
Industrious and wise."

Foreign Lands
By Robert Louis Stevenson

Up into the cherry tree
Who should climb but little me?
I held the trunk with both my hands
And looked abroad in foreign lands.

I saw the next door garden lie,
Adorned with flowers, before my eye,
And many pleasant places more
That I had never seen before.

I saw the dimpling river pass
And be the sky's blue looking-glass;
The dusty roads go up and down
With people tramping in to town.

If I could find a higher tree
Farther and farther I should see,
To where the grown-up river slips
Into the sea among the ships,

To where the roads on either hand
Lead onward into fairy land,
Where all the children dine at five,
And all the playthings come alive.

Blue Shoes
By Kate Greenaway

Little Blue Shoes
Mustn't go
Very far alone, you know
Else she'll fall down,
Or, lose her way;
Fancy--what
Would mamma say?
Better put her little hand
Under sister's wise command.
When she's a little older grown
 Blue Shoes may go quite alone.

Father
By Edgar Guest

My father knows the proper way
   The nation should be run;
He tells us children every day
   Just what should now be done.
He knows the way to fix the trusts,
   He has a simple plan;
But if the furnace needs repairs,
   We have to hire a man.

My father, in a day or two
   Could land big thieves in jail;
There's nothing that he cannot do,
   He knows no word like "fail."
"Our confidence" he would restore,
   Of that there is no doubt;
But if there is a chair to mend,
   We have to send it out.

All public questions that arise,
   He settles on the spot;
He waits not till the tumult dies,
   But grabs it while it's hot.
In matters of finance he can
   Tell Congress what to do;
But, O, he finds it hard to meet
   His bills as they fall due.

It almost makes him sick to read
   The things law-makers say;
Why, father's just the man they need,
   He never goes astray.
All wars he'd very quickly end,
   As fast as I can write it;
But when a neighbor starts a fuss,
   'Tis mother has to fight it.

In conversation father can
   Do many wondrous things;
He's built upon a wiser plan
   Than presidents or kings.
He knows the ins and outs of each
   And every deep transaction;
We look to him for theories,
   But look to ma for action.

_____
tumult—*a ruckus, causing commotion and noise*

Only a Dad
By Edgar Guest

Only a dad with a tired face,
Coming home from the daily race,
Bringing little of gold or fame
To show how well he has played the game;
But glad in his heart that his own rejoice
To see him come and to hear his voice.

Only a dad with a brood of four,
One of ten million men or more
Plodding along in the daily strife,
Bearing the whips and the scorns of life,
With never a whimper of pain or hate,
For the sake of those who at home await.

Only a dad, neither rich nor proud,
Merely one of the surging crowd
Toiling, striving from day to day,
Facing whatever may come his way,
Silent whenever the harsh condemn,
And bearing it all for the love of them.

Only a dad but he gives his all
To smooth the way for his children small,
Doing with courage stern and grim,
The deeds that his father did for him.
This is the line that for him I pen:
Only a dad, but the best of men.

The Good, Great Man
By Samuel Taylor Coleridge

"How seldom, friend! a good great man inherits
Honour or wealth with all his worth and pains!
It sounds like stories from the land of spirits
If any man obtain that which he merits
Or any merit that which he obtains."

REPLY TO THE ABOVE
For shame, dear friend, renounce this canting strain!
What would'st thou have a good great man obtain?
Place? titles? salary? a gilded chain?
Or throne of corses which his sword had slain?
Greatness and goodness are not *means*, but *ends*!
Hath he not always treasures, always friends,
The good great man? *three* treasures, LOVE, and LIGHT,
And CALM THOUGHTS, regular as infant's breath:
And three firm friends, more sure than day and night,
HIMSELF, his MAKER, and the ANGEL DEATH!

---

canting—*speaking with a whiny voice*
corses—*corpses, dead bodies*

July

"Fortune sides with him who dares."
—Virgil

Americans
Anonymous

You can always tell the English,
You can always tell the Dutch,
You can always tell the Yankees -
But you can't tell them *much!*

"The New Colossus"
By Emma Lazarus

Not like the brazen giant of Greek fame,
With conquering limbs astride from land to land;
Here at our sea-washed, sunset gates shall stand
A mighty woman with a torch, whose flame
Is the imprisoned lightning, and her name
Mother of Exiles. From her beacon-hand
Glows world-wide welcome; her mild eyes command
The air-bridged harbor that twin cities frame.
"Keep, ancient lands, your storied pomp!" cries she
With silent lips. "Give me your tired, your poor,
Your huddled masses yearning to breathe free,
The wretched refuse of your teeming shore.
Send these, the homeless, tempest-tossed to me,
I lift my lamp beside the golden door!"

---

astride—*to be stretched out from side to side*
beacon—*a light that is positioned up high that can be seen from afar like from a lighthouse*
tempest—*a wild and dangerous storm*

Forgotten
By Charles Harper

He shone in the senate, the camp, and the grove,
The mirror of manhood, the darling of love.
He fought for his country, the star of the brave,
And died for it's weal when to die was to save.
And Wisdom and Valour long over him wept,
And Beauty, for ages, strewed flowers where he slept.
And the bards of the people inwrought with their lays
The light of his glory, the sound of his praise.
But afar in the foreworld have faded their strains,
And now of his being what record remains?
Within a lone valley a tomb crumbles fast,
And the name of the Sleeper is lost in the past.

_____

weal—*republic or state; happiness or prosperity*
bard—*ancient Celtic singer and storyteller of epic tales, poet*
inwrought—*a fabric decoration that is embroidered with great detail*
foreworld—*ancient time or world*

Bivouac on a Mountain Side
By Walt Whitman

I see before me now a traveling army halting,
Below a fertile valley spread, with barns and the orchards of summer,
Behind, the terraced sides of a mountain, abrupt, in places rising high,
Broken, with rocks, with clinging cedars, with tall shapes dingily seen,
The numerous camp-fires scatter'd near and far, some away up on the mountain,
The shadowy forms of men and horses, looming, large-sized, flickering,
And over all the sky—the sky! far, far out of reach, studded, breaking out, the eternal stars

---

bivouac—*to camp without any tents or coverings, most often referring to soldiers or those surviving in the mountains*

Sonnet to Liberty
By Oscar Wilde

Not that I love thy children, whose dull eyes
See nothing save their own unlovely woe,
Whose minds know nothing, nothing care to know,—
But that the roar of thy Democracies,
Thy reigns of Terror, thy great Anarchies,
Mirror my wildest passions like the sea,—
And give my rage a brother——! Liberty!
For this sake only do thy dissonant cries
Delight my discreet soul, else might all kings
By bloody knout or treacherous cannonades
Rob nations of their rights inviolate
And I remain unmoved—and yet, and yet,
These Christs that die upon the barricades,
God knows it I am with them, in some things.

———————————————

democracies—*government ran by the people*
anarchies—*when there is no law or government in power*
knout—*a punishment inflicted by a whip*
cannonades—*continuous gun fire*

Old Ironsides
By Oliver Wendell Holmes Sr.

Ay, tear her tattered ensign down!
Long has it waved on high,
And many an eye has danced to see
That banner in the sky;
Beneath it rung the battle shout,
And burst the cannon's roar;—
The meteor of the ocean air
Shall sweep the clouds no more!

Her deck, once red with heroes' blood
Where knelt the vanquished foe,
When winds were hurrying o'er the flood
And waves were white below,
No more shall feel the victor's tread,
Or know the conquered knee;—
The harpies of the shore shall pluck
The eagle of the sea!

O, better that her shattered hulk
Should sink beneath the wave;
Her thunders shook the mighty deep,
And there should be her grave;
Nail to the mast her holy flag,
Set every thread-bare sail,
And give her to the god of storms,—
The lightning and the gale!

----

vanquished—*to be defeated*
foe—*enemy*
tread—*to walk on or set foot on the ground*
harpies—*a winged figure that has the body of a vulture and the head of a woman with
clawed feet and fingers*

Dover Beach
By Matthew Arnold

The sea is calm tonight.
The tide is full, the moon lies fair
Upon the straits; on the French coast, the light
Gleams and is gone; the cliffs of England stand,
Glimmering and vast, out in the tranquil bay.
Come to the window, sweet is the night-air!
Only, from the long line of spray
Where the sea meets the moon-blanched land,

Listen! you hear the grating roar
Of pebbles which the waves draw back, and fling,
At their return, up the high strand,
Begin, and cease, and then again begin,
With tremulous cadence slow, and bring
The eternal note of sadness in.

Sophocles long ago
Heard it on the Aegean, and it brought
Into his mind the turbid ebb and flow
Of human misery; we
Find also in the sound a thought,
Hearing it by this distant northern sea.

The Sea of Faith
Was once, too, at the full, and round earth's shore
Lay like the folds of a bright girdle furled.
But now I only hear
Its melancholy, long, withdrawing roar,
Retreating, to the breath
Of the night-wind, down the vast edges drear
And naked shingles of the world.

Ah, love, let us be true
To one another! for the world, which seems
To lie before us like a land of dreams,
So various, so beautiful, so new,
Hath really neither joy, nor love, nor light,
Nor certitude, nor peace, nor help for pain;
And we are here as on a darkling plain
Swept with confused alarms of struggle and flight,
Where ignorant armies clash by night.

---

spray—*a small shoot extending from a branch; small particles of water that leaves a wave and floats around in the air*

blanched—*whitened*

tremulous—*trembling with fear*

cadence—*music term meaning the rhythm or a fluctuation in a voice*

Sophocles—*an ancient Greek playwright who wrote over 120 plays and one of three greats who wrote tragedies; only seven complete plays survive; he died circa 406 BCE*

aegean—*a geographical area comprised of the aegean sea and surrounding islands and shores*

turbid—*to stir, liquid that is opaque due to having some sort of particle in it*

ebb—*to return like a wave returning back to the ocean*

melancholy—*a mood that is gloomy and depressed*

drear—*dreary and dismal*

certitude—*certain or sure*

darkling—*dark or void of light*

ignorant—*not knowing, uninformed*

A Sunbeam Stooped and Kissed a Wave
By Caroline W. Leakey

A SUNBEAM stooped and kissed a wave
That rippled o'er the sea,
And seemed its crystal cheek to lave
With roseate brilliancy.
The wave in gladness danced away,
Far, far adown its stream,
And, laughing, cast a pearl-white spray
Up to the bright sunbeam.
A ray of light shot o'er my way,
And I began to sing;
My heart as uncaged lark away
Upborne on joy's gay wing.
But why I sung I cannot tell,
Nor why my heart felt light,
Save that along my pathway fell
That little sunbeam bright.
But while such joy my heart did fill,
That I went singing on,
The sun had sunk behind the hill,
The little beam was gone!
And then I could no longer sing,
But this one feeling had,—
Joy's own fair form may shadows fling,
In thoughts funereal clad.

---

lave—*to wash (term most often used in poetry)*
roseate—*a rose like color*
spray—*a small shoot extending from a branch; small particles of water that leaves a wave and floats around in the air*
upborne—*to be supported or helped up*

In the Wood
By Sara Teasdale

I heard the water-fall rejoice
Singing like a choir,
I saw the sun flash out of it
Azure and amber fire.
The earth was like an open flower
Enamelled and arrayed,
The path I took to find its heart
Fluttered with sun and shade.
And while earth lured me, gently, gently,
Happy and all alone,
Suddenly a heavy snake
Reared black upon a stone.

_____

enamelled—*to be coated or covered*
azure—*the color of a blue sky, resembling the color of the sky*

Stones
By John Frederick Freeman

Small yellow stones
That, lifted, through my idle fingers fall
Leaving a score--
And these I toss between the parted lips
Of the lapping sea,
And the sea tosses again with millions more--
Yellow and white stones;
Then drawing back her snaky long waves all,
Leaves the stones
Yellow and white upon the sandy shore....
As they were bones
Yellow and white left on the silent shore
Of an unfoaming far unvisioned Sea.

A Midsummers Day
By Madison Julius

The locust gyres; the heat intensifies'
The rain-crow croaks from hot-leafed tree to tree:
The butterfly, a flame-fleck, aimlessly
Droops down the air and knows not where it flies.
Beside the stream, whose bed in places
The small green heron flaps; the minnows flee:
And mid the blackberry-lilies, wasp and bee
Drowse where the cattle pant with half-closed eyes.
The Summer Day, like some tired labourer,
Lays down her burden here and sinks to rest,
The tan of toil upon her face and hands:
She dreams, and lo, the heavens over her
Unfold her dream: Along the boundless West
Rolls gold the harvest of the sunset's lands.

---

gyres—*gyrate, to move quickly in a circular motion like a spiral*

Sanctuary
By Melissa Crowther

Breathless, I stumble to a halt in my own patch of woods
And claim, "Sanctuary".

Wooden spires lead my sight heavenward,
A reminder our souls share common radiance.

The choir, robed in feathers,
Sweetly lilts a blithesome hymn.

I inhale gratitude and exhale burden,
Praying with a hope of transformation.
Here
In my sanctuary.

---

blithesome—*gay and cheerful like the song of a bird*
lilt–to do something quickly with fine dexterity

The Whippoorwill and I
By Horatio Alger Jr

In the hushed hours of night, when the air quite still,
I hear the strange cry of the lone whippoorwill,
Who Chants, without ceasing, that wonderful trill,
Of which the sole burden is still, "Whip-poor-Will."

And why should I whip him? Strange visitant,
Has he been playing truant this long summer day?
I listened a moment; more clear and more shrill
Rang the voice of the bird, as he cried, "Whip-poor-Will."

But what has poor Will done? I ask you once more;
I'll whip him, don't fear, if you'll tell me what for.
I paused for an answer; o'er valley and hill
Rang the voice of the bird, as he cried, "Whip-poor-Will."

Has he come to your dwelling, by night or by day,
And snatched the young birds from their warm nest away?
I paused for an answer; o'er valley and hill
Rang the voice of the bird, as he cried, "Whip-poor-Will."

Well, well, I can hear you, don't have any fears,
I can hear what is constantly dinned in my ears.
The obstinate bird, with his wonderful trill,
Still made but one answer, and that, "Whip-poor-Will."

But what HAS poor Will done? I prithee explain;
I'm out of all patience, don't mock me again.
The obstinate bird, with his wonderful trill,
Still made the same answer, and that, "Whip-poor-Will."

Well, have your own way, then; but if you won't tell,
I'll shut down the window, and bid you farewell;
But of one thing be sure, I won't whip him until
You give me some reason for whipping poor Will.

I listened a moment, as if for reply,
But nothing was heard but the bird's mocking cry.
I caught the faint echo from valley and hill;
It breathed the same burden, that strange "Whip-poor-Will."

---

prithee—*a contraction of pray thee*
obstinate—*stubborn*

Lonely Airs
By John Frederick Freeman

Ah, bird singing late in the gloam
While the evening shadow thickens,
And the dizzy bat-wings roam,
And the faint starlight quickens;

And her bud eve's primrose bares
Before night's cold fingers come:
Thine are such lonely airs,
Bird singing late in the gloam!

_____

gloam—*sullen*

The Stars
By Madison Julius Cawein

These-the bright symbols of man's hope and fame,
In which he reads his blessing or his curse-
Are syllables with which God speaks His name
In the vast utterance of the universe

The Killamanine
By Isla Fairs-Billam

It lurks in the dark,
And feeds on the dead,
Got to be careful,
When it's not been fed.

It's eyes a blazing red,
It's skin as tough as leather,
I'd call it wise,
But mostly cunning and clever.

It's teeth razor sharp,
Claws covered in mud,
Once it's finished with you,
You'll be less than bones and blood.

Flesh is for dinner,
Blood is for lunch,
So stop shaking,
It won't help much.

It can pick up your scent,
From a mile away,
It then tracks you down,
And that's your last day.

So beware of that forest,
If you like the sunshine,
For down in its depths,
Lives the Killamanine.

The Moon
By Robert Louis Stevenson

The moon has a face like the clock in the hall;
She shines on thieves on the garden wall,
On streets and fields and harbour quays,
And birdies asleep in the forks of the trees.
The squalling cat and the squeaking mouse,
The howling dog by the door of the house,
The bat that lies in bed at noon,
All love to be out by the light of the moon.
But all of the things that belong to the day
Cuddle to sleep to be out of her way;
And flowers and children close their eyes
Till up in the morning the sun shall arise.

---

quay— *a wharf or structure onto which one secures a boat or ship*
squalling—*crying or screeching out loud*

A Rural Home
By Mei Yaochen

The cock crows three times; the sky is almost light.
Someone's lined up bowls of rice, along with flasks of tea.
Anxiously, the peasants rush to start the ploughing early,
I pull aside the willow shutter and gaze at the morning stars.

The Eagle
By Alfred Lord Tennyson

He clasps the crag with crooked hands;
Close to the sun in lonely lands,
Ringed with the azure world, he stands.

The wrinkled sea beneath him crawls;
He watches from his mountain walls,
And like a thunderbolt he falls.

---

crag—*a rough jagged rock*
azure—*the color of a blue sky, resembling the color of the sky*

Lessons from a River
By Steven Wesley Law

Run wild
Disappear around a bend
Slow down and reflect
Be free
Meander when needed
Push forward
Slow down and until things settle and grow clear
She will tell you her greatest secrets only when you reach her mouth

A Baby
By Madison Julius Cawein

Why speak of Rajah rubies,
And roses of the South?
I know a sweeter crimson
A baby's mouth.

Why speak of Sultan sapphires
And violet seas and skies?
I know a lovelier azure
A baby's eyes.

Go seek the wide world over!
Search every land and mart!
You 'll never find a pearl like this
A baby's heart.

_____

azure—*the color of a blue sky, resembling the color of the sky*

A Southern Girl
By Madison Cawein

Serious but smiling, stately and serene,
    And dreamier than a flower;
A girl in whom all sympathies convene
    As perfumes in a bower;
Through whom one feels what soul and heart may mean,
    And their resistless power.

Eyes, that commune with the frank skies of truth,
    Where thought like starlight curls;
Lips of immortal rose, where love and youth
    Nestle like two sweet pearls;
Hair, that suggests the Bible braids of RUTH,
    Deeper than any girl's.

When first I saw you, 't was as if within
    My soul took shape some song -
Played by a master of the violin -
    A music pure and strong,
That rapt my soul above all earthly sin
    To heights that know no wrong.

_____

bowers—*shaded covering under a tree caused by branches*
rapt—*transported, carried away, ravished*

The Tea Party
By Kate Greenaway

In the pleasant green Garden
We sat down to tea;
"Do you take sugar?" and
"Do you take milk?"
She'd got a new gown on
A smart one of silk.
We all were so happy
As happy could be,
On that bright Summer's day
When she asked us to tea.

Book of Nonsense Limerick 31
By Edward Lear

There was a Young Lady of Norway,
Who casually sat in a doorway;
When the door squeezed her flat,
She exclaimed, "What of that?"
This courageous Young Lady of Norway.

The Bubble
By William Allingham

See the pretty planet!
Floating sphere!
Faintest breeze will fan it
Far or near;

World as light as feather;
Moonshine rays,
Rainbow tints together,
As it plays.

Drooping, sinking, failing,
Nigh to earth,
Mounting, whirling, sailing,
Full of mirth;

Life there, welling, flowing,
Waving round;
Pictures coming, going,
Without sound.

Quick now, be this airy
Globe repelled!
Never can the fairy
Star be held.

Touched, it in a twinkle
Disappears!
Leaving but a sprinkle,
As of tears.

---

nigh—*something is near, happening soon*
mirth—*social excitement, gayety, showing amusement with laughter and noise*

Casey at the Bat
By Ernest L. Thayer

The outlook wasn't brilliant for the Mudville nine that day:
The score stood four to two, with but one inning more to play,
And then when Cooney died at first, and Barrows did the same,
A pall-like silence fell upon the patrons of the game.
A straggling few got up to go in deep despair. The rest
Clung to the hope which springs eternal in the human breast;
They thought, "If only Casey could but get a whack at that—
We'd put up even money now, with Casey at the bat
But Flynn preceded Casey, as did also Jimmy Blake,
And the former was a hoodoo, while the latter was a cake;
So upon that stricken multitude grim melancholy sat,
For there seemed but little chance of Casey getting to the bat.
But Flynn let drive a single, to the wonderment of all,
And Blake, the much despisèd, tore the cover off the ball;
And when the dust had lifted, and men saw what had occurred,
There was Jimmy safe at second and Flynn a-hugging third.
Then from five thousand throats and more there rose a lusty yell;
It rumbled through the valley, it rattled in the dell;
It pounded on the mountain and recoiled upon the flat,
For Casey, mighty Casey, was advancing to the bat.
There was ease in Casey's manner as he stepped into his place;
There was pride in Casey's bearing and a smile lit Casey's face.
And when, responding to the cheers, he lightly doffed his hat,
No stranger in the crowd could doubt 'twas Casey at the bat.
Ten thousand eyes were on him as he rubbed his hands with dirt;
Five thousand tongues applauded when he wiped them on his shirt;
Then while the writhing pitcher ground the ball into his hip,
Defiance flashed in Casey's eye, a sneer curled Casey's lip.
And now the leather-covered sphere came hurtling through the air,
And Casey stood a-watching it in haughty grandeur there.
Close by the sturdy batsman the ball unheeded sped—
"That ain't my style," said Casey. "Strike one!" the umpire said.
From the benches, black with people, there went up a muffled roar,
Like the beating of the storm-waves on a stern and distant shore;
"Kill him! Kill the umpire!" shouted someone on the stand;
And it's likely they'd have killed him had not Casey raised his hand.
With a smile of Christian charity great Casey's visage shone;
He stilled the rising tumult; he bade the game go on;
He signaled to the pitcher, and once more the dun sphere flew;
But Casey still ignored it and the umpire said, "Strike two!"
"Fraud!" cried the maddened thousands, and echo answered "Fraud!"
But one scornful look from Casey and the audience was awed.
They saw his face grow stern and cold, they saw his muscles strain,
And they knew that Casey wouldn't let that ball go by again.
The sneer is gone from Casey's lip, his teeth are clenched in hate,

He pounds with cruel violence his bat upon the plate;
And now the pitcher holds the ball, and now he lets it go,
And now the air is shattered by the force of Casey's blow.
Oh, somewhere in this favoured land the sun is shining bright,
The band is playing somewhere, and somewhere hearts are light;
And somewhere men are laughing, and somewhere children shout,
But there is no joy in Mudville—mighty Casey has struck out.

---

hoodoo—*bad luck*
melancholy—*a mood that is gloomy and depressed*
recoiled—*came back*
writhing—*to twist, contort, or squirm*
visage—*the way a person's face looks or their countenance*
tumult—*a ruckus, causing* commotion and noise
bade—*to ask or order someone, the past tense of bid*
dun—*gloomy, dark colored*

August

"Hold fast to dreams, For if dreams die Life is a broken-winged bird,
That cannot fly."
—Langston Hughes

Hope
By Thomas Campbell

At summer eve, when heaven's aerial bow
Spans with bright arch the glittering hills below,
Why to yon mountain turns the musing eye,
Whose sunbright summit mingles with the sky?
Why do those cliffs of shadowy tint appear
More sweet than all the landscape smiling near?
'Tis distance lends enchantment to the view,
And robes the mountain in its azure hue.

_____

aerial—*having to do with, being in, or created in the air*
musing—*to think, contemplate or meditate in silence*
azure—*the color of a blue sky, resembling the color of the sky*

An Evening
By William Allingham

A sunset's mounded cloud;
A diamond evening-star;
Sad blue hills afar;
Love in his shroud.

Scarcely a tear to shed;
Hardly a word to say;
The end of a summer day;
Sweet Love dead.

_____

shroud—*shelter, covering*

Evening Star
By Edgar Allen Poe

'Twas noontide of summer,
And mid-time of night;
And stars, in their orbits,
Shone pale, thro' the light
Of the brighter, cold moon,
'Mid planets her slaves,
Herself in the Heavens,
Her beam on the waves.
I gazed awhile
On her cold smile;
Too cold- too cold for me-
There pass'd, as a shroud,
A fleecy cloud,
And I turned away to thee,
Proud Evening Star,
In thy glory afar,
And dearer thy beam shall be;
For joy to my heart
Is the proud part
Thou bearest in Heaven at night,
And more I admire
Thy distant fire,
Than that colder, lowly light.

---

shroud—*shelter, covering*

The Tyger
By William Blake

Tyger! Tyger! burning bright
In the forests of the night,
What immortal hand or eye
Could frame thy fearful symmetry?
In what distant deeps or skies
Burnt the fire of thine eyes?
On what wings dare he aspire?
What the hand, dare sieze the fire?
And what shoulder, & what art,
Could twist the sinews of thy heart?
And when thy heart began to beat,
What dread hand? & what dread feet?
What the hammer? what the chain?
In what furnace was thy brain?
What the anvil? what dread grasp
Dare its deadly terrors clasp?
When the stars threw down their spears,
And water'd heaven with their tears,
Did he smile his work to see?
Did he who made the Lamb make thee?
Tyger! Tyger! burning bright
In the forests of the night,
What immortal hand or eye
Dare frame thy fearful symmetry?

---

symmetry—*the equal proportions of any item when comparing two sides of its axis*
sinew—*tendon, fibrous tissue that binds things together like muscles to a bone*

Delay
By Elizabeth Jennings

The radiance of the star that leans on me
Was shining years ago. The light that now
Glitters up there my eyes may never see,
And so the time lag teases me with how

Love that loves now may not reach me until
Its first desire is spent. The star's impulse
Must wait for eyes to claim it beautiful
And love arrived may find us somewhere else.

Four by the Clock
By Henry Wadsworth Longfellow

Four by the clock! and yet not day;
But the great world rolls and wheels away,
With its cities on land, and its ships at sea,
Into the dawn that is to be!

Only the lamp in the anchored bark
Sends its glimmer across the dark,
And the heavy breathing of the sea
Is the only sound that comes to me

A Dirge
By Percy Bysshe Shelley

Rough wind, that moanest loud
Grief too sad for song;
Wild wind, when sullen cloud
Knells all the night long;
Sad storm whose tears are vain,
Bare woods, whose branches strain,
Deep caves and dreary main, -
Wail, for the world's wrong!

---

knells—*ringing in a solemn and sad way*

The Aim Was Song
By Robert Frost

Before man came to blow it right
The wind once blew itself untaught,
And did its loudest day and night
In any rough place where it caught.

Man came to tell it what was wrong:
It hadn't found the place to blow;
It blew too hard—the aim was song.
And listen—how it ought to go!

He took a little in his mouth,
And held it long enough for north
To be converted into south,
And then by measure blew it forth.

By measure. It was word and note,
The wind the wind had meant to be—
A little through the lips and throat.
The aim was song—the wind could see.

My Voice
By Oscar Wilde

Within the restless, hurried, modern world
        We took our hearts' full pleasure—You and
And now the white sails of our ships are furled,
        And spent the lading of our argosy.

Wherefore my cheeks before their time are wan,
        For very weeping is my gladness fled,
Sorrow hath paled my lip's vermilion
        And Ruin draws the curtains of my bed.

But all this crowded life has been to thee
        No more than lyre, or lute, or subtle spell
Of viols, or the music of the sea
        That sleeps, a mimic echo, in the shell.

------

lading—*large load or cargo of a ship*
argosy—*large merchant ship*
wan—*a sickly pale hue*
vermilion—*a bright shade of red*

Give Me Freshening Breeze, My Boys
By Louisa May Alcott

'Give me freshening breeze, my boys,
A white and swelling sail,
A ship that cuts the dashing waves,
And weathers every gale.
What life is like a sailor's life,
So free, so bold, so brave?
His home the ocean's wide expanse,
A coral bed his grave.'

The Days When We Went Swimming
By Henry Lawson

The breezes waved the silver grass,
Waist-high along the siding,
And to the creek we ne'er could pass
Three boys on bare-back riding;
Beneath the sheoaks in the bend
The waterhole was brimming--
Do you remember yet, old friend,
The times we 'went in swimming'?

The days we 'played the wag' from school--
Joys shared--and paid for singly--
The air was hot, the water cool--
And naked boys are kingly!
With mud for soap the sun to dry--
A well planned lie to stay us,
And dust well rubbed on neck and face
Lest cleanliness betray us.

And you'll remember farmer Kutz--
Though scarcely for his bounty--
He leased a forty-acre block,
And thought he owned the county;
A farmer of the old world school,
That grew men hard and grim in,
He drew his water from the pool
That we preferred to swim in.

And do you mind when down the creek
His angry way he wended,
A green-hide cartwhip in his hand
For our young backs intended?
Three naked boys upon the sand--
Half buried and half sunning--
Three startled boys without their clothes
Across the paddocks running.

We've had some scares, but we looked blank
When, resting there and chumming,
One glanced by chance upon the bank
And saw the farmer coming!
And home impressions linger yet
Of cups of sorrow brimming;
I hardly think that we'll forget
The last day we went swimming.

---

wend—*to go or return when going someplace (used primarily in poetry)*

Bed in Summer
By Robert Louis Stevenson

In winter I get up at night
And dress by yellow candle-light.
In summer quite the other way,
I have to go to bed by day.

I have to go to bed and see
The birds still hopping on the tree,
Or hear the grown-up people's feet
Still going past me in the street.

And does it not seem hard to you,
When all the sky is clear and blue,
And I should like so much to play,
To have to go to bed by day?

The Men that Don't Fit In
By Robert W. Service

There's a race of men that don't fit in,
      A race that can't stay still;
So they break the hearts of kith and kin,
      And they roam the world at will.
They range the field and they rove the flood,
      And they climb the mountain's crest;
Theirs is the curse of the gypsy blood,
      And they don't know how to rest.

If they just went straight they might go far;
      They are strong and brave and true;
But they're always tired of the things that are,
      And they want the strange and new.
They say: "Could I find my proper groove,
      What a deep mark I would make!"
So they chop and change, and each fresh move
      Is only a fresh mistake.

And each forgets, as he strips and runs
      With a brilliant, fitful pace,
It's the steady, quiet, plodding ones
      Who win in the lifelong race.
And each forgets that his youth has fled,
      Forgets that his prime is past,
Till he stands one day, with a hope that's dead,
      In the glare of the truth at last.

He has failed, he has failed; he has missed his chance;
      He has just done things by half.
Life's been a jolly good joke on him,
      And now is the time to laugh.
Ha, ha! He is one of the Legion Lost;
      He was never meant to win;
He's a rolling stone, and it's bred in the bone;
      He's a man who won't fit in.

The Queen of Hearts
By Christina Rossetti

How comes it, Flora, that, whenever we
Play cards together, you invariably,
   However the pack parts,
   Still hold the Queen of Hearts?

I've scanned you with a scrutinizing gaze,
Resolved to fathom these your secret ways:
   But, sift them as I will,
   Your ways are secret still.

I cut and shuffle; shuffle, cut, again;
But all my cutting, shuffling, proves in vain:
   Vain hope, vain forethought too;
   The Queen still falls to you.

I dropped her once, prepense; but, ere the deal
Was dealt, your instinct seemed her loss to feel:
   'There should be one card more,'
   You said, and searched the floor.

I cheated once; I made a private notch
In Heart-Queen's back, and kept a lynx-eyed watch;
   Yet such another back
   Deceived me in the pack:

The Queen of Clubs assumed by arts unknown
An imitative dint that seemed my own;
   This notch, not of my doing,
   Misled me to my ruin.

It baffles me to puzzle out the clue,
Which must be skill, or craft, or luck in you:
   Unless, indeed, it be
   Natural affinity.

---

fathom—*deep thought*
prepence—thought of beforehand
affinity—when two different bodies unite into one

Mary's Lamb
By Sarah Josepha Hale

Mary had a little lamb,
Its fleece was white as snow,
And every where that Mary went
The lamb was sure to go;
He followed her to school one day—
That was against the rule,
It made the children laugh and play,
To see a lamb at school.
And so the Teacher turned him out,
But still he lingered near,
And waited patiently about,
Till Mary did appear;
And then he ran to her, and laid
His head upon her arm,
As if he said—"I'm not afraid—
You'll keep me from all harm."
"What makes the lamb love Mary so?"
The eager children cry—
"O, Mary loves the lamb, you know,"
The Teacher did reply;—
"And you each gentle animal
In confidence may bind,
And make them follow at your call,
If you are always kind."

Company Manners
By James Whitcomb Riley

When Bess gave her Dollies a Tea, said she, -
   "It's unpolite, when they's Company,
   To say you've drinked_two_cups, you see, -
   But say you've drinked_a couple_of tea.

As Created
By James Whitcomb Riley

There's a space for good to bloom in
Every heart of man or woman, -
And however wild or human,
Or however brimmed with gall,
ever heart may beat without it;
And the darkest heart to doubt it
Has something good about it
After all.

gall—*bitterness, anger*

Beards
Anonymous

There was an old man with a beard,
Who said, "It is just as I feared! -
   Two owls and a hen,
    Four larks and a wren,
Have all built their nests in my beard."

Miss Molly and the Little Fishes
By Kate Greenaway

Oh, sweet Miss Molly,
You're so fond
Of Fishes in a little Pond.
And perhaps they're glad
To see you stare
With such bright eyes
Upon them there.
And when your fingers and your thumbs
Drop slowly in the small white crumbs
I hope they're happy. Only this
When you've looked long enough, sweet miss.
Then, most beneficent young giver,
Restore them to their native river.

beneficent—*doing a good deed*

The Still River
By Elaena Amans-Lucas

The river is still,
as still as a painting,
yet just as a painting,
it is full of motion.
Upon the still river,
the round orb like shape of the Moon,
leading the stars
like a shepherd leads his sheep.
Then once a month,
when the shepherd goes to sleep,
the stars twinkle
and dance across the night sky.
Then, when the night turns to day,
the sun appears, a fiery maiden,
her golden hair rippling behind her.
Her dress and shoes made of gold,
riding in a orange chariot
pulled by fiery birds,
leading her army of clouds
against the armies of rain.
Just as they start to win the battle,
her own forces betray, and banish her.
All this reflected on the still river.

Still Will I Harvest Beauty Where It Grows
By Edna St. Vincent Millay

Still will I harvest beauty where it grows:
In coloured fungus and the spotted fog
Surprised on foods forgotten; in ditch and bog
Filmed brilliant with irregular rainbows
Of rust and oil, where half a city throws
Its empty tins; and in some spongy log
Whence headlong leaps the oozy emerald frog. . . .
And a black pupil in the green scum shows.
Her the inhabiter of divers places
Surmising at all doors, I push them all.
Oh, you that fearful of a creaking hinge
Turn back forevermore with craven faces,
I tell you Beauty bears an ultra fringe
Unguessed of you upon her gossamer shawl!

_____

craven—*scared, not having courage*

Song of the Queer Green Frog
By Louisa May Alcott

"No, no, come and fly
Through the sunny sky,
Or honey sip
From the rose's lip,
Or dance in the air,
Like spirits fair.
Come away, come away;
'Tis our holiday."

The Cry of the Cicada
By Matsuo Basho
Translated By William George Aston

The cry of the cicada
Gives us no sign
That presently it will die

The Best of the Best
By Max Lawrie

Stomp, crunch, whack! Crack!
Leathery, tough, mega, dangerous.
Stalk, attack, limp, ambush.
Big and small and scary and friendly.
Dinosaurs are the best.

Brontosaurus Divine
By Christine Owens

The Brontosaurus dinosaur is so cute
It's sweet rounded nose and its neck like a chute
Did you know this sweetheart was stripped of its name?
The poor little dinosaur, head hung in shame
They said that it was an Apatosaurus
Why make the change and cause such a great fuss?
Yes, they're both big and have long necks and tails
But one can't compare them for cuteness prevails
Its neck much more delicate its head shape more fine
The Thunder Lizards name is much more divine
It was first discovered in 1874
Inside the west Northern American floor
Thanks to Roger Benson in 2015
The sauropod Brontosaurus was redeemed.

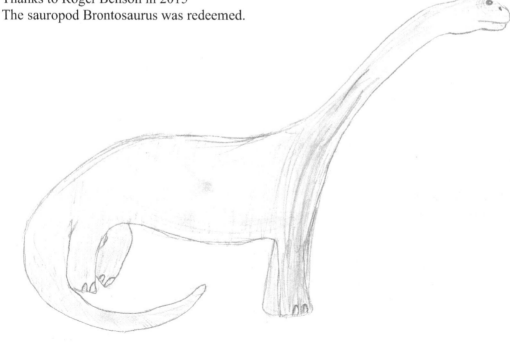

September

"Be yourself; everyone else is already taken."
—Oscar Wilde

Children of Liberty, Children of Mine
By Sarah Janisse Brown

Give them liberty, set them free
Let the become who they were meant to be,
Keep them safe from the lightening,
let them play in the rain
Let them walk through the trials, that bring your heart pain
Let them learn from life's lessons one day at a time
Let them feel the warmth of God's mercy shine
When they fall give them grace- with love on your face
Lift them up and restore them to love's highest place
When they weep let them know you weep too
When they walk through the valley- pray they'll make it though
When they break your rules, or break your heart
Have compassion to help them to make a new start
And let them always come running back to you...
No matter how much mud they've been running through.
Live a life of faith that that leads the way
And always shower them with hope and praise
Lead them and guide them and then set them free
That they would become who they were meant to be.

Arithmetic
By Carl Sandburg

Arithmetic is where numbers fly like pigeons in and out of your
head.
Arithmetic tells you how many you lose or win if you know how
many you had before you lost or won.
Arithmetic is seven eleven all good children go to heaven — or five
six bundle of sticks.
Arithmetic is numbers you squeeze from your head to your hand
to your pencil to your paper till you get the answer.
Arithmetic is where the answer is right and everything is nice and
you can look out of the window and see the blue sky — or the
answer is wrong and you have to start all over and try again
and see how it comes out this time.
If you take a number and double it and double it again and then
double it a few more times, the number gets bigger and bigger
and goes higher and higher and only arithmetic can tell you
what the number is when you decide to quit doubling.
Arithmetic is where you have to multiply — and you carry the
multiplication table in your head and hope you won't lose it.
If you have two animal crackers, one good and one bad, and you
eat one and a striped zebra with streaks all over him eats the
other, how many animal crackers will you have if somebody
offers you five six seven and you say No no no and you say
Nay nay nay and you say Nix nix nix?
If you ask your mother for one fried egg for breakfast and she
gives you two fried eggs and you eat both of them, who is
better in arithmetic, you or your mother?

To One Who Teaches Me
By Louisa May Alcott

"To one who teaches me
The sweetness and the beauty
Of doing faithfully
And cheerfully my duty."

Mentorlove
By Kathy Mellor

I look into
> your eyes
> and see endless possibilities

I listen to
> your laugh
> knowing it is payment enough

I hear
> your opinion
> and probe to its foundation

I accept
> your paper
feeling entrusted with your soul

I recognize
> your mistakes
> as a leap towards greatness

I place obstacles
> before you
> to demonstrate unfound strength

We walk together
> among the Greats
> and dare to believe the impossible

I watch
> you leave
> yet your place in my heart remains

Always

Advice to a Young Author
By Artur Conan Doyle

First begin
Taking in.
Cargo stored,
All aboard,
Think about
Giving out.
Empty ship,
Useless trip!

Never strain
Weary brain,
Hardly fit,
Wait a bit!
After rest
Comes the best.

Sitting still,
Let it fill;
Never press;
Nerve stress
Always shows.
Nature knows.

Critics kind,
Never mind!
Critics flatter,
No matter!
Critics curse,
None the worse.
Critics blame,
All the same!
Do your best.
Hang the rest!

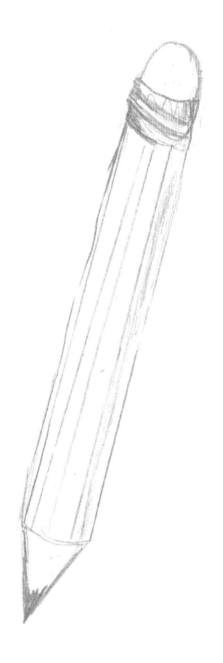

If You Were Coming in the Fall
By Emily Dickinson

If you were coming in the fall,
I'd brush the summer by
With half a smile and half a spurn,
As housewives do a fly.

If I could see you in a year,
I'd wind the months in balls,
And put them each in separate drawers,
Until their time befalls.

If only centuries delayed,
I'd count them on my hand,
Subtracting till my fingers dropped
Into Van Diemen's land.

If certain, when this life was out
That yours and mine should be,
I'd toss it yonder like a rind,
And taste eternity.
But now, all ignorant of the length
Of time's uncertain wing,
It goads me, like the goblin bee,
That will not state its sting.

---

spurn—*to push, brush, or kick away*
befalls—*occurs, happens*
Van Diemen's land—*the island of Tasmania, originally called this by most europeans; its name was changed in 1856*
ignorant—*not knowing, uninformed*
goad—*a pointed tool to encourage an animal to move*

Bells
By Sara Teasdale

At six o'clock of an autumn dusk
With the sky in the west a rusty red,
The bells of the mission down in the valley
Cry out that the day is dead.

The first star pricks as sharp as steel,
Why am I suddenly so cold?
Three bells, each with a separate sound
Clang in the valley, wearily tolled.

Bells in Venice, bells at sea,
Bells in the valley heavy and slow,
There is no place over the crowded world
Where I can forget that the days go.

When You Are Old
By W. B. Yeats

When you are old and grey and full of sleep,
And nodding by the fire, take down this book,
And slowly read, and dream of the soft look
Your eyes had once, and of their shadows deep;
How many loved your moments of glad grace,
And loved your beauty with love false or true,
But one man loved the pilgrim soul in you,
And loved the sorrows of your changing face;
And bending down beside the glowing bars,
Murmur, a little sadly, how Love fled
And paced upon the mountains overhead
And hid his face amid a crowd of stars.

Morning Song
By Sara Teasdale

A diamond of a morning
   Waked me an hour too soon;
Dawn had taken in the stars
   And left the faint white moon.

O white moon, you are lonely,
   It is the same with me,
But we have the world to roam over,
   Only the lonely are free.

Ever and Everywhere
By Johann Wolfgang von Goethe

Far explore the mountain hollow,
High in air the clouds then follow!

To each brook and vale the Muse

Thousand times her call renews.

Soon as a flow'ret blooms in spring,
It wakens many a strain;

And when Time spreads his fleeting wing,

The seasons come again.

Less Than a Cloud to the Wind
By Sara Teasdale

Less than the cloud to the wind,
Less than the foam to the sea,
Less than a rose to the storm
Am I to thee

More than the star to the night,
More than the rain to the lea,
More than heaven to earth
Art thou to me.

Lines Composed in a Wood on a Windy Day
By Anne Brontë

My soul is awakened, my spirit is soaring
And carried aloft on the wings of the breeze;
For above and around me the wild wind is roaring,
Arousing to rapture the earth and the seas.

The long withered grass in the sunshine is glancing,
The bare trees are tossing their branches on high;
The dead leaves, beneath them, are merrily dancing,
The white clouds are scudding across the blue sky.

I wish I could see how the ocean is lashing
The foam of its billows to whirlwinds of spray;
I wish I could see how its proud waves are dashing,
And hear the wild roar of their thunder today!

---

scudding—*moving quickly in a strait line*
spray—*a small shoot extending from a branch; small particles of water that leaves a wave and floats around in the air*

Daybreak
By Henry Wadsworth Longfellow

A wind came up out of the sea,
And said, "O mists, make room for me."

It hailed the ships, and cried, "Sail on,
Ye mariners, the night is gone."

And hurried landward far away,
Crying, "Awake! it is the day."

It said unto the forest, "Shout!
Hang all your leafy banners out!"

It touched the wood-bird's folded wing,
And said, "O bird, awake and sing."

And o'er the farms, "O chanticleer,
Your clarion blow; the day is near."

It whispered to the fields of corn,
"Bow down, and hail the coming morn."

It shouted through the belfry-tower,
"Awake, O bell! proclaim the hour."

It crossed the churchyard with a sigh,
And said, "Not yet! in quiet lie."

---

chanticleer—*rooster*

170

Wynken, Blynken, and Nod
By Eugene Field

Wynken, Blynken, and Nod one night
    Sailed off in a wooden shoe,—
Sailed on a river of crystal light
    Into a sea of dew.
"Where are you going, and what do you wish?"
    The old moon asked the three.
"We have come to fish for the herring-fish
    That live in this beautiful sea;
    Nets of silver and gold have we,"
            Said Wynken,
            Blynken,
            And Nod.
The old moon laughed and sang a song,
    As they rocked in the wooden shoe;
And the wind that sped them all night long
    Ruffled the waves of dew;
The little stars were the herring-fish
    That lived in the beautiful sea.
"Now cast your nets wherever you wish,—
    Never afraid are we!"
    So cried the stars to the fishermen three,
            Wynken,
            Blynken,
            And Nod.

All night long their nets they threw
   To the stars in the twinkling foam,—
Then down from the skies came the wooden shoe,
   Bringing the fishermen home:
'Twas all so pretty a sail, it seemed
   As if it could not be;
And some folk thought 'twas a dream they'd dreamed
   Of sailing that beautiful sea;
   But I shall name you the fishermen three:
        Wynken,
        Blynken,
        And Nod.

Wynken and Blynken are two little eyes,
   And Nod is a little head,
And the wooden shoe that sailed the skies
   Is a wee one's trundle-bed;
So shut your eyes while Mother sings
   Of wonderful sights that be,
And you shall see the beautiful things
   As you rock in the misty sea
   Where the old shoe rocked the fishermen three:—
        Wynken,
        Blynken,
        And Nod.

I Love All Beauteous Things
By Robert Bridges

I love all beauteous things,
I seek and adore them;
God hath no better praise,
And man in his hasty days
Is honoured for them.

I too will something make
And joy in the making;
Altho' to-morrow it seem
Like the empty words of a dream
Remembered on waking.

The Cow
By Robert Louis Stevenson

The friendly cow all red and white,
    I love with all my heart:
She gives me cream with all her might,
    To eat with apple-tart.

She wanders lowing here and there,
    And yet she cannot stray,
All in the pleasant open air,
    The pleasant light of day;

And blown by all the winds that pass
    And wet with all the showers,
She walks among the meadow grass
    And eats the meadow flowers.

A Late Walk
By Robert Frost

When I go up through the mowing field,
The headless aftermath,
Smooth-laid like thatch with the heavy dew,
Half closes the garden path.

And when I come to the garden ground,
The whir of sober birds
Up from the tangle of withered weeds
Is sadder than any words

A tree beside the wall stands bare,
But a leaf that lingered brown,
Disturbed, I doubt not, by my thought,
Comes softly rattling down.

I end not far from my going forth
By picking the faded blue
Of the last remaining aster flower
To carry again to you.

---

whir—*a continuous sound*

September
By Helen Hunt Jackson

The golden-rod is yellow;
The corn is turning brown;
The trees in apple orchards
With fruit are bending down.
The gentian's bluest fringes
Are curling in the sun;
In dusty pods the milkweed
Its hidden silk has spun.
The sedges flaunt their harvest,
In every meadow nook;
And asters by the brook-side
Make asters in the brook.
From dewy lanes at morning
the grapes' sweet odors rise;
At noon the roads all flutter
With yellow butterflies.
By all these lovely tokens
September days are here,
With summer's best of weather,
And autumn's best of cheer.
But none of all this beauty
Which floods the earth and air
Is unto me the secret
Which makes September fair.
'T is a thing which I remember;
To name it thrills me yet:
One day of one September
I never can forget.

---

gentian—*a specific genus of plant commonly found in the mountains of Germany*
sedges—*a tall grass plant*

The Mirror
By A. A. Milne

Between the woods the afternoon
Its fallen in a golden swoon,
The sun looks down from quiet skies
To where a quiet water lies,
And silent trees stoop down to the trees.
And there I saw a white swan make
Another white swan in the lake;
And, breast to breast, both motionless,
They waited for the wind's caress. . .
And all the water was at ease.

---

swoon—*to collapse into a fainting induced by extreme emotion*

Elegant Grey
By Christine Owens

She sits there in the water, massive elegant grey
Bubbles rising from her nose enjoying a bright day
Her gapping wide mouth opens, to welcome water plants
Her rear goes up, tail starts to spin, her feces fly and dance

Song of Myself
By Walt Whitman

Not I, not any one else can travel that road for you,
You must travel it for yourself.
It is not far, it is within reach,
Perhaps you have been on it since you were born and did not know,
Perhaps it is everywhere on water and on land.

The Banjo Player
By Fenton Johnson

There is music in me,
the music of a peasant people.
I wander through the levee,
picking my banjo
and singing my songs
of the cabin and the field.
At the Last Chance Saloon
I am as welcome as the violets in March;
there is always food and drink for me there,
and the dimes of those who love honest music.
Behind the railroad tracks
the little children clap their hands
and love me as they love Kris Kringle.
But I fear that I am a failure.
Last night a woman called me a troubadour.

What is a troubadour?

---

levee—*an embankment made to stop the overflow of river water*
troubadour—*a French musical poet from the 11th to 13th centuries (medieval era), love being a common lyrical theme*

Travel
By Edna St. Vincent Millay

The railroad track is miles away,
And the day is loud with voices speaking,
Yet there isn't a train goes by all day
But I hear its whistle shrieking.

All night there isn't a train goes by,
Though the night is still for sleep and dreaming,
But I see its cinders red on the sky,
And hear its engine steaming.

My heart is warm with the friends I make,
And better friends I'll not be knowing;
Yet there isn't a train I wouldn't take,
No matter where it's going.

Holidays
By Henry Wadsworth Longfellow

The holiest of all holidays are those
       Kept by ourselves in silence and apart;
       The secret anniversaries of the heart,
       When the full river of feeling overflows;—
The happy days unclouded to their close;
       The sudden joys that out of darkness start
       As flames from ashes; swift desires that dart
       Like swallows singing down each wind that blows!
White as the gleam of a receding sail,
       White as a cloud that floats and fades in air,
       White as the whitest lily on a stream,
These tender memories are;— a Fairy Tale
       Of some enchanted land we know not where,
       But lovely as a landscape in a dream.

When Imagination Takes Role
By Adison Thomas

Waves and water with marine,
Valleys and meadows all in green.
Flowers of red, pink, and gold,
The mountains and rocks of old.
Palaces, cottages, and castles,
Tall tapestries of color with tassels.
Brave knights and fair ladies,
Fierce dragons and dainty fairies.
Something you've always wanted to be,
That inside yourself you cannot see.
But in your head you are better than best,
To imagine this is truly the test.
When you think of new things,
Your mind clearly rings.
It soars from pole to pole,
That's when imagination takes role!

The Cats Have Come to Tea
By Kate Greenaway

What did she see oh, what did she see,
As she stood leaning against the tree?
Why all the Cats had come to tea.

What a fine turn out from round about,
All the houses had let them out,
And here they were with scamper and shout.

"Mew mew mew!" was all they could say,
And, "We hope we find you well to-day."

Oh, what should she do oh, what should she do?
What a lot of milk they would get through;
For here they were with "Mew mew mew!"

She didn't know oh, she didn't know,
If bread and butter they'd like or no;
They might want little mice, oh! oh! oh!

Dear me oh, dear me,
All the cats had come to tea.

Fog
By Carl Sandberg

The fog comes
On little cat feet.
It sits looking
over harbor and city
On silent haunches
And then moves on.

———————————

haunches—*on a animal or human it is referring to the area of the body including both the buttock and thigh.*

October

"Expose yourself to your deepest fear; after that, fear has no power, and the fear of freedom shrinks and vanishes. You are free."
—Jim Morrison

Late Autumn
By William Allingham

October - and the skies are cool and gray
O'er stubbles emptied of their latest sheaf,
Bare meadow, and the slowly falling leaf.
The dignity of woods in rich decay
Accords full well with this majestic grief
That clothes our solemn purple hills to-day,
Whose afternoon is hush'd, and wintry brief
Only a robin sings from any spray.

And night sends up her pale cold moon, and spills
White mist around the hollows of the hills,
Phantoms of firth or lake; the peasant sees
His cot and stockyard, with the homestead trees,
Islanded; but no foolish terror thrills
His perfect harvesting; he sleeps at ease.

---

sheaf—*a bundle of straw, to be collected and bound*
spray—*a small shoot extending from a branch*
cot—*a small house or hut*

The Road Not Taken
By Robert Frost

Two roads diverged in a yellow wood,
And sorry I could not travel both
And be one traveler, long I stood
And looked down one as far as I could
To where it bent in the undergrowth;

Then took the other, as just as fair,
And having perhaps the better claim,
Because it was grassy and wanted wear;
Though as for that the passing there
Had worn them really about the same,

And both that morning equally lay
In leaves no step had trodden black.
Oh, I kept the first for another day!
Yet knowing how way leads on to way,
I doubted if I should ever come back.

I shall be telling this with a sigh
Somewhere ages and ages hence:
Two roads diverged in a wood, and I—
I took the one less traveled by,
And that has made all the difference.

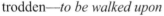

diverged—*two lines that are not parallel, to proceed in two different directions*
trodden—*to be walked upon*

A Leaf
By Emily Mary Barton

OH Mother Linden, hold me fast,
I tremble in the vernal blast,
Lest, with its ice-drops cold and keen,
It rend my new-made robe of green;
Rudely it threatens to divide
The link that binds me to thy side.
> "Fear not, my child, the Hand that made
> The breeze and sunshine, light and shade,
> Has bid thee on my branch to grow,
> And taught me not to let thee go."
A summer storm obscures the skies,
The thunder growls, the lightning flies,
Nature lets loose in sudden ire,
Her streams of water and of fire;
And, wildly flutt'ring in the strife.
Mother, I cling to thee for life.
> "Be comforted, this whirling blast
> But cleanses as it hurries past;
> The Voice that bids the tempest blow
> Will tell me when to let thee go."
Now Autumn, with her rustling train,
Has swept the fields of golden grain,
And tinted me with amber hues,
And spangled me with diamond dews;
My stem is weak, my veins are dry,
My crimson brethren round me fly.
> In bright attire they hover round,
> Or dance in circles on the ground;
> Caressing breezes whisper low,
> "Mother, sweet mother, let me go!"
We know not where the leaflet lies,
But we believe that genial skies
Are bending o'er her mossy bed,
With kindred relies overspread.
We brush them in our morning ride,
And o'er them muse at eventide.
> We marvel why so gaily drest
> The children left their mother's breast,
> But not in sorrow, for we know
> The wither'd leaf was glad to go!

---

vernal—*belonging to Spring*   genial—*merry, cheerfulness*
ire—*wrath or anger*   muse—*to think, contemplate, ponder or meditate in silence*
tempest—*a wild and dangerous storm*
spangle—*to glisten or shine, to be decorated in with small, shiny details*

Autumn Thoughts
By John Greenleaf Whittier

Gone hath the Spring, with all its flowers,
And gone the Summer's pomp and show,
And Autumn, in his leafless bowers,
Is waiting for the Winter's snow.

I said to Earth, so cold and gray,
An emblem of myself thou art.
Not so, the Earth did seem to say,
For Spring shall warm my frozen heart.
I soothe my wintry sleep with dreams
Of warmer sun and softer rain,
And wait to hear the sound of streams
And songs of merry birds again.

But thou, from whom the Spring hath gone,
For whom the flowers no longer blow,
Who standest blighted and forlorn,
Like Autumn waiting for the snow;

No hope is thine of sunnier hours,
Thy Winter shall no more depart;
No Spring revive thy wasted flowers,
Nor Summer warm thy frozen heart.

———————————————

bowers—*shaded covering under a tree caused by branches*
blighted—*disease happening to a plant, to stop growth, to frustrate, to be blasted*

Dusk in Autumn
By Sara Teasdale

The moon is like a scimitar,
A little silver scimitar,
A-drifting down the sky.
And near beside it is a star,
A timid twinkling golden star,
That watches likes an eye.

And thro' the nursery window-pane
The witches have a fire again,
Just like the ones we make,—
And now I know they're having tea,
I wish they'd give a cup to me,
With witches' currant cake.

---

scimitar—*a curved short sword used in Prussia and Turkey*

Autumn Dusk
By Sara Teasdale

I saw above a sea of hills
        A solitary shine,
And there was no one, near or far,
        To keep the world from being mine.

Mountain Travel
By Du Mu

Far away on the cold mountain, a stone path slants upwards,
In the white clouds is a village, where people have their homes.
I stop the carriage, loving the maple wood in the evening,
The frosted leaves are redder than the second month's flowers.

The Two Streams
By Oliver Wendell Holmes Sr.

Behold the rocky wall
That down its sloping sides
Pours the swift rain-drops, blending, as they fall,
In rushing river-tides!

Yon stream, whose sources run
Turned by a pebble's edge,
Is Athabasca, rolling toward the sun
Through the cleft mountain-ledge.

The slender rill had strayed,
But for the slanting stone,
To evening's ocean, with the tangled braid
Of foam-flecked Oregon.

So from the heights of Will
Life's parting stream descends,
And, as a moment turns its slender rill,
Each widening torrent bends,—

From the same cradle's side,
From the same mother's knee,—
One to long darkness and the frozen tide,
One to the Peaceful Sea!

————————————————
Athabasca—*a river in Alberta, Canada*
rill—*a small brook*

The Kraken
By Alfred Lord Tennyson

Below the thunders of the upper deep,
Far, far beneath in the abysmal sea,
His ancient, dreamless, uninvaded sleep
The Kraken sleepeth: faintest sunlights flee
About his shadowy sides; above him swell
Huge sponges of millennial growth and height;
And far away into the sickly light,
From many a wondrous grot and secret cell
Unnumbered and enormous polypi
Winnow with giant arms the slumbering green.
There hath he lain for ages, and will lie
Battening upon huge sea worms in his sleep,
Until the latter fire shall heat the deep;
Then once by man and angels to be seen,
In roaring he shall rise and on the surface die.

---

abysmal—*extremely deep, appalling*
millennial—*referring to a thousand years*
grot—*can be short for grotesque, to be very ugly, disfigured*
polypi (polyp)—*a sea creature with a mouth at the center that is surrounded by tentacles,
like a sea anemone*
winnow—*to fan or beat about*
battening—*becoming fatter*

A Noiseless Patient Spider
By Walt Whitman

A noiseless patient spider,
I mark'd where on a little promontory it stood isolated,
Mark'd how to explore the vacant vast surrounding,
It launch'd forth filament, filament, filament, out of itself,
Ever unreeling them, ever tirelessly speeding them.

And you O my soul where you stand,
Surrounded, detached, in measureless oceans of space,
Ceaselessly musing, venturing, throwing, seeking the spheres to connect them,
Till the bridge you will need be form'd, till the ductile anchor hold,
Till the gossamer thread you fling catch somewhere, O my soul.

---

promontory—*high elevated land that is jutting out into a large body of water like the Rock of Gibraltar*
filament—*a fine fiber*
musing, muse—*to think, contemplate, ponder or meditate in silence*
ductile—*in Latin it means to lead, can also mean flexible*
gossamer—*a substance that is fine like cobwebs*

Theme in Yellow
By Carl Sandburg

I spot the hills
With yellow balls in autumn.
I light the prairie cornfields
Orange and tawny gold clusters
And I am called pumpkins.
On the last of October
When dusk is fallen
Children join hands
And circle round me
Singing ghost songs
And love to the harvest moon;
I am a jack-o'-lantern
With terrible teeth
And the children know
I am fooling.

Ruth
By Thomas Hood

She stood breast high amid the corn,
Clasped by the golden light of morn,
Like the sweetheart of the sun,
Who many a glowing kiss had won.

On her cheek an autumn flush,
Deeply ripened;—such a blush
In the midst of brown was born,
Like red poppies grown with corn.

Round her eyes her tresses fell,
Which were blackest none could tell,
But long lashes veiled a light,
That had else been all too bright.

And her hat, with shady brim,
Made her tressy forehead dim;—
Thus she stood amid the stooks,
Praising God with sweetest looks:—

Sure, I said, heaven did not mean,
Where I reap thou shouldst but glean,
Lay thy sheaf adown and come,
Share my harvest and my home.

---

tresses—*sections of hair that are in curls or ringlets*
glean—*to collect what little is left*
sheaf—*a bundle of straw, to be collected and bound*

Calling
By Steven Wesley Law

a button lying in a box amongst others
buttons look natural, quite comfortable
looks like it belongs

but what the button really wants is
to be
sewn to the shirt and pushed through
the button hole

Little Phillis
By Kate Greenaway

I am a very little girl,
    I think that I've turned two;
And if you'd like to know my name
    I'd like to tell it you.

They always call me Baby,
    But Phillis is my name.
No no one ever gave it me,
    I think it only came.

I've got a pretty tulip
    In my little flower-bed;
If you would like I'll give it you
    It's yellow, striped with red.

I've got a little kitten, but
    I can't give that away,
She likes to play with me *so* much;
    She's gone to sleep to-day.

And I've got a nice new dolly,
    Shall I fetch her out to you?
She's got such pretty shoes on,
    And her bonnet's trimmed with blue.

You'd like to take her home with you?
    Oh, *no*, she mustn't go;
Good-bye I want to run now,
    You walk along so slow.

When I Shall Sleep
By Emily Bronte

Oh, for the time when I shall sleep
Without identity,
And never care how rain may steep,
Or snow may cover me!
No promised heaven these wild desires
Could all, or half, fulful;
No threatened hell, with quenchless fires,
Subdue this quenchless will!

So said I, and still say the same;
Still, to my death, will say –
Three gods within this little frame
Are warring night and day:
Heaven could not hold them all, and yet
They all are held in me;
And must be mine till I forget
My present entity!

Oh, for the time when in my breast
Their struggles will be o'er!
Oh, for the day when I shall rest,
And never suffer more!

To Sleep
By John Keats

O soft embalmer of the still midnight!
  Shutting with careful fingers and benign
Our gloom-pleased eyes, embower'd from the light,
  Enshaded in forgetfulness divine;
O soothest Sleep! if so it please thee, close,
  In midst of this thine hymn, my willing eyes,
Or wait the amen, ere thy poppy throws
  Around my bed its lulling charities;
  Then save me, or the passèd day will shine
Upon my pillow, breeding many woes;
Save me from curious conscience, that still lords
  Its strength for darkness, burrowing like a mole;
Turn the key deftly in the oilèd wards,
  And seal the hushèd casket of my soul.

---

embalmer—*a person that preserved dead bodies*
benign—*kind and gentle disposition*
embower'd—*sheltered or covered*
enshaded—*to be kept in shade*
deftly—*to work in neat and skillful way with great dexterity*

Deadly Dreams
By Kylie Liu

Journeying through my horrid nightmares,
I meet many zombies on wild night tears.
Monsters who are both smart and tricky,
Seeking for brains which are very icky.

Following them is a group of vampires,
Avoiding men with pitchforks and fires.
Feasting on stray mortals with vigor,
They tower high over my small figure.

Sanguinary blood drips from their fangs,
I watch, heart beating with pangs.
The scene shifts into a garden lush,
I think a witch is causing it in a rush.

The witch then curses me with a rash.
Finally, she whips me with a lash.
She calls a man to slowly me dead make,
A killer who will toss me in a lake.

I'm stretched on burning torture racks.
Then, the man starts to sharpen his axe.
As my life he's about to take,
I suddenly awake.

---

vigor—*with strength and enthusiasm*
sanguinary—*accompanied with much blood shed, cruel, murderous*
pangs—*extreme bodily pains, spasms*

Jabberwocky
By Lewis Carroll

'Twas brillig, and the slithy toves
Did gyre and gimble in the wabe:
All mimsy were the borogoves,
And the mome raths outgrabe.
"Beware the Jabberwock, my son!
The jaws that bite, the claws that catch!
Beware the Jubjub bird, and shun
The frumious Bandersnatch!"
He took his vorpal sword in hand:
Long time the manxome foe he sought
So rested he by the Tumtum tree,
And stood a while in thought.
And, as in uffish thought he stood,
The Jabberwock, with eyes of flame,
Came whiffling through the tulgey wood,
And burbled as it came!
One two! One two! And through and through
The vorpal blade went snicker-snack!
He left it dead, and with its head
He went galumphing back.
"And hast thou slain the Jabberwock?
Come to my arms, my beamish boy!
Oh frabjous day! Callooh! Callay!"
He chortled in his joy.
'Twas brillig, and the slithy toves
Did gyre and gimble in the wabe:
All mimsy were the borogoves,
And the mome raths outgrabe.

NOTE: *Many words in this poem are nonsensical and have many interpretations. Have fun and look up the different literary explanations for many of the words.*
gyre—*gyrate, to move quickly in a circular motion like a spiral*

Fire and Ice
By Robert Frost

Some say the world will end in fire,
Some say in ice.
From what I've tasted of desire
I hold with those who favor fire.
But if it had to perish twice,
I think I know enough of hate
To say that for destruction ice
Is also great
And would suffice.

A Train Went Through a Burial Gate
By Emily Dickinson

A train went through a burial gate,
A bird broke forth and sang,
And trilled, and quivered, and shook his throat
Till all the churchyard rang ;

And then adjusted his little notes,
And bowed and sang again.
Doubtless, he thought it meet of him
To say good-by to men.

Invictus
By William Earnest Henley

Out of the night that covers me,
    Black as the pit from pole to pole,
I thank whatever gods may be
    For my unconquerable soul.

In the fell clutch of circumstance
    I have not winced nor cried aloud.
Under the bludgeonings of chance
    My head is bloody, but unbowed.

Beyond this place of wrath and tears
    Looms but the Horror of the shade,
And yet the menace of the years
    Finds and shall find me unafraid.

It matters not how strait the gate,
    How charged with punishments the scroll,
I am the master of my fate,
    I am the captain of my soul.

The Little Ghost
By Edna St. Vincent Millay

I knew her for a little ghost
    That in my garden walked;
The wall is high—higher than most—
    And the green gate was locked.
And yet I did not think of that
    Till after she was gone—
I knew her by the broad white hat,
    All ruffled, she had on.
By the dear ruffles round her feet,
    By her small hands that hung
In their lace mitts, austere and sweet,
    Her gown's white folds among.
I watched to see if she would stay,
    What she would do—and oh!
She looked as if she liked the way
    I let my garden grow!
She bent above my favourite mint
    With conscious garden grace,
She smiled and smiled—there was no hint
    Of sadness in her face.
She held her gown on either side
    To let her slippers show,
And up the walk she went with pride,
    The way great ladies go.
And where the wall is built in new
    And is of ivy bare
She paused—then opened and passed through
    A gate that once was there.

---

austere—*rigid*

The Night Wind
By Eugene Field

Have you ever heard the wind go "Yoooo"?
  'Tis a pitiful sound to hear!
It seems to chill you through and through
  With a strange and speechless fear.
'Tis the voice of the night that broods outside
  When folks should be asleep,
And many and many's the time I've cried
To the darkness brooding far and wide
  Over the land and the deep:
"Whom do you want, O lonely night,
  That you wail the long hours through?"
And the night would say in its ghostly way,
  "Yoooooooo!
  Yoooooooo!
  Yoooooooo!"

My mother told me long ago
  (When I was a little lad)
That when the night went wailing so,
  Somebody had been bad;
And then, when I was snug in bed,
  Whither I had been sent,
With the blankets pulled up round my head,
I'd think of what my mother'd said,
  And wonder what boy she meant!
And, "Who's been bad today?" I'd ask
  Of the wind that hoarsely blew,
And the voice would say in its meaningful way,
  "Yoooooooo!
  Yoooooooo!
  Yoooooooo!"

That this was true I must allow —
  You'll not believe it, though!
Yes, though I'm quite a model now,
  I was not always so.
And if you doubt what things I say,
  Suppose you make the test;
Suppose, when you've been bad some day
And up to bed are sent away
  From mother and the rest —
Suppose you ask, "Who has been bad?"
  And then you'll hear what's true,
For the wind will moan in its ruefulest tone:
  "Yoooooooo!
  Yoooooooo!
  Yoooooooo!"

"Double, Double Toil and Trouble"
(Song of the witches from *Macbeth*)
By William Shakespeare

Double, double toil and trouble;
Fire burn and caldron bubble.
Fillet of a fenny snake,
In the caldron boil and bake;
Eye of newt and toe of frog,
Wool of bat and tongue of dog,
Adder's fork and blind-worm's sting,
Lizard's leg and howlet's wing,
For a charm of powerful trouble,
Like a hell-broth boil and bubble.

Double, double toil and trouble;
Fire burn and caldron bubble.
Cool it with a baboon's blood,
Then the charm is firm and good.

The Raven
By Edgar Allan Poe

Once upon a midnight dreary, while I pondered, weak and weary,
Over many a quaint and curious volume of forgotten lore—
      While I nodded, nearly napping, suddenly there came a tapping,
As of some one gently rapping, rapping at my chamber door.
"'Tis some visitor," I muttered, "tapping at my chamber door—
      Only this and nothing more."

      Ah, distinctly I remember it was in the bleak December;
And each separate dying ember wrought its ghost upon the floor.
      Eagerly I wished the morrow;—vainly I had sought to borrow
      From my books surcease of sorrow—sorrow for the lost Lenore—
For the rare and radiant maiden whom the angels name Lenore—
      Nameless *here* for evermore.

      And the silken, sad, uncertain rustling of each purple curtain
Thrilled me—filled me with fantastic terrors never felt before;
      So that now, to still the beating of my heart, I stood repeating
      "'Tis some visitor entreating entrance at my chamber door—
Some late visitor entreating entrance at my chamber door;—
      This it is and nothing more."

      Presently my soul grew stronger; hesitating then no longer,
"Sir," said I, "or Madam, truly your forgiveness I implore;
      But the fact is I was napping, and so gently you came rapping,
      And so faintly you came tapping, tapping at my chamber door,
That I scarce was sure I heard you"—here I opened wide the door;—
      Darkness there and nothing more.

      Deep into that darkness peering, long I stood there wondering, fearing,
Doubting, dreaming dreams no mortal ever dared to dream before;
      But the silence was unbroken, and the stillness gave no token,
      And the only word there spoken was the whispered word, "Lenore?"
This I whispered, and an echo murmured back the word, "Lenore!"—
      Merely this and nothing more.

      Back into the chamber turning, all my soul within me burning,
Soon again I heard a tapping somewhat louder than before.
      "Surely," said I, "surely that is something at my window lattice;
      Let me see, then, what thereat is, and this mystery explore—
Let my heart be still a moment and this mystery explore;—
      'Tis the wind and nothing more!"

Open here I flung the shutter, when, with many a flirt and flutter,
In there stepped a stately Raven of the saintly days of yore;
　　Not the least obeisance made he; not a minute stopped or stayed he;
　　But, with mien of lord or lady, perched above my chamber door—
Perched upon a bust of Pallas just above my chamber door—
　　Perched, and sat, and nothing more.

Then this ebony bird beguiling my sad fancy into smiling,
By the grave and stern decorum of the countenance it wore,
"Though thy crest be shorn and shaven, thou," I said, "art sure no craven,
Ghastly grim and ancient Raven wandering from the Nightly shore—
Tell me what thy lordly name is on the Night's Plutonian shore!"
　　Quoth the Raven "Nevermore."

　　Much I marvelled this ungainly fowl to hear discourse so plainly,
Though its answer little meaning—little relevancy bore;
　　For we cannot help agreeing that no living human being
　　Ever yet was blessed with seeing bird above his chamber door—
Bird or beast upon the sculptured bust above his chamber door,
　　With such name as "Nevermore."

　　But the Raven, sitting lonely on the placid bust, spoke only
That one word, as if his soul in that one word he did outpour.
　　Nothing farther then he uttered—not a feather then he fluttered—
　　Till I scarcely more than muttered "Other friends have flown before—
On the morrow *he* will leave me, as my Hopes have flown before."
　　Then the bird said "Nevermore."

　　Startled at the stillness broken by reply so aptly spoken,
"Doubtless," said I, "what it utters is its only stock and store
　　Caught from some unhappy master whom unmerciful Disaster
　　Followed fast and followed faster till his songs one burden bore—
Till the dirges of his Hope that melancholy burden bore
　　Of 'Never—nevermore'."

　　But the Raven still beguiling all my fancy into smiling,
Straight I wheeled a cushioned seat in front of bird, and bust and door;
　　Then, upon the velvet sinking, I betook myself to linking
　　Fancy unto fancy, thinking what this ominous bird of yore—
What this grim, ungainly, ghastly, gaunt, and ominous bird of yore
　　Meant in croaking "Nevermore."

　　This I sat engaged in guessing, but no syllable expressing
To the fowl whose fiery eyes now burned into my bosom's core;
　　This and more I sat divining, with my head at ease reclining
　　On the cushion's velvet lining that the lamp-light gloated o'er,
But whose velvet-violet lining with the lamp-light gloating o'er,
　　She shall press, ah, nevermore!

Then, methought, the air grew denser, perfumed from an unseen censer
Swung by Seraphim whose foot-falls tinkled on the tufted floor.
"Wretch," I cried, "thy God hath lent thee—by these angels he hath sent thee
Respite—respite and nepenthe from thy memories of Lenore;
Quaff, oh quaff this kind nepenthe and forget this lost Lenore!"
Quoth the Raven "Nevermore."

"Prophet!" said I, "thing of evil!—prophet still, if bird or devil!—
Whether Tempter sent, or whether tempest tossed thee here ashore,
Desolate yet all undaunted, on this desert land enchanted—
On this home by Horror haunted—tell me truly, I implore—
Is there—*is* there balm in Gilead?—tell me—tell me, I implore!"
Quoth the Raven "Nevermore."

"Prophet!" said I, "thing of evil!—prophet still, if bird or devil!
By that Heaven that bends above us—by that God we both adore—
Tell this soul with sorrow laden if, within the distant Aidenn,
It shall clasp a sainted maiden whom the angels name Lenore—
Clasp a rare and radiant maiden whom the angels name Lenore."
Quoth the Raven "Nevermore."

"Be that word our sign of parting, bird or fiend!" I shrieked, upstarting—
"Get thee back into the tempest and the Night's Plutonian shore!
Leave no black plume as a token of that lie thy soul hath spoken!
Leave my loneliness unbroken!—quit the bust above my door!
Take thy beak from out my heart, and take thy form from off my door!"
Quoth the Raven "Nevermore."

And the Raven, never flitting, still is sitting, *still* is sitting
On the pallid bust of Pallas just above my chamber door;
And his eyes have all the seeming of a demon's that is dreaming,
And the lamp-light o'er him streaming throws his shadow on the floor;
And my soul from out that shadow that lies floating on the floor
Shall be lifted—nevermore!

---

surcease—*to stop*
implore—*to ask or petition earnestly, beg*
mien—*one's look or manner*
Pallas—*a Greek Titan god*
decorum—*how one speaks or behaves*
obeisance—*to bow or curtsey*
melancholy—*a mood that is gloomy and depressed*
Plutonian—*referring to or comparing to the underworld*
ominous—*implying a future act or event*
nepenthe—*a medication or drug that eliminates pain*
quaff—*to swallow large amounts of liquid at a time, to gulp down*
Aidenn—*the Arabic word for 'paradise'*

November

"Happiness is a choice that requires effort at times."
—Aeschylus

A Caution to Poets
By Matthew Arnold

What poets feel not, when they make,
A pleasure in creating,
The world, in its turn, will not take
Pleasure in contemplating

A Plea to the King
By Elena Cutler

How could the earth be a boring abyss
With all the people such as this:
The soldiers who never say a word?
Or the dancer whose music is always heard?
What of the storyteller whose shows are worthwhile,
Bringing to the children smile upon smile?
Or the workers who seem not to have names
Yet always have time for the children's games?
Or the little toddlers with two left feet
Who follow their parents like little lost sheep?
They might seem like stepping stones in the ground.
But with them here the earth is crowned.
Not with the metal that you may believe
But with all of the things that they can achieve.
So, I ask of thee- right here, right now,
If thou wilt hear my pleaded vow;
To see the world as it really should be
Not things in the way of thy decree.
And while they need not show their worth-
(As that has been useless since their birth),
I ask of thee, O' King O' Mine,
If thou wilt see this as a sign-

To have error is human and that's all we can be,
To change is divine so that's what I ask of thee.

Each Road
By Johann Wolfgang von Goethe

 Each road to the proper end
   Runs straight on, without a bend.

City Trees
By Edna St. Vincent Millay

The trees along this city street,
    Save for the traffic and the trains,
Would make a sound as thin and sweet
    As trees in country lanes.

And people standing in their shade
    Out of a shower, undoubtedly
Would hear such music as is made
    Upon a country tree.

Oh, little leaves that are so dumb
    Against the shrieking city air,
I watch you when the wind has come,--
    I know what sound is there.

I Dream'd in a Dream
Walt Whitman

I dream'd in a dream, I saw a city invincible to the
attacks of the whole of the rest of the earth;
I dream'd that was the new City of Friends;
Nothing was greater there than the quality of robust love - it led the rest;
It was seen every hour in the actions of the men of that city,
And in all their looks and words.

----

robust—*strong, sinewy*

If I Can Stop One Heart From Breaking
By Emily Dickinson

If I can stop one heart from breaking,
I shall not live in vain ;
If I can ease one life the aching,
Or cool one pain,
Or help one fainting robin
Unto his nest again,
I shall not live in vain.

Lodged
By Robert Frost

The rain to the wind said,
'You push and I'll pelt.'
They so smote the garden bed
That the flowers actually knelt,
And lay lodged, though not dead.
I know how the flowers felt.

Life
By Charlotte Bronte

Life, believe, is not a dream
So dark as sages say;
Oft a little morning rain
Foretells a pleasant day.
Sometimes there are clouds of gloom,
But these are transient all;
If the shower will make the roses bloom,
O why lament its fall?
Rapidly, merrily,
Life's sunny hours flit by,
Gratefully, cheerily
Enjoy them as they fly!
What though Death at times steps in,
And calls our Best away?
What though sorrow seems to win,
O'er hope, a heavy sway?
Yet Hope again elastic springs,
Unconquered, though she fell;
Still buoyant are her golden wings,
Still strong to bear us well.
Manfully, fearlessly,
The day of trial bear,
For gloriously, victoriously,
Can courage quell despair!

---

transient—*not being in one place, not in a permanent place*
lament—*to cry out, to grieve or mourn about something*
buoyant—*floating or able to float*
quell—*to make quiet, to crush, to create peace*

My Books
By Henry Wadsworth Longfellow

Sadly as some old mediaeval knight
   Gazed at the arms he could no longer wield,
   The sword two-handed and the shining shield
   Suspended in the hall, and full in sight,
While secret longings for the lost delight
   Of tourney or adventure in the field
   Came over him, and tears but half concealed
   Trembled and fell upon his beard of white,
So I behold these books upon their shelf,
   My ornaments and arms of other days;
   Not wholly useless, though no longer used,
For they remind me of my other self,
   Younger and stronger, and the pleasant ways
   In which I walked, now clouded and confused.

Four Things Make Us Happy Here
By Robert Herrick

Health is the first good lent to men;
A gentle disposition then:
Next, to be rich by no by-ways;
Lastly, with friends t' enjoy our days.

To Market, To Market
Anonymous (nursery rhyme)
19th Century version

To market, to market, to buy a fat pig,
Home again, home again, jiggety-jig.
To market, to market, to buy a fat hog,
Home again, home again, jiggety-jog.
To market, to market, to buy a plum bun,
Home again, home again, market is done.

The Custard
By Robert Herrick

For second course, last night, a custard came
To th' board, so hot as none could touch the same:
Furze three or four times with his cheeks did blow
Upon the custard, and thus cooled so;
It seem'd by this time to admit the touch,
But none could eat it, 'cause it stunk so much.

**Custard recipe on page 283

---

furze—*another term for the gorse plant, a plant within the pea family with yellow flowers*

Cock-A-Doodle-Doo
Anonymous (English rhyme)

Cock a doodle do!
What is my dame to do?
Till master's found his fiddling stick,
She'll dance without her shoe.

Gathering Leaves
By Robert Frost

Spades take up leaves
No better than spoons,
And bags full of leaves
Are light as balloons.

I make a great noise
Of rustling all day
Like rabbit and deer
Running away.

But the mountains I raise
Elude my embrace,
Flowing over my arms
And into my face.

I may load and unload
Again and again
Till I fill the whole shed,
And what have I then?

Next to nothing for weight,
And since they grew duller
From contact with earth,
Next to nothing for color.

Next to nothing for use,
But a crop is a crop,
And who's to say where
The harvest shall stop?

Autumn Fires
By Robert Louis Stevenson

In the other gardens
       And all up the vale,
From the autumn bonfires
       See the smoke trail!

Pleasant summer over
       And all the summer flowers,
The red fire blazes,
       The grey smoke towers.

Sing a song of seasons!
       Something bright in all!
Flowers in the summer,
       Fires in the fall!

Sleeping on a Night of Autumn Rain
By Bai Juyi

It's cold this night in autumn's third month,
Peacefully within, a lone old man.
He lies down late, the lamp already gone out,
And beautifully sleeps amid the sound of rain.
The ash inside the vessel still warm from the fire,
Its fragrance increases the warmth of quilt and covers.
When dawn comes, clear and cold, he does not rise,
The red frosted leaves cover the steps.

Symphony in Yellow
By Oscar Wilde

An omnibus across the bridge
Crawls like a yellow butterfly
And, here and there, a passer-by
Shows like a little restless midge.

Big barges full of yellow hay
Are moored against the shadowy wharf,
And, like a yellow silken scarf,
The thick fog hangs along the quay.

The yellow leaves begin to fade
And flutter from the Temple elms,
And at my feet the pale green Thames
Lies like a rod of rippled jade.

---

omnibus—*another name for a bus*
midge—*a tiny two winged fly*
moored—*when a boat is anchored or roped in place; an English moore is an open area of land that is covered in plants like heather*
quay— *a wharf or structure onto which one secures a boat or ship*
Thames—*a river that runs through London to the North Sea*

Autumn Birds
By John Clare

The wild duck startles like a sudden thought,
And heron slow as if it might be caught.
The flopping crows on weary wings go by
And grey beard jackdaws noising as they fly.
The crowds of starnels whizz and hurry by,
And darken like a clod the evening sky.
The larks like thunder rise and suthy round,
Then drop and nestle in the stubble ground.
The wild swan hurries hight and noises loud
With white neck peering to the evening clowd.
The weary rooks to distant woods are gone.
With lengths of tail the magpie winnows on
To neighbouring tree, and leaves the distant crow
 While small birds nestle in the edge below.

---

clowd—*another spelling of cloud*
winnow—*to fan or beat about*

Autumn Within
By Henry Wadsworth Longfellow

It is autumn; not without,
    But within me is the cold.
Youth and spring are all about;
    It is I that have grown old.

Birds are darting through the air,
    Singing, building without rest;
Life is stirring everywhere,
    Save within my lonely breast.

There is silence: the dead leaves
    Fall and rustle and are still;
Beats no flail upon the sheaves
    Comes no murmur from the mill.

---

flail—*To hit or strike something*
sheaf, sheaves—*a bundle of straw, to be collected and bound*

Fall, Leaves, Fall
By Emily Brontë

Fall, leaves, fall; die, flowers, away;
Lengthen night and shorten day;
Every leaf speaks bliss to me
Fluttering from the autumn tree.

I shall smile when wreaths of snow
Blossom where the rose should grow;
I shall sing when night's decay
Ushers in a drearier day.

A Vision of Rest
By Alexander Posey

Some day this quest
  Shall cease;
Some day,
  For aye,
This heart shall rest
 In peace.
Sometimes—ofttimes—I almost feel
The calm upon my senses steal,
So soft, and all but hear
The dead leaves rustle near
And sign to be
At rest with me.
Though I behold
  The ashen branches tossing to and fro,
  Somehow I only vaguely know
The wind is rude and cold.

A Song of the Navajo Weaver
By Bertrand N. O. Walker (Hen-Toh)

For ages long, my people have been
    Dwellers in this land;
For ages viewed these mountains,
    Loved these mesas and these sands,
That stretch afar and glisten,
    Glimmering in the sun
As it lights the mighty canons
    Ere the weary day is done.
Shall I, a patient dweller in this
    Land of fair blue skies,
Tell something of their story while
    My shuttle swiftly flies?
As I weave I'll trace their journey,
    Devious, rough and wandering,
Ere they reached the silent region
    Where the night stars seem to sing.
When the myriads of them glitter
    Over peak and desert waste,
Crossing which the silent runner and
    The gaunt of co-yo-tees haste.
Shall I weave the zig-zag pathway
    Whence the sacred fire was born;
And interweave the symbol of the God
    Who brought the corn—
Of the Rain-god whose fierce anger
    Was appeased by sacred meal,
And the trust that my brave people
    In him evermore shall feel?
All this perhaps I might weave
    As the woof goes to and fro,
Wafting as my shuttle passes,
    Humble hopes, and joys and care,
Weaving closely, weaving slowly,
    While I watch the pattern grow;
Showing something of my life:
    To the Spirit God a prayer.
Grateful that he brought my people
    To the land of silence vast
Taught them arts of peace and ended
    All their wanderings of the past.
Deftly now I trace the figures,
    This of joy and that of woe;
And I leave an open gate-way
    For the Dau to come and go.

mesa(s)—*an isolated mountain or land mass with a flat top*
devious—*wandering off the common or more direct path*
myriads—*an extremely high number*
gaunt—*thin and starved looking, appearing to have sunken in cheeks and starving*
waft—*to be carried through water or air*
deftly—*to work in neat and skillful way with great dexterity*

Pilgrims
By Henry David Thoreau

'Have you not seen
  In ancient times
Pilgrims pass by
  Toward other climes?
With shining faces,
  Youthful and strong,
Mounting this hill
  With speech and with song?'
'Ah, my good sir,
  I know not those ways:
Little my knowledge,
  Tho' many my days.
When I have slumbered,
  I have heard sounds
As of travelers passing
  These my grounds:
'Twas a sweet music
  Wafted them by,
I could not tell
  If afar off or nigh.
Unless I dreamed it,
  This was of yore:
I never told it
  To mortal before;
' Never remembered
  But in my dreams,
What to me waking
  A miracle seems."

waft—*to be carried through water or air*
yore—*a long time past*

Thanksgiving
By Edgar Guest

Gettin' together to smile an' rejoice,
An' eatin' an' laughin' with folks of your choice;
An' kissin' the girls an' declarin' that they
Are growin' more beautiful day after day;
Chattin' an' braggin' a bit with the men,
Buildin' the old family circle again;
Livin' the wholesome an' old-fashioned cheer,
Just for awhile at the end of the year.

Greetings fly fast as we crowd through the door
And under the old roof we gather once more
Just as we did when the youngsters were small;
Mother's a little bit grayer, that's all.
Father's a little bit older, but still
Ready to romp an' to laugh with a will.
Here we are back at the table again
Tellin' our stories as women an' men.

Bowed are our heads for a moment in prayer;
Oh, but we're grateful an' glad to be there.
Home from the east land an' home from the west,
Home with the folks that are dearest an' best.
Out of the sham of the cities afar
We've come for a time to be just what we are.
Here we can talk of ourselves an' be frank,
Forgettin' position an' station an' rank.

Give me the end of the year an' its fun
When most of the plannin' an' toilin' is done;
Bring all the wanderers home to the nest,
Let me sit down with the ones I love best,
Hear the old voices still ringin' with song,
See the old faces unblemished by wrong,
See the old table with all of its chairs
An' I'll put soul in my Thanksgivin' prayers.

Autumn
By Emily Dickinson

The morns are meeker than they were,
The nuts are getting brown ;
The berry's cheek is plumper,
The rose is out of town.

The maple wears a gayer scarf,
The field a scarlet gown.
Lest I should be old-fashioned,
I 'll put a trinket on.

Alchemy
By Sara Teasdale

I lift my heart as spring lifts up
A yellow daisy to the rain;
My heart will be a lovely cup
Altho' it holds but pain.

For I shall learn from flower and leaf
That color every drop they hold,
To change the lifeless wine of grief
To living gold

'Tis the First Snow
By Matsuo Basho
Translated By William George Aston

'Tis the first snow
Just enough to bend
The gladiolus leaves

Autumn's Pall
By Clark Ashton Smith

But yesterday 'twas Autumn, and the leaves,
All aureate and vermeil, strewed the ground
And lay in drifted banks the trees around -
A fair and gorgeous sight. Night's hours, like thieves
Have stol'n them all, and now the Winter weaves
Where erst they lay, an ermine pall of snow.
Yon woods, where some lone bird for Autumn grieves,
And hills and fields, that pallid covering know.

---

aureate—*having the appearance of gold, made of or having gold*
vermeila—*a French term: a certain quality of jewelry that must meet very specific criteria*
ermine—*a ferret like animal popular for its snow-white winter coat*
pall—*a cloak, a cloth that is placed over a dead body or casket*

December

"Those who don't believe in magic will never find it."
—Roald Dahl

A Winter Scene
By Henry David Thoreau

The rabbit leaps,
The mouse out-creeps,
The flag out-peeps
Beside the brook;
The ferret weeps,
The marmot sleeps,
The owlet keeps
In his snug nook.
The apples thaw,
The ravens caw,
The squirrels gnaw
The frozen fruit.
To their retreat
I track the feet
Of mice that eat
The apple's root.
The snow-dust falls,
The otter crawls,
The partridge calls,
Far in the wood.
The traveller dreams,
The tree-ice gleams,
The blue-jay screams
In angry mood.
The willows droop,
The alders stoop,
The pheasants group
Beneath the snow.
The catkins green
Cast o'er the scene
A summer's sheen,
A genial glow.

First Fig
By Edna St. Vincent Millay

My candle burns at both ends;
    It will not last the night ;
But ah, my foes, and oh, my friends--
    It gives a lovely light!

Chanukah Dreams
By Judith Ish-Kishor

Chanukah I think most dear
Of the feasts of all the year.
I could sit and watch all night
Every twinkling baby light.

Father lights the first one—green;
Hope it always seems to mean;
Hope and Strength to glow anew
In the heart of every Jew.

Jacob lights the blue for Truth.
Pink for Love is lit by Ruth.
Then the white one falls to me,
White that shines for Purity.

How the story of those days
Fills my wondering heart with praise!
And in every flame one sees
The heroic Maccabees.

The Feast of Lights
By Emma Lazarus

Kindle the taper like the steadfast star
Ablaze on evening's forehead o'er the earth,
And add each night a lustre till afar
An eightfold splendor shine above thy hearth.
Clash, Israel, the cymbals, touch the lyre,
Blow the brass trumpet and the harsh-tongued horn;
Chant psalms of victory till the heart takes fire,
The Maccabean spirit leap new-born.

Remember how from wintry dawn till night,
Such songs were sung in Zion, when again
On the high altar flamed the sacred light,
And, purified from every Syrian stain,
The foam-white walls with golden shields were hung,
With crowns and silken spoils, and at the shrine,
Stood, midst their conqueror-tribe, five chieftains sprung
From one heroic stock, one seed divine.

Five branches grown from Mattathias' stem,
The Blessed John, the Keen-Eyed Jonathan,
Simon the fair, the Burst-of Spring, the Gem,
Eleazar, Help of-God; o'er all his clan
Judas the Lion-Prince, the Avenging Rod,
Towered in warrior-beauty, uncrowned king,
Armed with the breastplate and the sword of God,
Whose praise is: "He received the perishing."

They who had camped within the mountain-pass,
Couched on the rock, and tented neath the sky,
Who saw from Mizpah's heights the tangled grass
Choke the wide Temple-courts, the altar lie
Disfigured and polluted--who had flung
Their faces on the stones, and mourned aloud
And rent their garments, wailing with one tongue,
Crushed as a wind-swept bed of reeds is bowed,

Even they by one voice fired, one heart of flame,
Though broken reeds, had risen, and were men,
They rushed upon the spoiler and o'ercame,
Each arm for freedom had the strength of ten.
Now is their mourning into dancing turned,
Their sackcloth doffed for garments of delight,
Week-long the festive torches shall be burned,
Music and revelry wed day with night.

Still ours the dance, the feast, the glorious Psalm,
The mystic lights of emblem, and the Word.
Where is our Judas? Where our five-branched palm?
Where are the lion-warriors of the Lord?
Clash, Israel, the cymbals, touch the lyre,
Sound the brass trumpet and the harsh-tongued horn,
Chant hymns of victory till the heart take fire,
The Maccabean spirit leap new-born!

---

doffed—*to be removed*

Spellbound
By Emily Brontë

The night is darkening round me,
The wild winds coldly blow;
But a tyrant spell has bound me
And I cannot, cannot go.

The giant trees are bending
Their bare boughs weighed with snow.
And the storm is fast descending,
And yet I cannot go.

Clouds beyond clouds above me,
Wastes beyond wastes below;
But nothing drear can move me;
I will not, cannot go.

---

boughs—*branches of a tree (but not shoots of a tree)*

Winter
By Jordan Henrie

The Winter air blows in my face,
The snow that storms down is as white as lace.

No birds fill the air with their joyous spring calls,
And the bears are all resting in their winter walls.

But i am here now outside in the snow,
And the snowy owls did not have to go.

They fill the night sky with their lovely soft hoot,
Well the little small lemmings go scooty scoot scoot.

But now I must put my sleep to the test,
And dream all the dreams that behind my eyes rest.

Winter Is Good – His Hoar Delights
By Emily Dickinson

Winter is good — his Hoar Delights
Italic flavor yield—
To Intellects inebriate
With Summer, or the World —
Generic as a Quarry
And hearty — as a Rose —
Invited with Asperity
But welcome when he goes.

---

hoar(y)—*hair that is white and grey*
inebriate—*to be intoxicated or drunk*
quarry—*a place, potentially a large deep pit, where stone is dug up*

The Winter Pear
By William Allingham

Is always Age severe?
Is never Youth austere?
Spring-fruits are sour to eat;
Autumn's the mellow time.
Nay, very late in the year,
Short day and frosty rime,
Thought, like a winter pear,
Stone-cold in summer's prime,
May turn from harsh to sweet.

_____

austere—*rigid, strict in attitude and appearance*

Stopping by Woods on a Snowy Evening
By Robert Frost

Whose woods these are I think I know.
His house is in the village though;
He will not see me stopping here
To watch his woods fill up with snow.

My little horse must think it queer
To stop without a farmhouse near
Between the woods and frozen lake
The darkest evening of the year.

He gives his harness bells a shake
To ask if there is some mistake.
The only other sound's the sweep
Of easy wind and downy flake.

The woods are lovely, dark and deep,
But I have promises to keep,
And miles to go before I sleep,
And miles to go before I sleep.

Snowflakes
By Henry Wadsworth Longfellow

Out of the bosom of the Air,
    Out of the cloud-folds of her garments shaken,
Over the woodlands brown and bare,
    Over the harvest-fields forsaken,
        Silent, and soft, and slow
        Descends the snow.

Even as our cloudy fancies take
    Suddenly shape in some divine expression,
Even as the troubled heart doth make
    In the white countenance confession,
        The troubled sky reveals
        The grief it feels.

This is the poem of the air,
    Slowly in silent syllables recorded;
This is the secret of despair,
    Long in its cloudy bosom hoarded,
        Now whispered and revealed
        To wood and field.

_____

countenance—*the expression a person's face is making*

The Ballad of the Harp-Weaver
By Edna St. Vincent Millay

"Son," said my mother,
When I was knee-high,
"You've need of clothes to cover you,
And not a rag have I.

"There's nothing in the house
To make a boy breeches,
Nor shears to cut a cloth with
Nor thread to take stitches.

"There's nothing in the house
But a loaf-end of rye,
And a harp with a woman's head
Nobody will buy,"
And she began to cry.

That was in the early fall.
When came the late fall,
"Son," she said, "the sight of you
Makes your mother's blood crawl,—

"Little skinny shoulder-blades
Sticking through your clothes!
And where you'll get a jacket from
God above knows.

"It's lucky for me, lad,
Your daddy's in the ground,
And can't see the way I let
His son go around!"
And she made a queer sound.

That was in the late fall.
When the winter came,
I'd not a pair of breeches
Nor a shirt to my name.

I couldn't go to school,
Or out of doors to play.
And all the other little boys
Passed our way.

"Son," said my mother,
"Come, climb into my lap,
And I'll chafe your little bones

While you take a nap."

And, oh, but we were silly
For half an hour or more,
Me with my long legs
Dragging on the floor,

A-rock-rock-rocking
To a mother-goose rhyme!
Oh, but we were happy
For half an hour's time!

But there was I, a great boy,
And what would folks say
To hear my mother singing me
To sleep all day,
In such a daft way?

Men say the winter
Was bad that year;
Fuel was scarce,
And food was dear.

A wind with a wolf's head
Howled about our door,
And we burned up the chairs
And sat on the floor.

All that was left us
Was a chair we couldn't break,
And the harp with a woman's head
Nobody would take,
For song or pity's sake.

The night before Christmas
I cried with the cold,
I cried myself to sleep
Like a two-year-old.

And in the deep night
I felt my mother rise,
And stare down upon me
With love in her eyes.

I saw my mother sitting
On the one good chair,
A light falling on her
From I couldn't tell where,

Looking nineteen,
And not a day older,
And the harp with a woman's head
Leaned against her shoulder.

Her thin fingers, moving
In the thin, tall strings,
Were weav-weav-weaving
Wonderful things.

Many bright threads,
From where I couldn't see,
Were running through the harp-strings
Rapidly,

And gold threads whistling
Through my mother's hand.
I saw the web grow,
And the pattern expand.

She wove a child's jacket,
And when it was done
She laid it on the floor
And wove another one.

She wove a red cloak
So regal to see,
"She's made it for a king's son,"
I said, "and not for me."
But I knew it was for me.

She wove a pair of breeches
Quicker than that!
She wove a pair of boots
And a little cocked hat.

She wove a pair of mittens,
She wove a little blouse,
She wove all night
In the still, cold house.

She sang as she worked,
And the harp-strings spoke;
Her voice never faltered,
And the thread never broke.
And when I awoke,—

There sat my mother
With the harp against her shoulder
Looking nineteen
And not a day older,

A smile about her lips,
And a light about her head,
And her hands in the harp-strings
Frozen dead.

And piled up beside her
And toppling to the skies,
Were the clothes of a king's son,
Just my size.

---

queer—*odd, whimsical*

A Christmas Dream
By Joseph B. Soldano

A Christmas dream is what we wish.
The tree is trimmed with heavenly bliss.
Children asleep within their dreams,
Dancing on silver moonbeams.

Velvet Red and snowy white
Venturing into the magical night.
Snowy white and velvet red
He's plump and round and well fed.

Sparkling stars light his way
Into the night a speeding sleigh.
All the toys now under the tree,
One for you and one for me.

Fluffy white and crimson red,
A tassel cap on his head.
Quiet as a mouse and swift as a dear,
Jolly old Nick is finally here.

His bulging bag is full of wishes
For mom it may be a set of dishes,
For dad it might be a shirt of tie,
Children were so happy, they could cry.

Little children looking up high,
At the silver streak in the sky.
Waving to Santa and saying goodbye.
"Next year we'll see you" they said with a sigh.

A Visit from St. Nicholas
By Clement Clarke Moore

'Twas the night before Christmas, when all through the house
Not a creature was stirring, not even a mouse;
The stockings were hung by the chimney with care,
In hopes that St. Nicholas soon would be there;
The children were nestled all snug in their beds,
While visions of sugar-plums danced in their heads;
And mamma in her 'kerchief, and I in my cap,
Had just settled our brains for a long winter's nap,
When out on the lawn there arose such a clatter,
I sprang from the bed to see what was the matter.
Away to the window I flew like a flash,
Tore open the shutters and threw up the sash.
The moon on the breast of the new-fallen snow
Gave the lustre of mid-day to objects below,
When, what to my wondering eyes should appear,
But a miniature sleigh, and eight tiny reindeer,
With a little old driver, so lively and quick,
I knew in a moment it must be St. Nick.
More rapid than eagles his coursers they came,
And he whistled, and shouted, and called them by name;
"Now, Dasher! now, Dancer! now, Prancer and Vixen!
On, Comet! on, Cupid! on, Donder and Blitzen!
To the top of the porch! to the top of the wall!
Now dash away! dash away! dash away all!"
As dry leaves that before the wild hurricane fly,
When they meet with an obstacle, mount to the sky;
So up to the house-top the coursers they flew,
With the sleigh full of Toys, and St. Nicholas too.
And then, in a twinkling, I heard on the roof
The prancing and pawing of each little hoof.
As I drew in my head, and was turning around,
Down the chimney St. Nicholas came with a bound.
He was dressed all in fur, from his head to his foot,
And his clothes were all tarnished with ashes and soot;
A bundle of Toys he had flung on his back,
And he looked like a pedler just opening his pack.
His eyes—how they twinkled! his dimples how merry!
His cheeks were like roses, his nose like a cherry!
His droll little mouth was drawn up like a bow
And the beard of his chin was as white as the snow;
The stump of a pipe he held tight in his teeth,
And the smoke it encircled his head like a wreath;
He had a broad face and a little round belly,
That shook when he laughed, like a bowlful of jelly.
He was chubby and plump, a right jolly old elf,

And I laughed when I saw him, in spite of myself;
A wink of his eye and a twist of his head,
Soon gave me to know I had nothing to dread;
He spoke not a word, but went straight to his work,
And filled all the stockings; then turned with a jerk,
And laying his finger aside of his nose,
And giving a nod, up the chimney he rose;
He sprang to his sleigh, to his team gave a whistle,
And away they all flew like the down of a thistle,
But I heard him exclaim, ere he drove out of sight,
"Happy Christmas to all, and to all a good-night."

Gingerbread
By Louisa May Alcott

"Gingerbread,
Go to the head.
Your task is done;
A soul is won.
Take it and go
Where muffins grow,
Where sweet loaves rise
To the very skies,
And biscuits fair
Perfume the air.
Away, away!
Make no delay;
In the sea of flour
Plunge this hour.
Safe in your breast
Let the yeast-cake rest,
Till you rise in joy,
A white bread boy!"

Under the Mistletoe
By George Francis Shults

She stood beneath the mistletoe
   That hung above the door,
Quite conscious of the sprig above,
   Revered by maids of yore.
A timid longing filled her heart;
   Her pulses throbbed with heat;
He sprang to where the fair girl stood.
"May I, just one, my sweet?"
He asked his love, who tossed her head,
"Just do it, if, you dare!" she said.

He sat before the fireplace
   Down at the club that night.
"She loves me not," he hotly said,
   "Therefore she did but right!"
She sat alone within her room,
   And with her finger-tips
She held his picture to her heart,
Then pressed it to her lips.
"My loved one!" sobbed she, "if you cared
You surely would have, would have, dared."

---

yore—*a long time past*

Christmas in Australia
By Victor James Daley

O day, the crown and crest of all the year!
Thou comest not to us amid the snows,
But midmost of the reign of the red rose;
Our hearts have not yet lost the ancient cheer
That filled our fathers' simple hearts when sere
The leaves fell, and the winds of Winter froze
The waters wan, and carols at the close
Of yester-eve sang the Child Christ anear.
And so we hail thee with a greeting high,
And drain to thee a draught of our own wine,
Forgetful not beneath this bluer sky
Of that old mother-land beyond the brine,
Whose gray skies gladden as thou drawest nigh,
O day of God's good-will the seal and sign!

The Evening Darkens Over
By Robert Bridges

The evening darkens over
After a day so bright
The windcapt waves discover
That wild will be the night.
There's sound of distant thunder.

The latest sea-birds hover
Along the cliff's sheer height;
As in the memory wander
Last flutterings of delight,
White wings lost on the white.

There's not a ship in sight;
And as the sun goes under
Thick clouds conspire to cover
The moon that should rise yonder.
Thou art alone, fond lover.

Carol
By Kenneth Grahame

Villagers all, this frosty tide,
Let your doors swing open wide,
Though wind may follow, and snow beside,
Yet draw us in by your fire to bide;
      Joy shall be yours in the morning!
Here we stand in the cold and the sleet,
Blowing fingers and stamping feet,
Come from far away you to greet —
You by the fire and we in the street —
      Bidding you joy in the morning!
For ere one half of the night was gone,
Sudden a star has led us on,
Raining bliss and benison —
Bliss tomorrow and more anon,
      Joy for every morning!
Goodman Joseph toiled through the snow —
Saw the star o'er a stable low;
Mary she might not further go —
Welcome thatch, and litter below!
      Joy was hers in the morning!
And then they heard the angels tell,
"Who were the first to cry Nowell?
Animals all, as it befell,
In the stable where they did dwell!
      Joy shall be theirs in the morning!"

---

benison—*blessing*
anon—*shortly or soon*

Now the Day Is Over
By Sabine Baring-Gould

Now the day is over,
Night is drawing nigh,
Shadows of the evening
Steal across the sky.
Now the darkness gathers,
Stars began to peep,
Birds and beasts and flowers
Soon will be asleep.
Jesus, give the weary
Calm and sweet repose;
With thy tenderest blessing
May our eyelids close.
Grant to little children
Visions bright of thee;
Guard the sailors tossing
On the deep blue sea.
Comfort every sufferer
Watching late in pain;
Those who plan some evil
From their sin restrain.
Through the long night-watches
May thine angels spread
Their white wings above me,
Watching round my bed.
When the morning wakens,
Then may I arise
Pure and fresh and sinless
In thy holy eyes.
Glory to the Father,
Glory to the Son,
And to thee, blest Spirit,
Whilst all ages run.

The Star
Jane Taylor

Twinkle, twinkle, little star,
How I wonder what you are!
Up above the world so high,
Like a diamond in the sky.

When the blazing sun is gone,
When he nothing shines upon,
Then you show your little light,
Twinkle, twinkle, all the night.

Then the traveler in the dark,
Thanks you for your tiny spark,
He could not see which way to go,
If you did not twinkle so.

In the dark blue sky you keep,
And often through my curtains peep,
For you never shut you eye,
Till the sun is in the sky.

As your bright and tiny spark,
Lights the traveler in the dark-
Though I know not what you are,
Twinkle, twinkle, little star.

On This Silent Night (Mary's Song)
By Sarah Beth Watson

I see the firelight gleaming in the snow
Iced like a white cake with a candle just for show
The hills are silent the earth hold its breath and waits... anticipates
Oh the silence is screaming, "Stay quiet, keep dreaming the dreams that only you know."

On this Silent Night

I feel you moving there isn't much room left inside
You're such a mystery more than any before and forevermore
But I stay silent and hold my breath... I wait, anticipate
Now the cattle are lowing, my pain is growing like I've never felt before

On this Silent Night

Away on the hillsides the shepherds watch over their sheep, fast asleep
Suddenly, a bright light brings a great fright here, but, "Do not fear."
"I bring you good news that will cause great joy, your Savior is born. He is the Lord!"
Oh the angels are singing, "Glory to God!" and "Peace on the earth!"

On this Silent Night

Now the shepherds come and see you lying in the manger
And go to spread the good news that there is born a Savior
But I hold you oh so tight and bury deep this treasure
Inside my heart, this gift beyond all measure

On this Silent Night

Falling Asleep
By Caroline W. Leakey

FADING, fading into mistiness,
A sweet half-conscious blessedness
Of love and loved ones round;
A murm'ring yet a soothing sound
Of pleasant voices falling:
Dropping asleep beneath a song of love,
To waken—singing it above,
Upon a Father's breast!
Bright angel forms, and faces blest—
Happy cherubs clustering!
And only thus awakening to know
Of having fallen asleep! So may I go,
And so awaken!

Midnight
By Sara Teasdale

Now at last I have come to see what life is,
Nothing is ever ended, everything only begun,
And the brave victories that seem so splendid
Are never really won.

Even love that I built my spirit's house for,
Comes like a brooding and a baffled guest,
And music and men's praise and even laughter
Are not so good as rest.

Carving a Name
By Horatio Alger Jr.

I wrote my name upon the sand,
And trusted it would stand for aye;
But, soon, alas! the refluent sea
Had washed my feeble lines away.

I carved my name upon the wood,
And, after years, returned again;
I missed the shadow of the tree
That stretched of old upon the plain.

To solid marble next, my name
I gave as a perpetual trust;
An earthquake rent it to its base,
And now it lies, o'erlaid with dust.

All these have failed. In wiser mood
I turn and ask myself, "What then?"
If I would have my name endure,
I'll write it on the hearts of men,

In characters of living light,
Of kindly deeds and actions wrought.
And these, beyond the touch of time,
Shall live immortal as my thought.

---

rent—*to rip or tear*
refluent—*to flow backwards*
wrought—*worked; to work metal*

If
By Rudyard Kipling

If you can keep your head when all about you
  Are losing theirs and blaming it on you;
If you can trust yourself when all men doubt you,
  But make allowance for their doubting too;
If you can wait and not be tired by waiting,
  Or, being lied about, don't deal in lies,
Or, being hated, don't give way to hating,
  And yet don't look too good, nor talk too wise;

If you can dream—and not make dreams your master;
  If you can think—and not make thoughts your aim;
If you can meet with triumph and disaster
  And treat those two impostors just the same;
If you can bear to hear the truth you've spoken
  Twisted by knaves to make a trap for fools,
Or watch the things you gave your life to broken,
  And stoop and build 'em up with worn-out tools;

If you can make one heap of all your winnings
  And risk it on one turn of pitch-and-toss,
And lose, and start again at your beginnings
  And never breathe a word about your loss;
If you can force your heart and nerve and sinew
  To serve your turn long after they are gone,
And so hold on when there is nothing in you
  Except the Will which says to them: "Hold on";

If you can talk with crowds and keep your virtue,
  Or walk with kings—nor lose the common touch;
If neither foes nor loving friends can hurt you;
  If all men count with you, but none too much;
If you can fill the unforgiving minute
With sixty seconds' worth of distance run—
  Yours is the Earth and everything that's in it,
And—which is more—you'll be a Man, my son!

The Old Year
By John Clare

The Old Year's gone away
To nothingness and night:
We cannot find him all the day
Nor hear him in the night:
He left no footstep, mark or place
In either shade or sun:
The last year he'd a neighbour's face,
In this he's known by none.
All nothing everywhere:
Mists we on mornings see
Have more of substance when they're here
And more of form than he.
He was a friend by every fire,
In every cot and hall–
A guest to every heart's desire,
And now he's nought at all.
Old papers thrown away,
Old garments cast aside,
The talk of yesterday,
Are things identified;
But time once torn away
No voices can recall:
The eve of New Year's Day
Left the Old Year lost to all.

Poetry Corner

It's now your turn to be the poet.
Use this space to either write your own poetry
or
write down other poems that you love.

A Sip & Delicate Bite

RECIPES

While tea and poetry are the main attraction, food is a wonderful feature of the poetry tea time. Here you will find recipes that are staples of English tea time—no need to go searching for them. I've also included some other tasty treats that are sure to please little taste buds and refined palates alike. If cooking is your quiet time then enjoy some time creating a tasty menu for your event. If you are wanting to use cooking time as a moment to educate, then get your kids involved and help them learn valuable kitchen life skills.

Allergies

I have indicated which recipes can accommodate food allergies. Gluten Free (GF), Dairy Free (DF), Egg Free (EF), and Nut Free (NF). But please remember, if a person has a severe allergy you will need to find out what precautions will need to be taken. They may just choose to bring their own food even if you try to prepare for them. I only say this from experience since my husband and one of my sons cannot eat gluten. But if you do make "safe" food for your friend with allergies, make sure to check the ingredients and for where it is prepared. Also, lay out the allergy safe food in an area separate from the other food. This will help in two ways. The allergy safe food will not become cross contaminated and the allergen free treats won't be eaten up by your other guests. I hope these indicators will help those with allergies.

Budget Friendly

You will also find a "$" next to some recipes. This is to indicate which recipes are extremely budget friendly. I determined this designation by the price of the ingredients and by the typical ingredients most homes would have.

Now let's get into the kitchen.

Scones

Scones

The Traditional English scone sits tall and hides a wonderful fluffy texture on the inside. You won't find any glazes or icings adorning the English scone, because it's the job of the jams or curd to bring the sweet. You will also find the recipe for clotted cream, jam, and curd just below. Now you can create the ultimate British tea experience with homemade goodness. **(GF, NF)**

Servings 9 scones with a 2.5 inch circle cutter
Prep time 10 minutes
Cook Time 15 minutes

INGREDIENTS
- 2 cups (500ml, 10oz) all-purpose flour or cup for cup GF flour
- 4 tsp baking powder
- 1/2 tsp salt
- 1/4 cup (50g, 1 ¾ oz) sugar
- 6 Tbsp unsalted butter **at room temperature**
- 2/3 cup (128 ml, 5 ½ oz) whole milk
- 1 large egg

INSTRUCTIONS
1. Preheat your oven to 425° F (218° C).
2. Add to your food processor the flour, baking powder, salt, and sugar.
3. Pulse the ingredients a couple times until combined.
4. Cut the butter into chunks and add them to the food processor. Pulse at least 8 times to combine the ingredients. It should have a soft crumbly texture. If not, pulse a couple more times.
5. Transfer mixture to a large bowl.
6. In a separate small bowl whisk your eggs with the milk.
7. Set aside about ⅛ cup of the egg-milk mixture and pour the rest into the large bowl with the dry ingredients.
8. Using your hands or a spoon, combine the wet and dry ingredients until it comes together into a dough.
9. Transfer the dough to a floured surface and knead until a smooth ball forms. Make sure not to knead too much or your scones will be squaty and not as fluffy. It should take about 9–10 kneads for the right consistency.
10. Roll out your dough to 1 inch (2.5 cm) thick and cut out the rounds with a 2.5 inch (6 cm) cutter. Once you run out of cutout space, roll the leftovers together and roll out again. If you don't have a 2.5 inch cutter then make sure to adjust your cooking time to accommodate for larger or smaller scones.
11. Place them on a parchment covered (or a well greased) pan.
12. Using your fingers or a pastry brush, thinly coat the top of each scone with the egg/milk wash.
13. Bake 13–15 minutes. They should rise three times taller and be golden brown on the bottom and the top.

Jams

Jam is one of the traditional additions to the English scone. But homemade jam is so much better than store bought. Of course, I purchase jam from the store, but making it fresh would make your scone that much more wonderful. Jams can be made from so many different fruits and combinations of fruit. I have included small batches so you can try different kinds of jam and to keep costs down. You can also use these jam recipes to make jam for any desserts that call for jam. If you happen to be a canner, I have included the amount of time needed to process the jars of jam in a waterbath canner. Don't forget that jam can not be left unattended for long at any point, so make sure you are not multitasking when you start cooking the jam. I love making jam and once you see how simple it is, I think you will too.

Berry Jam

You can use Blackberry, Blueberry, Boysenberry, Dewberry, Loganberry, Raspberries or any other berries similar to them. You can either use one kind of berry or combine different berries to make a unique jam. **(GF, EF, DF, NF)**

Yield 2 pints (about 1 liter)
Canning process time is 15 minutes in a water bath canner

INGREDIENTS
- 6 cups berries
- 4 cups (512 grams) sugar

INSTRUCTIONS
1. Add berries and sugar to a large saucepan or small pot.
2. Bring the mixture to a boil while stirring constantly to avoid burning. You want to dissolve all of the sugar.
3. You want it to cook hot (a rapid boil) to cause the jam to thicken. Make sure to keep stirring, especially now.
4. You will keep going until the jam sticks to your spoon when you lift it out of the jam and slowly runs off.
5. Remove the jam from the heat and you are done. If a foam has formed then just skim it off the top. (I love to just eat this.)

Blueberry-Lime Jam
This jam is like a party in the mouth. The lime gives it a super refreshing flavor. It is by far one of my favorit jams. If this is in my house I'll buy food just to smear it on so I can eat it. **(GF, EF, DF, NF)**

Yields 1.5 pints (about ¾ liter)
Canning process time is 15 minutes in a water bath canner (using ½ pint jars)

INGREDIENTS
- 2 ¼ cup (225g) blueberries
- 2 Tbsp powdered pectin (½ of a packet)
- 2 1/2 cups (500 g) sugar
- ½ Tbsp grated lime zest (peel without the white pith)
- 2 ½ Tbsp lime juice

INSTRUCTIONS
1. Crush your blueberries until they are all broken up.
2. Put the berries and pectin into your large saucepan and start to heat them.
3. Stirring frequently, bring the mixture to a boil.
4. Add sugar and continue to stir as the sugar dissolves.
5. Add lime zest and lime juice and bring back up to a hard boil and boil for 60 seconds and KEEP stirring.
6. Remove from heat and remove any foam that has formed on the top.

Strawberry Jam without Pectin $
Strawberry jam is a classic and just as easy as the berry jam. No pectin is needed. Pectin free jams will have a slightly different taste due to the extended cooking time. **(GF, EF, DF, NF)**

Yields 2 pints
Canning process time is 15 minutes in a water bath canner (1 pint jars)

INGREDIENTS
W/O pectin
- 1 quart strawberries
- 3 cups (600g) sugar

INSTRUCTIONS
1. Wash and destem your strawberries leaving no leaves behind.
2. Crush the strawberries.
3. Add strawberries and sugar to a large saucepan or small pot.
4. Slowly bring to a boil and dissolve sugar while stirring constantly.
5. Stir rapidly while it thickens. Once the jam sticks to the spoon and runs off slowly.
6. Remove from heat and remove any foam that has formed on the top.

Strawberry Jam with Pectin
Here is a strawberry jam that uses pectin. Pectin helps to set the Jam faster which means less cooking time. This can save some of the volume of your jam and preserve the fresh fruit taste better since you're not cooking it for so long. **(GF, EF, DF, NF)**

Yields 2 pints
Canning process time is 15 minutes in a water bath canner (4-½ pint jars)
INGREDIENTS
- 1 quart strawberries
- 2 Tbsp pectin (1/2 a package)
- ⅛ cup lemon juice (30ml, 1oz)
- 3 ½ cups (700g, 25oz) sugar

INSTRUCTIONS
1. Wash and destem your strawberries leaving no leaves behind.
2. Crush the strawberries.
3. Add strawberries, pectin, and lemon juice to the large saucepan or small pot.
4. Slowly bring to a boil while stirring occasionally.
5. Add sugar and stir until it is dissolved.
6. Bring to a boil and boil hard for 60 seconds stirring constantly.
7. Once it sticks to the spoon and runs off slowly, remove from the heat.

Apricot Jam
Apricot jam is a special treat. It adds a bit of summer to your scone any time of year if it's canned and saved. It can also be a great addition to a layered jam cake both in flavor and in color. By far one of my favorite fruits and the jam does not disappoint. **(GF, EF, DF, NF)**

Yields 2 ½ pints
Canning process time is 15 minutes in a water bath canner (4-½ pint jars)
INGREDIENTS
- 1 quart (about 760g) peeled and crushed apricots
- ⅛ cup (1 oz) lemon juice
- 3 cups (600g) sugar

INSTRUCTIONS
1. Mix together the apricots and lemon juice in a large saucepan or small pot.
2. Add sugar stirring until it dissolves.
3. Bring slowly to a boil.
4. Cook rapidly until it thickens and the jam sticks to the spoon and slowly drips off.
5. Remove from heat.

Lemon Curd $

Lemon curd is such a treat. Silky in texture and bursting with the aroma and flavor of lemon. Curd is another welcome addition to a scone. There is nothing like it. Other uses: for toast, as an ice cream topping, to add flavor to whipped cream, or in a tart. It is a true treat. **(GF, NF)**

Yield 2 cups
Will store in the fridge for 2 weeks in an airtight container

INGREDIENTS
- The zest of 2 large lemons, grated
- About 7 Tbsp of lemon juice
- ¼ pound (56g, 2oz) of butter
- 1 cup (200g, 7oz) sugar
- 4 eggs

INSTRUCTIONS
1. In a small bowl beat the 4 eggs until they are incorporated. Set aside.
2. Bring water in a double boiler to a simmer.
3. Place the zest, juice, and sugar into the top section of a double boiler. If you don't have a double boiler—no problem. Use a metal bowl that you can rest in the water.
4. Add the butter, and as it melts, make sure to stir as the sugar dissolves.
5. Now, while stirring the eggs constantly, slowly pour in a small amount of the hot lemon mixture. This will help to warm the eggs.
6. Now slowly pour the warmed egg mixture into the lemon mixture stirring constantly. You don't want scrambled eggs.
7. Continue stirring until it thickens, up to 20 minutes. It should coat the spoon when poured off.

Clotted Cream $

Clotted cream is native to the UK. Australians top their scones with whipped cream, as a variant. And in the US the scone is so sweet on its own that there is no need to add anything to it. Clotted cream is a process but it's simple. Just make sure you are using a cream that is not ultra-pasteurized and that you give yourself plenty of time to complete this 20-hour process. Yep, I said 20 hours. But in the end you will be left with a nutty, smooth spread that normally would require travel all the way to the UK for this experience. **(GF, EF, NF)**

Yields 2 cups (about 8 servings)

INGREDIENTS
- 4 cups (32oz, 960g) of heavy cream (NOT ultra-pasteurized)

INSTRUCTIONS
1. Preheat your oven to 180° F (80°C)
2. In a 8–9 inch square pan pour in the cream. You will want it to be between 1 ½ –2 inches deep.
3. Now place it in the oven and leave it for 12 hours, and do not stir it.
4. At the end of the 12 hours, remove the baked cream from the oven and let cool until it reaches room temperature.
5. Cover it and place it in the fridge until completely cooled. (This step can be done overnight.)
6. Fold back a small piece in the corner of the pan and carefully drain any leftover liquid hiding underneath your baked cream.
7. Place the clotted cream into a bowl and stir it gently to reveal its creamy smooth texture. If it's too thick, you can add some of the runoff back into it.
8. Pack the clotted cream into a jar or ceramic container that you can cover. It will stay good for up to 14 days.

TIP:*If your oven runs hot, then you may want to check on it at 8 and 10 hours. You don't want the top of your clotted cream to become any darker than a tan color. Also, some ovens are programmed to shut off if left on for too long. If your oven does this you may want to do the baking during the day so you can keep an eye on it.*

Savory

Tea sandwiches are the cute savory little finger sandwiches that you see in the movies, a lace-gloved hand gingerly holding the triangle as a delicate bite is taken. They are demure, irresistible, and leaves you wondering what each one will taste like.

You can use fresh white or wheat bread to make these sandwiches. Some sandwiches are better paired with pumpernickel. Here you will find the basic, classic finger sandwiches to get you started.

When preparing them for the party, you want to prep them just before the party to prevent the bread from going dry; you can make them an hour or two in advance and cover with plastic wrap to keep them fresh.

Cucumber Sandwich $
This is a fresh-tasting, delicate sandwich.
The ingredients marked as optional will change this from a plain, cucumber cream cheese sandwich to a lemony, cucumber sandwich. **(GF, NF)**

Yields 9-12 tea sandwiches

INGREDIENTS
- 4 ounces (112g) cream cheese, at room temperature
- 2 Tbsp mayo (optional)
- 2 Tbsp chopped fresh dill (optional)
- Zest and juice of one lemon (optional)
- Salt and pepper (optional)
- 6 slices fresh white bread or 10 slices of GF bread
- ½ english seedless cucumber very thinly sliced

INSTRUCTIONS
Cucumber sandwich
1. Spread cream cheese over each slice of bread. (skip to step 3)
2. Assemble the cucumber slices over ½ of the bread slices and place the other bread slices on top. Cut off the crust and cut the sandwich either into 3 rectangles or into 4 triangles.
Variation:
Lemony Cucumber—Mix the cream cheese, mayo, dill, lemon zest, and juice before following the steps above.

Egg Salad Sandwich $

Egg salad is a common finger sandwich that many people enjoy. Of course, if you have your own favorite egg salad recipe, that will work too. Just make sure anything you add is finely chopped. **(GF, NF)**

Yields 15 tea sandwiches
- 1 dozen, boiled eggs peeled and chilled in the fridge
- ½ cup (115g, 4oz) mayo
- 2 Tbsp chopped chives (optional)
- 2 Tbsp yellow mustard
- Salt and pepper
- 10 slices of fresh white bread or 15 slices gluten free bread

INSTRUCTIONS
1. Chop up all the eggs with a knife or egg slicer.
2. Add the mayo, chives (optional), and mustard, and stir until well combined.
3. Apply egg mixture to ½ of the bread.
4. Put a slice of bread on top of each sandwich.
5. Cut off crusts.
6. Cut each sandwich into 3 rectangles or 4 triangles.

Chicken-Cran Curry Sandwich

This little sandwich and its touch of curry will introduce children to a new flavor with enough sweetness that they will be asking for more. Make sure to chop things up small so its easy to take a bite without making a mess. There are so many great flavors in this sandwich. That being said, if you happen to have the celery and apple, but not the pecans and cranberries, you will still have a great tasting sandwich. **(GF, DF)**

Yields 18 tea sandwiches

INGREDIENTS
- 1 cup (6 oz, 140g) chopped, cook chicken
- ½ red apple, chopped
- 6 Tbsp dried cranberries
- ⅛ cup (14g, 1/2oz) chopped pecans (optional)
- ¼ cup (27g, 1oz) thinly sliced celery
- 1 Tbsp chopped green onion
- 6 Tbsp mayo
- 1/4 Tbsp lime juice
- 1/4 tsp curry powder
- 6 slices of fresh bread or 10 slices Gluten Free Bread

INSTRUCTIONS
1. Combined the first 6 ingredients into a bowl.
2. In another small bowl mix the mayo, lime juice, and curry powder.
3. Combine all ingredients together.
4. Just before serving, place the mixture on 3 slices of bread.
5. Top each half with a slice of bread, remove the crust, cut into 3 rectangles or desired shape.

Ranch and Turkey Sandwich
Here is a super simple sandwich you can make with what you may already have in the fridge. Fancy them up with a cute small cookie cutter in the shape of a circle, flower, or any other cutter shape you may have. **(GF, NF)**

Yields 16 tea sandwiches

INGREDIENTS
- 4 slices of white bread or 5 slices of gluten free bread
- 4 slices of wheat bread or 5 slices of gluten free wheat bread
- 2 Tbsp ranch dressing
- 6 oz (180g) cream cheese
- Finely sliced cucumber, celery or other vegetable. (optional)
- ½ pound (227g, 16oz) of smoked turkey sliced and chopped.
- Mayo
- ½ pound (235g, 8 oz) of cheese (choose a variety of cheese like, swiss, cheddar, colby).
- ½ cup (113g, 4oz) softened butter

INSTRUCTIONS
1. In a small bowl mix together the ranch, cream cheese, and chopped cucumbers if you choose.
2. In another bowl, combine turkey, chopped celery, and enough mayo to dress it.
3. Thinly coat one side of each bread slice with butter. Chill in the freezer for a short time to set butter.
4. Spread the ranch mixture on each white slice and top with turkey mixture.
5. Top each one with the wheat slice, cut off the crust, and cut into 4 triangles.

Smoked Salmon Medallions
Here is something a little more sophisticated. It's always fun to try something new. This sandwich is both bold and refreshing with the salmon cucumber combo. If you don't have a 2 inch round cutter you could just cut off the crust and cut into smaller pieces.
(GF, EF, NF)

Yield 24 tea sandwiches

INGREDIENTS
- 8 oz (250g) cream cheese
- 4 Tbsp fresh dill, chopped (some extra for garnish)
- 2 Tbsp flat leaf parsley, finely chopped
- ¼ tsp salt
- ⅛ tsp pepper
- ⅛ tsp garlic powder or ¼ tsp freshly chopped
- 1 tsp lemon zest
- Pumpernickel bread, either full sized slices or you could purchase the mini loaf. For a gluten free option you could purchase a bread that is on the dryer side.
- Cucumber sliced into ¼ inch thick pieces
- Smoked Salmon

INSTRUCTIONS
1. Combined the first 7 ingredients in a bowl.
2. Using a 2 inch cutter, cut circles from the bread. If you prefer, you can use a mini loaf and not worry about cutting the sandwiches.
3. Spread cream cheese mixture onto each circle and sprinkle with a little salt and pepper to taste.
4. Top with a small piece of smoked salmon and garnish with dill.

Under the Sea Tea Sandwich
This is the tea sandwich for those who enjoy shrimp and want to elevate their tea fare. The best part is that it is super easy to make. You can choose to make them open-face too. If you are doing open-face, make sure to cut your bread before you top it. **(GF, EF, NF)**

Yields 24 (12 if GF bread slices are small)

INGREDIENTS
- ½ cup (50g, 4oz) cooked shelled medium shrimp, finely chopped
- 1 Tbsp finely chopped flat leaf parsley
- Finely grated zest of 1 lemon
- 1 tsp lemon juice (freshly squeezed is recommended)
- ½ tsp Worcestershire sauce
- 2 ½ Tbsp mayo
- Salt and pepper (if available, use coarse salt and freshly ground pepper)
- 4 Tbsp of stick butter
- 1 ½ ounces (16 ½ g)sprouts (optional)
- 12 (6 for open-face sandwiches) slices of white bread or 12 (6) slices of GF bread

INSTRUCTIONS
1. In a bowl mix together the first 6 ingredients. Once combined add salt and pepper to taste.
2. Spread the butter on the 12 slices of bread (only 6 is doing open-face).
3. IF you are doing open-face sandwiches, cut the crust off your bread and cut the bread into quarters (in half for GF bread if it is small).
4. Top your bread with shrimp mixture and with the sprouts if you are using them.
5. For closed sandwiches you will now add your second slice of bread, cut off the crusts and cut your sandwiches in quarters. Either squares or triangles.

Peanut Butter Banana Squares

OK, don't knock it until you try it. I grew up on peanut butter banana sandwiches. I included this one to give a new, but easy, sandwich to make. However, with the variations, this can work as a great little sandwich that is also a treat. Fancy them up by cutting your bread into circles. **(GF, DF, EF)**

Yields 12

INGREDIENTS
- 2 peeled bananas cut into ½ inch slices
- Creamy peanut butter
- 6 slices of bread (6 slices of GF bread)

INSTRUCTIONS
1. Spread peanut butter in each slice of bread.
2. Place banana slices on 3 bread slices to cover the entire surface.
3. Top with a piece of bread.
4. Cut off crusts with a sharp knife and cut into 4 squares. Bananas can be slippery, so make sure to actually cut through the banana and do not just press down or your bananas may shoot out from between the bread slices.

Variations:

Cocoa Butter Nana—Sprinkle 3 of the bread slices with mini chocolate chips before adding the banana.

Nutella Monkey—Use Nutella to spread on the bread in place of the peanut butter.

Chunky Monkey—Use chunky peanut butter instead of creamy.

Peanut Free—Use any kind of nut butter you would like.

Sweet

Sweets are a quintessential part of the tea that adds a touch of elegance—a tiny bite of whimsical fare to tantalise your taste buds. Who doesn't love seeing a display of tiny, beautiful desserts. That's why I have included desserts that can be made in small batches to accommodate families, and so making more than one treat isn't overwhelming. If you need more, just double or triple the recipe.

Meringues $
Have you ever had Meringues? These delicate little bites are crisp, but they will melt in your mouth. This recipe is not one for last-minute preparation. It will take 7 hours to complete the process, but they are for the most part hands off once they are in the oven. I have also included some different variations. **(GF, DF, NF)**

Yields 12 small meringues

INGREDIENTS
- 2 eggs whites
- 8 Tbsp sugar
- 1tsp vanilla
- Pinch of cream of tartar (optional)

INSTRUCTIONS
1. Preheat your oven to 250°F (121° C).
2. Cover a cookie sheet with parchment paper.
3. Beat your egg whites until they hold stiff peaks. You will know when this has happened when there is no egg white liquid in the bottom of the bowl and when you turn off the beaters and lift it straight up, the egg whites will hold a strong peak sticking up in the air.
4. 1 spoonful at a time, add the 6 tablespoons of sugar, beating well after each spoonful.
5. Fold in the vanilla and last two spoonfuls of sugar.
6. Using a spoon or a pastry bag (with a plain or large star tip) place the 12 meringues 1 inch apart. They will be shaped like a large hershey kiss. Wide on the bottom and pointed on the top.
7. Bake for 1 hour.
8. Next, DO NOT OPEN THE OVEN DOOR. Leave the meringues in the over for another 6 hours so they can dry out.

Variations
Candy Cane Meringues—sprinkle with crushed candy cane (peppermint stick) just before baking.
Nut Meringues—add ½ chopped nuts of your choice. Pistachios would both look and taste amazing.
Chocolate Meringues—Fold 4 Tbsp of unsweetened cocoa with the last two tablespoons of sugar. These may turn out a little flatter.
Chocolate chip Meringues—fold in 2.5 Tbsp mini chocolate chips with the last two tablespoons of sugar.

Whimsy Meringues—melt 4 ounces of chocolate and drizzle some of it over the white egg mixture just before spooning it onto the cookie sheet. DO NOT MIX IT UP. Just take a scoop with a spoon and place it on the cookie sheet. Once the first layer of chocolate is gone from the bowl, then drizzle some more and keep spooning it onto the cooky sheet. Add a little more fun by folding in some gel food coloring into the meringue before drizzling the chocolate.If you have never used gel food coloring before, it takes a very small amount to color. Use a toothpick to add it. Use a new toothpick each time.

Colored Rose Meringues—fold in a tiny bit of gel food coloring. Using a Wilton 1M star tip, pipe meringues onto the pan. Pipe a Hershey kiss size amount of meringue and then continue piping it in a circle to create a round rose shape.

Mad Hatters Meringues—With an icing bag, take a little gel icing on the tip of a toothpick and draw a line of color on the inside from the tip pulling back until about ¾ way up the bag. Do this with 2–3 other colors on different locations. Now fill your bag with the meringue, being as careful as possible not to smear the colors. Now pipe your meringues onto the cookie sheet. Either make rosettes with the 1M star tip or use the more simple, plain tip and make the Hershey kiss shape.

English Digestive Biscuits $
This is a crunchy, English cookie that is traditionally dunked into tea. It is akin to scottish shortbread, but uses wheat flour—this gives it a nuttier taste. **(EF, NF)**

Yields 3–4 dozen

INGREDIENTS
- 1 ⅓ cup (171g, 5.5oz) whole wheat flour
- ⅔ cup (85g, 3oz) white flour
- 1 tsp baking soda
- ¾ cup (3oz/85g) confectioners sugar
- ½ cup (4oz/115g) butter cut into cubes
- ¼ cup (2floz/57ml) milk

INSTRUCTIONS
- Line a cookie sheet with parchment paper.
- Preheat oven to 350°F (180°C).
- Put all dry ingredients in a bowl and mix until combined.
- Using a dough blender, or your fingers, work the butter into the dough until it's soft and crumbly. Work quickly so the butter does not get too warm.
- Add the milk and incorporate to form a dough.
- Place on a floured surface and work into a nice ball. If it's too sticky add a sprinkle of flour. If it's too dry add a tiny bit of milk.
- Now take a rolling pin and flour it a lot. Roll out the dough until it's about ⅛ of an inch thick.
- Cut into 2 ½ inch (6cm) rounds. Once you run out of space to cut then, roll all of the remaining dough back into a ball and roll it out again. Now cut more.
- Place your biscuits on the lined pan and poke a pattern into the biscuits with a fork.
- Bake for 20 minutes or until they are a light golden color.

Mini Cheesecakes
Cheesecake is a classic, and it can be dressed up in so many ways. One thing for sure, there won't be any of these left over. Not only are they a nice bite size, they're easy to make.
(GF, NF)

Yields 24

INGREDIENTS
- ⅔ cup (134g, 5oz) graham cracker crumbs or Gf graham cracker crumbs, or finely chopped walnuts or pecans
- 2 Tbsp butter, melted
- ½ cup (100g, 3 ½ oz) plus 1 Tbsp granulated sugar, divided
- 1 ½ packages cream cheeses (336g, 12 oz), softened
- 1egg

INSTRUCTIONS
1. Heat oven to 325° F (162° C).
2. Place 24 mini muffin papers inside the mini muffin pan.
3. Mix together the graham crackers, butter, and 1 Tbsp of sugar until it is all damp.
4. Press the crumb mixture into each cute, little paper. A little less than ½ Tbsp each.
5. In a small mixing bowl beat the cream cheese and remaining sugar until blended.
6. Add the egg and mix until blended.
7. Put about 1 Tbsp mixture onto each crust.
8. Bake 12–14 minutes. They are done when the center is almost set.
9. Cool all the way and then refrigerate.
10. Serve with or without papers removed.

Variations:
Raspberry on a cloud—top with a mini dab of whipped cream and a raspberry
Jam Swirl—swirl ⅛ tsp of a favorit jam before putting them in the oven. You can even do a couple different jams to have a variety of flavors.
Creamy Oreo Bites—Use ⅔ cup crumbled oreo (to include the creamy centers) with the butter for the crust.
Fruit topped—put a tiny dollop of a pie filling on top before serving (like cherry or blueberry).
Zebra Bite—melt chocolate and drizzle the melted chocolate in a zigzag pattern to create stripes.

Pumpkin Spice Cheesecake

Is it fall yet? No matter what time of the year it is, these will make the perfect addition to a Fall themed tea time. Pumpkin spice is for sure a classic fall flavor that everyone goes crazy for. With real pumpkin added into it will make it a crowd pleaser. **(GF, NF)**

Yields 24

INGREDIENTS
- ⅓ cup (86g, 3oz) canned pure pumpkin (no pie mix)
- 1 egg
- 1 ⅓ cups (160g, 5.75 oz) Cream Cheese
- ½ cup (100g, 3 ½ oz) granulated sugar
- 1 tsp pumpkin pie spice
- ⅔ cup (85g, 3oz) finely chopped pecans or crushed graham cracker crumbs
- 2 tablespoons butter, melted

INSTRUCTIONS
1. Heat oven to 300° F (148° C)
2. Line mini muffin tin with paper liners.
3. Mix butter with chopped pecans together and then press the crust into the bottom of the paper liners.
4. Beat cream cheese on medium-high until it is smooth and has no lumps.
5. Reduce speed and slowly add the sugar.
6. Beat in each egg one at a time until it's just incorporated.
7. With a rubber spatula, scrape down the sides of the bowl as well as the very bottom of the bowl. Cream cheese will stick to the bottom of the bowl. Then beat for an additional 40 seconds in high.
8. Use 1 ½ cups of the mixture to start filling the liners.
9. Stir the pure pumpkin and spice into the remaining cream cheese and whisk it together.
10. Pour the pumpkin mix on top of the cream cheese layer.
11. Bake for 25–30 minutes. Remove from the oven and let cool to room temperature.
12. Chill for 2 hours

Variations:

Top with whipped cream OR top with a tiny drizzle of caramel sauce

Mini Key Lime Bites
Key lime is one of the boldest flavors that you will find in the kitchen. It is a true show stopper. Key lime anything will make your mouth both water and pucker as your taste buds make sense of all the flavor it is experiencing. **(GF, NF))**

Yield 24

INGREDIENTS
- 12 whole graham crackers crushed or 12–14 GF graham crackers crushed
- 6 Tbsp (85g, 3oz) butter
- 2 Tbsp granulated sugar
- 1 key lime, zest removed and saved
- 2 large egg yolks
- 1 - 14 ounce can sweetened condensed milk
- ½ cup (118ml, 4oz) key lime juice

INSTRUCTIONS
1. Preheat the oven to 350° F (176° C).
2. Spray the mini muffin pan with cooking spray or butter. Coat it well.
3. In a bowl, mix together the first four ingredients until it is all damp. If it does not stick together then add a little more melted butter.
4. Put about 1 Tbsp of the crust mixture into each cup.
5. Place the pan into the oven and bake for 20 minutes.
6. Combines the last three ingredients.
7. Once the shells are out of the oven and have cooled for about 10 minutes, fill each cup to about ¾ full.
8. Bake for 10 more minutes.

Variations:
Top with whipped cream and an itty bitty lime wedge or Top with whipped cream and sprinkle with lime zest.

Lemon Pound Cakes Bites $

Lemon is so amazing in baked goods. Especially when you use freshly squeezed lemons. With this recipe you can make a delicious pound cake and make it into a tiny little bite that will fit perfectly on your tea time platter. **(GF, NF)**

Yields 24

INGREDIENTS

The Cake
- ¾ cups (90g, 6oz) all purpose flour OR ¾ cup-for-cup gluten free flour
- 1 tsp lemon zest
- ⅛ tsp salt
- 4 Tbsp butter, softened
- 2 ounces (567g) cream cheese, at room temperature
- ¾ cup (150g, 5oz) granulated sugar
- 4 ½ Tbsp whisked egg (this is equal to about 1.5 eggs)
- 1 Tbsp lemon juice (about ½ a medium lemon)

The Glaze
- 1 cup (120g, 3 ½ oz) powdered sugar, sifted
- 1 tsp lemon zest
- 1 Tbsp lemon juice (use the other half of the lemon)
- 1 Tbsp milk

INSTRUCTIONS
1. Preheat oven to 350° F (176° C).
2. Grease 24 of the mini muffin pan cups.
3. With a whisk, stir the flour, zest, and salt.
4. In another bowl beat together the butter, cream cheese, and sugar until it is fluffy and light.
5. Add ½ of the eggs and mix well. Then add the rest of the egg.
6. Mix in the lemon juice
7. On low speed, slowly add the flour. Mix until it is just combined.
8. Scoop the batter into the 24 well-greased cups. Fill them until they are about ¾ full.
9. Bake for 16–18 minutes. Test with a toothpick to see if it's done—the toothpick should come out clean.
10. Let it cool in the pan for about 10 minutes and then move to a rack to finish cooling.
11. In a bowl mix the powdered sugar, lemon zest, lemon juice, and ½ Tbsp of the milk. Stir until smooth.
12. Add a tiny amount of milk until the glaze is pourable, but still has some thickness to it.
13. With the wire rack sitting over a cookie sheet or parchment paper, poor the glaze over the cakes with a spoon. This will allow the extra glaze to drip off.
14. Let the glaze set.

Variation:

Garnish with candied lemon rind before glaze sets.

Chocolate-Apricot Petit Fours

Here is a sophisticated taste that you and the children will enjoy. Chocolate cake with a hint of almond, hiding a sweet apricot jam filling will satisfy any sweet tooth. **(GF)**

Yields about 18 round OR 30 square

INGREDIENTS
- 6 Tbsp butter, softened
- 1-8oz (227g) can almond paste
- ¾ cup (150g, 5oz) granulated sugar
- 4 eggs
- ¾ cups (85g, 3oz) flour OR cup-for-cup gf flour
- ½ of a 12 oz can of cake filling (like SOLO brand)
- ½ cup (120g, 4oz) heavy whipping cream
- 1 cup (170g, 6oz) semisweet chocolate chips
- Dried apricots (optional for garnish)

INSTRUCTIONS
1. Preheat the oven to 400° F (204° C).
2. Grease the bottom of a 15X10 inch (38cmX25cm) jelly-roll pan, and then line it with wax paper, and then grease and flour the wax paper.
3. In a mixing bowl, beat together the almond paste until it is creamy.
4. Slowly add sugar and beat it well. Add eggs one at a time, beating after each egg.
5. Stir in the flour.
6. Spread the mix into the prepared pan.
7. Bake for 8–10 minutes and then remove from the oven.
8. Cool for 10 minutes on a wire rack. Using the paper carefully slide the cake out onto the wired rack and cool and hour more, or until completely cool.
9. Place the cake on a flat surface and remove the paper.
10. Cut the cake in half and trim off the crisp edges making sure to keep the edge as straight as possible.
11. Spread the apricot filling over ½ of the cake.
12. Top with the other half of the cake.
13. Loosely cover and chill in the freezer for 1 hour or in the fridge for 2 hours. This step will help with the next step.
14. For little round cakes cut with 1 ½ inch (4cm) round cutter. For square cakes use a ruler and gently mark the edges and create a 1.5 inch (3.8cm) grid and use a long sharp knife to cut out the cakes. Wipe off the blade between each cut.
15. To make the ganache you can use a double boiler or a microwave.
    Microwave: In a 2 cup glass bowl or measuring cup heat ½ cup of cream on high for about 1 minute. If the cream does not seem to be hot, heat for 1 more minute. Once it is hot add the 1 cup chocolate chips and stir until they are melted.
    Double Boiler: Simmer water in lower pan and place double boiler on top. Add the cream and heat through until hot, but not simmering. Add the chocolate chips and stir until melted. Remove from heat.
16. Place a wire rack over a shallow pan and place cakes on the wire rack. Using a spoon, pour ganache over each cake. Once you run out scoop up the drippings and heat again to continue layering the ganache onto the petit fours. To avoid running out, you can make the ganache with 1 cup cream and 2 cups chocolate chips.

17. After your last layer of ganache, sprinkle diced-up dried apricots on top. Or add an almond sliver so your guests will know it contains nuts.

Glacé Petit Fours (4 different flavors)
Petit fours means "little oven" in French. I remember my mother loved these tiny cakes when I was a child and would purchase some for my brothers and me to try. You will need to have a 12'X17" sheet cake pan to make this. This recipe is larger than all the others, but you can make four different flavors of petit fours from this one batch. **(GF, NF)**

Yields 48

INGREDIENTS
- 1 ½ cups (345g, 12oz) butter at room temperature
- 8 ounce (226g) package cream cheese (not whipped), at room temperature
- 2 cups (400g, 14oz) granulated sugar
- ⅓ cup (80g, 3oz) sour cream, at room temperature
- 2 ½ tsp vanilla
- 6 large eggs at room temperature
- 3 cups (345g, 12oz) cake flour (you can use cup-for-cup gf flour, but density may be different). To keep flour light, spoon the flour into the measuring cup and then level it off with the back of a knife.
- 1 tsp baking powder
- ⅛ tsp salt
- 1 ½ tsp vanilla
- ¼ cup (80g, 3oz) each raspberry jam, blackberry jam, orange marmalade, and cherry preserves
- ¼ cup (72g, 3oz) lemon curd (lemon curd recipe in the scone section)
- ½ cup (80g, 3oz) chocolate ganache (ganache recipe in the Chocolate-Apricot Petit Fours recipe)
- ¼ cup sweetened cream cheese (¼ cup (56g, 2oz) cream cheese beaten with ½ Tbsp powdered sugar and ⅛ tsp vanilla)
- ¾ cup (170g, 1 ½ sticks) unsalted butter
- 2 Tbsp whole milk or heavy cream
- Pinch of salt
- 12 cups (1440g, 51oz) powdered sugar, sifted
- ¾ cup (177ml, 6oz) water
- 3 Tbsp light corn syrup
- 1 tsp almond or vanilla extract
- Food coloring of your choice

Instructions
1. Preheat oven to 325° F (162 ° C).
2. Line a 12X17 inch pan with parchment paper (you can not change the pan size).
3. Beat butter on high speed until smooth.
4. Scrape down sides of the bowl and bottom and add the cream cheese. Beat for about 1 minute on medium/high speed until smooth and creamy. Scrape the bowl down again.
5. With the beater on low, beat the eggs in one at a time.
6. Now add the flour, baking powder, and salt and beat at medium speed only until it is just combined. You do not want to over beat the batter.
7. Mix in 1 ½ tsp vanilla.

8. Pour batter into the prepared pan and spread out evenly. Tap the pan out the counter a couple times to urge air bubbles to rise to the top.
9. Bake for 25–31 minutes. Poke a toothpick into the center of the cake to see if it is done cooking. If your toothpick comes out with nothing on it, or a moist crumb, your cake is done.
10. Let the cake cool completely while in the pan.
11. Time to make the buttercream icing!
Butter Cream—Beat the butter until creamy on medium speed. Add 3 cups powdered sugar, heavy cream, pinch of salt, and vanilla. Mix on low until the powdered sugar starts to incorporate. Then start to increase the speed and beat for 3 minutes on high. If the icing is too thin then add small amounts of powdered sugar until it is thick and creamy. If it is too thick then add up to a Tbsp of cream. Spread a thin layer of this icing on top of every cake. No more than an ⅛ of an inch. Let it sit for 15 minutes.
12. Once the cake is cool invert the cake onto the counter, long side parallel to the counters edge, and remove the paper.
13. Now trim any hard edges off the cake.
14. With a sharp knife, cut the cake in half long ways. Now you have two long rectangles. Then cut both long rectangles into thirds (vertically). This will leave you with 6 rectangles. Now, with a long knife and a steady hand, split each rectangle in half to create two even layers (while cutting, your knife will be parallel to the countertop). This will leave you with 12 equal cake layers.
15. Lay out 4 layers. Put a different jam on each one. You do not need to use the full ¼ cup. Use just enough to create a thin layer. Too much will cause the top layer to slide around.
16. Add a cake layer on top of each jam layer. Press gently, but firmly down on the layer.
17. Add a lemon curd layer to the raspberry cake, add a chocolate ganache layer to the blackberry and orange marmalade cakes, and add the cream cheese layer to the cherry cake. Top off each cake with the unused cake layer and press down gently but firmly. If there is a ton of over spill of fillings then take a knife and remove it from the edges.
18. Wrap your layered cakes individually in plastic wrap and place in the freezer for 1 hour.
19. Now to make the easy pourable fondant icing, place the sugar into a saucepan or small pot with the water and corn syrup. Cook over low heat while stirring, but do not allow the temperature to exceed 100° F (37° C). You can also do this in a double boiler if you have one big enough.
20. Once smooth and runny (but not too liquidy because it needs to be thick enough to stick to the cakes), remove from the heat and add flavoring. Either vanilla or almond (almond is a traditional petit four icing flavor). If you make it all almond keep the flavoring light so it doesn't over power the flavors in the cakes. You could also add color to the entire batch or divide it into three different bowls, each with a different color if you like.
21. Remove one layered cake from the freezer. Using a ruler, mark where you will be cutting your squares. With a sharp knife cut each layered cake into squares. Wipe your knife after each cut to keep your little squares clean.

22. Prepare a place where your wire rack can be elevated above the counter with a large pan underneath.
23. Using a toothpick, stick it into the bottom of a cake square, hold over the bowl of warm icing and spoon icing over the entire piece. Give it a gentle shake to help remove some of the excess icing and then place it on the rack with the toothpick pointing down. Now remove the toothpick by pulling down.
24. Repeat the processes until you have iced all of the cakes. Set aside the petit fours, leaving the icing to set.

Almond Buds

These are a twist on the more common peanut butter blossom. So, if you would rather use peanut butter, you can, but these have a very unique flavor. **(GF)**

Yields 20 cookies

INGREDIENTS
- ¼ cup (40g, 1 ½ oz) dark chocolate baking chunks (not processed with wheat for the GF option)
- 1 cup (240g, 8 ½ oz) almond butter (or any nut butter you would like to try)
- ⅓ cup (67g, 2 ½ oz) granulated sugar
- ⅓ cup (200g, 7 oz) packed brown sugar
- ½ tsp vanilla extract
- ½ tsp baking soda
- ¼ tsp salt
- 1 egg
- Additional sugar for rolling the dough in

Other variations: peanut butter with a Hershey Kiss OR peanut butter with butterscotch chips

INSTRUCTIONS
1. Preheat the oven to 350° F (176° C).
2. In a large mixing bowl beat together the almond butter, sugars, vanilla, baking soda, and salt.
3. Add the egg and beat well.
4. Shape dough into 20 small balls.
5. Roll each ball of dough in the extra granulated sugar.
6. Place onto an ungreased baking sheet.
7. Bake for 8–10 minutes or until they are slightly browned.
8. Remove from the oven immediately and press 2–3 dark chocolate chunks into the top of each cookie.
9. Place cookies onto a cooling rack.

Mini Glazed Fruit Tart

Fruit tarts are so yummy with their fruit and custard combo. And these are absolutely adorable sitting in their little shortbread-inspired crusts. What will make them look extremely festive and impressive is if you add an extra flare by putting a miniature fruit trio on top like raspberry, kiwi and blueberry. **(GF, NF)**

Yields 18–24

INGREDIENTS
- 1 ¼ (150g, 5 ⅓ oz) cups flour OR GF cup-for-cup flour
- ⅓ (35g, 1 ¼ oz) powdered sugar
- ¼ tsp salt
- ½ cup (113g, 4oz) butter (1 sick cut into cubes)
- 1 Tbsp cold water
- 1 Cup (237ml, 8oz) milk
- ¾ Tbsp pure vanilla extract
- 3 egg yolks
- ⅓ cup (67g, 2 ⅓ oz) sugar
- 2 Tbsp corn starch
- ½ Tbsp butter
- A variety of fruits (whatever is in season) strawberry, blueberry, raspberry, blackberries, mango, kiwi, mandarin oranges, well drained.
- ¼ cup apricot raspberry jelly (NOT JAM).
- Mint leaves for added garnish (optional)

INSTRUCTIONS
1. The Crust: Preheat the oven to 375° F (190° C) and grease a mini muffin tin.
2. In a food processor blend the flour, powdered sugar, and salt.
3. Add the cubes of butter and pulse until it is moist but crumbly. Then add the cold water and pulse until it starts to look more like a dough. If it's too dry, then add water 1 tsp at a time.
4. Put about 1 Tbsp dough into each mini muffin pan space. Then press the dough down into the bottom and pinch it up the sides.
5. Bake for 15 minutes until golden brown. Let them cool for 5 minutes and then remove from the pan to a wire rack to finish cooling. You may need to use a knife to loosen them from the pan.
6. The Custard: In a medium saucepan bring the milk to a boil over medium heat.
7. In another bowl, whisk the egg yolks and sugar until light and fluffy.
8. Add the corn starch and whisk until there are no lumps.
9. Now you are going to temper the eggs with the hot milk mixture. Slowly pour ¼ cup of the hot milk mixture into the egg mixture while stirring the egg mixture (avoiding scrambled eggs). When incorporated, slowly pour the tempered egg mixture back into the hot milk mixture, while stirring.
10. Increase the heat to a medium-high temp and whisking continuously until thickened. Continue until it has a slow boil.
11. Remove from the heat and add the butter and vanilla.
12. Place crusts into a container for going into the fridge and fill the crusts with custard.

13. Place ¼ cup jelly into the microwave and melt it by heating in 20-second intervals. This is your fruit glaze.
14. Decorate with fruit and optional mint leaf.
    Simple: place a single fruit on top and brush with glaze.
    Fun and tasty: dice up a collection of different fruits or different colors and garish each tart with fruit and brush with glaze.
    Elegant: Cut fruit in tiny, thin slices and arrange in layers for a traditional tart, just in miniature. Brush with glaze.
    Triple Berry: top with three berries and glaze.

Kid Friendly Bag Pudding $
(AKA Boiled Bag Pudding)
Bag pudding mentioned in the poem "Good King Arthur" (JAN) p27
I take every opportunity I can to explore things we learn from books. Even if it's learning how to boil a pudding in a bag for hours. For this recipe we won't be using a pudding steamer (popular in England for making things like a figgy pudding or Christmas pudding). We will be using cloth and a big pot of boiling water like in the 17th and 18th centuries. Why? The poem "Good King Arthur" was first published in 1872. I love giving my kids a taste of history. This pudding would be fun to serve at a Christmas poetry tea. This recipe does not include any alcohol (which is traditional) to make it kid friendly. Also, good to know is that this is about ¼ the size of a normal bagged pudding. Perfect for trying something new.

For this recipe you will need a very clean, naturally colored piece of cloth. 24"X24" square should work fine. You will also need a second piece of cloth, about 1"X12", to tie the cloth shut. These cloths should be washed beforehand with a dish detergent and not clothing detergent to avoid any undesirable flavors being added to this dessert. **(NF)**

INGREDIENTS

The pudding
- 1 cup (120g, 4oz) flour
- 8 Tbsp (1 stick, 4oz) butter (or beef suet to make it more authentic).
- 1 egg
- 1 egg yolk
- ½ cup (125 mil, 4 oz) milk
- 1 Tbsp sugar
- 1 tsp ginger
- 1 tsp mace
- 1 tsp nutmeg
- ½ tsp salt
- ½ cup raisins (you can also add dried currants)

Sauce
- 8 Tbsp (1 stick, 4oz) butter
- 3/4 cup packed brown sugar
- 1 egg yolk beaten
- ¾ cup melted grape jelly
- 1 dash grated nutmeg

INSTRUCTIONS
1. Start a pot with about a gallon or more (about 4 liters) of water and set the heat to high to bring it to a boil. Throw your square of cloth into the pot with the water.
2. In a bowl whisk together the egg, egg yolk, and milk.
3. In a separate bowl combine the flour, sugar, spices, and salt.
4. Chop up the butter and add it to the dry ingredients.
5. Using your fingers, incorporate the dry ingredients until it is all moist and there are no longer butter chunks left. It should feel crumbly.

6. Add the wet ingredients. As usual, if it's too wet add a little more flour and if it's too dry then add a little milk.
7. Add the raisins and currents.
8. Get a small/medium mixing bowl, remove cloth from boiling water, and drape the wet square of cloth over the bowl and push the cloth down into it with the edges hanging over the side.
9. Flour the inside of the cloth well.
10. Shape the dough into a ball and place the dough inside the cloth and gather the cloth tightly at the top to create the bag. (Make sure not to have any openings around the sides exposing the dough to the boiling water.) Tie off the top with the 1X12 inch piece of cloth.
11. Place the bag pudding into the boiling water and let it boil for 2 hours at least. Make sure to keep an eye on the water level so you don't lose too much water.
12. When the two hours are almost up, beat the butter, brown sugar and yolk until it is light and fluffy.
13. Place the mixture into a sauce pan and simmer for 5 minutes over medium-low heat stirring constantly.
14. Add the jelly and once it is melted pour into a bowl and sprinkle with the nutmeg.
15. After 2 hours remove the bagged pudding from the boiling water.
16. Place on a plate and slice it. Serve with the sauce poured over it.

Custard $

Custard is mentioned in the poem "Custard" in the month of November. This is an easy, stove-top custard that you could use as a filling for other desserts or as a tasty treat all on its own. With very basic ingredients this is an easy treat that can be whipped up in no time. You can chill it as the directions suggest or let it cool for a shorter time on the counter and have a very satisfying warm treat. **(GF, NF)**

INGREDIENTS
- 2 cups (237ml, 16oz) milk
- 2 Tbsp cornstarch
- 1/2 cup (100g, 3 ½ oz) sugar
- 4 egg yolks
- 1 tsp vanilla

INSTRUCTIONS
1. In a bowl add ¼ cup milk and the corn starch. Whisk until the corn starch becomes incorporated (no lumps).
2. Add the sugar and whisk until most of it has dissolved.
3. In a saucepan, turn on the stove to medium heat, whisking constantly to keep anything from burning on the bottom of the pan. Heat until the milk is scalded (milk begins to steam and you see tiny bubbles forming).
4. Whisk while adding one yolk at a time. Make sure it is well combined.
5. Heat the mixture for an additional 2–3 minutes and then remove from the heat once it has thickened. Do not let it boil.
6. Mix in vanilla
7. Pour into small serving dishes and chill for 30 minutes. If you don't have small serving dishes you can pour into a baking dish and chill all of it together.
8. Before serving you can top it with fresh fruit, or sprinkle with powdered sugar or nutmeg if you want a hint of fall or Christmas

Strawberries and Cream $

This is a quick, relatively healthy treat, all you need are strawberries and some whipping cream, and some sugar (wink, wink). **(GF, EF, NF)**

Yields 4–6 servings

INGREDIENTS
- 3 dozen strawberries
- 2 cups whipping cream
- Flavoring of choice: vanilla, coconut, or almond (optional)

INSTRUCTIONS
1. Wash strawberries and let dry or pat dry
2. In a large mixing bowl whip whipping cream on high until thick and creamy with soft peaks. Add ½ Tbsp powdered sugar and 1/4 tsp vanilla, coconut, or almond extract and beat to incorporate. If you would like more flavor or would like it sweeter, just add more flavoring or sugar to taste.
3. Serve strawberries in a dish and put whip cream into another bowl with a spoon or portion the strawberries and add a dollop of whipped cream.

Types of Tea

Green Tea—made from young buds and leaves that have not been bruised. Growers hand pick the bud and the first two leaves of the plant. It is then withered a little while under the sun and then it is pan baked. This stops the oxidation of the leaves. This tea is the highest in caffeine.

Black Tea—in China it is called Red Tea. It is 90%–95% oxidized. Young tea leaves are picked and then hand or machine rolled to bruise the leaves and release a lot of their natural oils. Tannins develop and it creates a stronger flavor. Tannins are a chemical compound that create the bitter tones and coloring of the tea.

Breakfast Tea—a black tea blend that is extremely popular in Britain and Ireland. The blend comes from black tea leaves grown in Kenya, Ceylon, and Assam. In Australia they have their own version of breakfast tea that adds a bit of lemon myrtle, also known as sweet verbena, and eucalyptus.

Blossoming Tea—long white tea buds are sewn together and hiding inside is a mini floral arrangement that will reveal itself once it is steeped in hot water. It looks like a little flower blossoming right in your cup. You can even find an herbal dandelion blooming tea online.

Earl Grey—a black tea tossed with bergamot oil. Bergamot is a pear-shaped, green-colored orange. The oil has a citrusy flavor and adds depth to the tea.

Herbal Tea—tea made from herbs, flowers, barks, fruits, and roots of plants. This type of tea does not include leaves from the tea plant Camellia Sinensis. In other countries these teas are referred to as tisanes. Since you can make herbal tea from just about any plant that is edible, the possibilities are endless. Popular herbal teas are mint, chamomile, echinacea, hibiscus, and ginger. For more info on this type of tea, refer to the Herbal Tea section below.

Oolong Tea—a semi-oxidized tea. Large tea leaves are picked and withered under the sun. The leaves are rolled and bruised, causing some of the natural oils to escape. The leaves are then pan fried to stop the oxidation process. The fried level can be anywhere from 15% to 85% oxidized, creating a wide range in flavor. The leaves are then processed with more rolling and drying. When the process is finished the leaves will either be a "ball roll" or left straight. The higher the oxidation, the darker it will be.

Pu-Erh Tea (Post Fermented Tea)—a fermented tea. It is made from the leaves of the tea plant that has grown into a full-sized tree. It is processed like green tea, but then pressed into a cake and left to age. These more mature leaves have live organisms that cause a natural fermentation process. This changes the properties of the tea and the flavor. The aging time is around 20–25 years. Tea producers have created a new method of fermenting the tea to produce it faster by adding heat and moisture so they can produce it within two months. It has a very earthy taste.

Scented Tea—tea that has been flavored with a flower such as jasmine tea. The green tea is processed and then laid out. Thousands and thousands of flower buds are then picked and sprinkled over the tea leaves. At night the flowers will open and release their scent on the leaves. The next morning, every single flower is removed by hand. The leaves are left to dry out and the entire process is repeated at least 3–5 times. A poor-quality scented tea will have flowers still left in it.

White Tea—the least processed tea that is dried out in the sun (solar weathered). It is called white tea because the little tea bud leaves have a fuzzy white downy on them. It has a light flavor.

Yellow Tea—originally the tea of the emperor. The process of making yellow tea was lost for about 100 years. In the1970's it was rediscovered and small amounts are now made. It is considered a gifting tea for politicians and other people of importance. Similar to green tea, the bud and first two leaves are withered in the sun and then pan fried. The leaves are steamed and heaped into a pile. The leaves are covered and left to sit. This creates a flavor that is between the white tea and the green tea.

Herbal Tea

Herbal teas have been used for thousands of years. Unlike the tea made from Camellia Sinensis, also known as the Tea plant/Tea tree, herbal tea is made from a whole variety of things. Herbal tea can be made from fruit, spices, herbs, barks, roots and more. An herbal tea is quite literally hot water that has been infused with other spices, herbs, and other plant material. Besides cooking, spices, and herbs have also been used for medical purposes. In recent years herbal remedies and the use of essential oils (created from extracting oils from herbs and other plants) have become more popular as people are looking for alternative ways to improve their health. Herbal teas are a fun and tasty way to warm your belly and improve your health at the same time.

The best part is that they are super easy. When I was a child my brother, William, and I used to heat rocks in a fire, put water and tea leaves in a ziplock bag and then heat the bag on the rocks (don't ask me how the bag didn't melt on the rock). We called it tea water, but we were actually making tea. Did you know that lemon squeezed into hot water makes tea? Smashed up mint leaves with hot water poured over it and left to steep for three to five minutes makes a mint tea. It's that simple, give it a try.

Healing Properties of Common Herbs
You likely have these right in your kitchen or growing in a garden. These have benefits beyond just tasting good.

Anis (Pimpinella anisum)—the flavor is similar to licorice and sweet. It is fragrant and spicy, creating a warming sensation. This power house with health benefits to depression, menopause, blood sugar, and more.

Camomile (Matricaria chamomilla)—if you are in need of some calm in your life, then camomile is your new best friend. It also helps with settling upset tummies and great for when people have the flu. In a study published in the *Journal of Advanced Nursing* (Chang & Chen 2015) German Camomile showed signs of reducing depression and improving the sleep quality of women postpartum. The German Camomile was steeped for an extended amount of time, fifteen minutes). German Camomile has cute dainty white flowers that are used for making the tea.

Cardamom (Elettaria cardamomum)—a few pods of this and some honey will make a great tea to battle the flu. It warms the body and aids with digestion. It can also help with ulcers, inflammation, blood sugar, oral health, liver health, heart health, and more.

Cinnamon (Cinnamomum verum)—made from the bark of the cinnamon tree, its oils are full of benefits. It has many different antioxidants such as polyphenols, and when compared to twenty-six other spices it was number one. It even beat out oregano and garlic. So only eating when a candy flavor is almost an insult to its awesomeness! It has also been shown to have wonderful anti-inflammatory properties.

Cloves (Syzygium aromaticum)—simmering whole cloves in water for five to ten minutes will make a tea that will warm you from the inside out. It has a hint of spiciness and helps bone and liver health, as well as regulating blood sugar.

Echinacea (Echinacea purpurea)—another mighty tea flower. Called a coneflower. Some of the more popular ones are the black-eyed Susan and the purple coneflower. All parts of the plant have been used for medical purposes for centuries. It has been used to help with the common cold.

Ginger (Zingiber officinale)—a rhizome (underground stem) and is native to hot humid climates in South Asia. It is for sore throats and has a warming effect. It can be made into a tea just by dropping a clean cutting of fresh ginger into a cup and pouring hot water over it and letting it steep until you reach your desired flavor intensity.

Lavender (Lavandula angustifolia)—one of the most calming of the herb world. A field of its cute purple flowers swaying in a breeze is calming alone. It can improve sleep, reduce inflammation, detox the body, and boost your immune system. Lavender is amazing!

Lemon Myrtle (backhousia citriodora australian)—also known as sweet verbena, it is native to Australia and this plant has been used for flavoring and medical purposes for hundreds of years. It is a wonder plant that is high in vitamin C, is antibacterial, anti-microbial, anti-biotic, antiseptic, and anti-inflammatory. That's a lot of bang for one plant.

Mint (mentha)—many different kinds of mint that you may not even know exist. Peppermint, spearmint, chocolate mint, mojito mint, and then a whole variety of fruit flavor mints like pineapple, orange, strawberry, and more. Mint has a cooling effect when you drink it. Spearmint is good for digestive problems. Peppermint will help cough and colds. Chocolate mint is just fun to drink.

Turmeric (Curcuma longa)—a rhizome that has a subtle but unique flavor. It has been used for medical purposes for thousands of years and drinking it in a tea is a popular way of consuming it. Its yellow color comes from the curcumin. It aids in boosting the immune system, heart health, and is an anti-inflammatory. The National Cancer Institute has recognized curcumin as a strong anti-carcinogen and can help prevent cancer.

Fun herbal tea blends to try!
When you add fresh herbs for a tea make sure to muddle (break and smash the leaves to release their oils) them before pouring the water over them.

TIP: *If sipping your tea with herbs floating in it doesn't fit your fancy, then pour it through a tea strainer into another cup before drinking or put the herbs into a tea ball strainer.*

Cinnamon stick, slice of ginger, and a pinch of turmeric
Lavender, camomile, lemon, ginger, and peppermint
Lemon and honey
Lemon, ginger, and camomile
Peppermint, lavender, and ginger
Peppermint and lemon
Clove and cinnamon
Ginger and cardamom
Turmeric, ginger, and cinnamon
Turmeric and lemon myrtle
Chocolate mint and honey
Echinacea, lemon myrtle, and mint
Cinnamon and anis

Have fun making your own herbal tea blends.

The Poetry Tea Time

TEA ETIQUETTE

It is time to learn the ins and outs of tea etiquette. There are many different rules and many ways people choose to follow them. Do you eat with your fingers or a fork? Does the clotted cream go on your scone before or after your jam? The following internationally accepted rules of etiquette taught by International etiquette consultant Jamila Musayeva and English Etiquette expert William Hanson will prepare you for any level of formality. Of course, if all else fails, do as your host does and you will be fine.

Afternoon Tea

As we learned in the history of tea, Anna Russell, Duchess of Bedford, popularized the Afternoon Tea. It is traditionally held between 3 and 5 pm. One would dress nicer for afternoon tea. If attending an afternoon tea, you would want to confirm with your host what the expected dress code will be. It can be smart casual (dressed up jeans) to cocktail dresses, depending on the event you are attending.

Food to expect at afternoon tea will include tea sandwiches, scones, and small desserts. If small desserts are not served you may enjoy a cake, such as sponge cake.

The Place Setting
When you sit down to tea you will place the napkin, folded in half, onto your lap, with the folded side towards yourself. When you need to use your napkin you will dab your mouth, not wipe. At your place setting you will have at least a plate, pastry fork, knife, tea cup and saucer, tea spoon, and possibly a tea strainer if your host is using loose-leaf tea (tea that is not in a tea bag). The knife is not for cutting things, rather for spreading.

Pouring the Tea
Typically the host or hostess will pour the tea unless they have given the honor to someone else. In England this person is referred to as the "Mother." You will be asked "would you like your tea strong or weak." If you want it strong then your tea cup will be filled ¾ full. If you say weak, your cup will be filled half way, leaving room for additional hot water to be added.

Next you will be asked if you would like milk, lemon, or sugar. If you want nothing added to your tea you will just say "plain please" or if in England "blank please." Sugar is always added to the tea first so it can dissolve well. As for the milk, some people argue whether milk should go into the cup before or after the tea. Jamila Musayeva explained that in the past, cups could possibly crack if hot tea were to be poured straight into them. The milk was used to temper the delicate cups. Tea cups no longer have this problem. So I would suggest doing tea first so the hot tea can dissolve the sugar. Then you can add your milk.

If you will be pouring your own tea, you would place the strainer on your cup and pour the tea through it. Once you place the strainer back on its holder, you will add your sugar. You do not drop your sugar into the center of the cup. That could cause your tea to splash and would be poor manners. Instead, you place it in closer to the edge of the cup. After this you will "stir" your tea by gently moving your spoon back and forth in a 6 o'clock to 12 o'clock motion until the sugar has dissolved. Place your spoon behind your cup, on your saucer once you are done. Now you can add your milk or lemon.

Drinking the Tea

If you are sitting at a high table, like a dining table, then the saucer remains on the table and you only pick up the cup. If you are standing or sitting at a low table, like a coffee table, then you will pick up the saucer with the cup. When drinking you will bring the cup to your mouth and you will tilt the cup towards your mouth. You never tilt your head or lean towards the cup. While you are drinking your tea, never look over the edge of the cup, but look into the cup and maintain your elegance.

How to Hold the Tea Cup

Yes, there is a way to hold the tea cup. You will NOT put your index finger all the way through the tea cups handle. It will meet your thumb just on the other side of the handle and the underside of the handle will rest upon the side of your middle finger. There is no need to lift your pinky finger. This was something that may have been done when tea cups had no handle. An elegant lady holds her pinky in. But of course, if you're holding a tea party at your house and those little girls want to feel fancy and lift up their pinky, then let them have their fun.

Eating Etiquette

The food may be served on a three-tier tray. There will either be one for each person or ones for all guests to share. Sandwiches on the bottom, scones in the middle, and desserts on the top. First you will eat sandwiches. This is to be light and fresh to clear your palate. Will foods be picked up with tongs or the fingers? Observe the table (are there tongs?) and do as your host does. Finger sandwiches are just that, little sandwiches to be eaten with one's fingers. Some might say that you should eat the tea sandwich with a fork and knife; William Hanson says one should eat your finger sandwiches with your fingers. But as I have mentioned before, do as the host does. One should not start eating the scones until everyone else has eaten their sandwiches. If you don't want to eat sandwiches then you will just wait until the other guests finish so everyone starts with the scones at the same time.

The Scone

The word scone is pronounced two different ways depending on where you are in the world. Scone can either rhyme with gone or cone. And now to eating the yummy little scone. A scone is not to be cut in half with a knife, but pulled apart by hand. There should be clotted cream and jam to put on top of your scone. You will first dish up a little clotted cream and jam onto your own plate. Then you will spread them onto the scone with your knife. There is a debate on whether you are supposed to put cream or jam on your scone first. Unless you are having afternoon tea in the English counties of Devon or Cornwall it can be done either way. But for your information, the Queen of England does jam first. If you happen to be served a scone with cheese, then you will have butter and relish to put on it. The scone is also meant to be eaten with your hands. William Hanson does warn to "never sandwich the two together, and eat as a whole." Again, if you're not interested in eating a scone, then wait for everyone else to finish their scone before eating a dessert.

The Dessert
You can expect to have a tart, mini cakes, petit fours, macaron, or biscuits (an english tea cookie), but cupcakes are not an English tea dessert. The dessert will be removed by hand and then placed on your plate. Then you will use the small fork or pastry fork to eat unless it is traditionally eaten with your fingers, like a macaron. When using your fork, it should be "upturned and in the right hand" suggests William Hanson. When using your fork remember, your saucer is only for your tea cup. So, make sure to use your other plate to prepare your scone and for eating your other desserts.

When You Are Done
Once you are done eating and ready to leave the table, you place your napkin neatly on the table to the left of your place setting.

Some other common variations of tea time include:

High Tea
High Tea is held around noon. It originated from when a person would have tea with lunch. This tea is eaten at a normal dining table which sits higher than a coffee table. This is the reason for the term "high" tea. It includes things like meats, cheeses, fruits, bread, and other meal fare.

Royal Tea
Royal Tea is like the afternoon tea, but you also have a glass of champagne.

Cream Tea
Cream Tea is the most basic tea. It includes scones, clotted cream, and jam.

Other Tips:
- Never place your elbows on the table.
- When you are not using a hand, you should rest it in your lap on top of your napkin.
- Never slurp while drinking your tea.
- Keep both legs in front of you when sitting in your chair.
- Do not talk while your fork is in your hand. You are supposed to put your fork down between bites.
- Do not reach across for items on the table, but ask others to hand them to you.
- Don't talk while there is food in your mouth.
- Sit up straight and do not slouch.
- Do not check your cell phone while sitting at the table.
-

If you would like to learn more about etiquette, then check out William Hanson's book *Bluffer's Guide to Etiquette: Instant Wit and Wisdom*

The Gracious Host: Planning Your Poetry Tea Time

Now it is time to plan your poetry tea time. There are a few things you need to keep in mind. First you will have to decide if you are planning a poetry tea time for your own children or if you plan on inviting other guests to join you.

Private Poetry Tea Time

If you are planning to do a poetry tea time with your own family you can make it as simple or elaborate as you would like. Getting your children involved is great fun and helps to teach responsibility. Assign each child a task like, reciting a poem, creating a menu, setting the table, learning how to fold napkins in a fancy way, choosing a theme, decorations, tea selection, and so on. Not only will they be excited to do their best, but feel proud about what they contributed to the tea time.

If you are planning on doing it every week, then I suggest to either do a simple tea or tea and snack poetry time to keep things simple and not overwhelming. You don't want to skip tea time just because you don't have freshly baked scones each week. A simple snack can be as easy as some fruit, like strawberries (with whipped cream to be a little fancy), some cookies you already have made or purchased, or some other simple snack you may have on hand. In my home I keep the weekly tea time to just having tea with milk, sugar, or honey. I read outloud a few poems and we discussed its meaning. It's that simple. You can also use the weekly poetry tea time as a chance for your children to practice reciting for an upcoming event.

Once a month or every other month we may make it a little more special. Children would be assigned a poem to memorize and recite. If you have any children who have trouble memorizing, or you would like a certain child to practice reading, then you could opt for children to read a poem, but practice using good expression (voice inflection, correct pauses, eye contact, and such). With this tea time you could hold a full afternoon tea. Children could help you plan and prepare the menu and determine your dress code. Depending on the age of your children, you could even assign things like dessert chef, place settings creator, poetry selector, finger sandwich maker and so on—everyone can do his or her part. Or you could decide to create a surprise theme now and then and create an extra special experience. Keep reading to see how.

Poetry Tea Time with Guests

Are you ready to host a poetry tea for guests? Just go through this guide and you will be ready. Even better, go to www.AYearofPoetryTeaTime.com and print the Poetry Tea Time Planner guide. How many people can you comfortably seat?

- Do you have all of the tableware needed?
- What is your budget?
- How long do you want your tea time to last?
- What will the order of events be?
- What will the dress code be?
- How formal will tea service be?
- Will there be a theme?
- Will guests be reciting poetry? Or will your children be reciting?
- How old will your guests be?
- How will you invite your guests?
- Will you have party favors?
- Do any of your guests have food allergies?
- How will you get it done?

Seating

First things first, you need to be aware of how many people you can accommodate. Keep the following in mind.

- Will everyone be sitting at a single table? How many people can comfortably sit there?
- Will guests be mingling and carrying their tea and treats to different visiting areas?
- Are there places to set down one's tea in a casual setting (coffee table, side tables, etc)?

TASK: *Sit down and decide how many guests you can realistically fit comfortably.*

Tableware

You need to decide if you have the amount of place settings you need for all of your guests, and what you will want to include in your settings. This step will determine if you will be buying actual dishware or if you will need to purchase paper or plastic plates, forks, spoons, and so on.

A basic tea setting will be set up as follows:

- Cover your table in a tablecloth if you would like.
- Place the dessert plate at the center of your place setting.
- Either place the saucer and teacup on top of the dessert plate or to the right of the plate, cup handle facing right and spoon set on the saucer behind the cup. If your table does not have room for the plates to be side by side then you could place it a little back in the traditional place of a drinking cup.
- Fold the napkin and either place it to the left (if the cup is on the plate) or on top of the bare dessert plate.

- Place the fork to the left of the dessert plate and the knife to the right, between your dessert plate and saucer.
- Teapot, foods, sugar, creamer, jam, and clotted cream can all be placed in the center of the table.

On a Budget

Use whatever you have. Don't be discouraged by what you don't have; your kids won't care. The most important part is getting your kids involved and the atmosphere you create. Really the poetry and the time spent together is the most important. So, pull out your mugs, ladle the water from a pot and curl up with a blanket. Or gather around the table with a homemade construction paper centerpiece and a slice of grandma's famous apple pie. Poetry tea time is your own creation.

Big Spender

If you are ready to drop some money on a tea party, then here is what I feel the order of importance is:
- Tea Kettle for boiling water and for extra hot water (this just makes it easier to heat your water)
- A Tea set (teapot, tea cups, saucers, sugar bowl and creamer)
- Tea strainers (if you plan on using loose-leaf tea)
- Tea spoons
- Dessert plates
- Three-tier server
- Serving dishes for clotted cream and jam
- Dessert forks
- Cloth napkins
- Mini vases for flowers

The list can go on and on with all sorts of niceties.

Money Saving Tip

Thrift store: dessert or salad plates are often sold and you may even be able to put together a nice collection of mismatched tea cups and saucers.

Borrow: borrow from others. Just be aware that if anything gets broken you will be responsible to replace it and that could be very pricey. So keep in mind the ages of your guests when contemplating this option.

Paper Plates: use pretty paper plates to eat off of if you don't have dessert plates.

BYOTC: Invite your guests to bring their own tea cup and saucer.

TASK: *Take inventory of what you have and decide what is still needed.*

Menu

The food is a big part of the afternoon tea. It's the very reason afternoon tea was started. Having a combo of savory and sweet is key. Finger sandwiches are supposed to be light and refreshing. Traditional sandwiches would be cucumber, egg salad, smoked salmon, and more. Scones can either be plain or have a simple something added to them. English and Australian scones do not have elaborate sweet flavors because they are to be topped with a jam and clotted cream. They are also traditionally round. These are different from the dense triangular glaze covered scones served up in America. Desserts are meant to be a sweet treat to finish off the event.

If you have a very small budget don't let that stop you. You can still put on a very nice poetry tea time on a tight budget. Lucky for you, tea fare isn't costly to begin with. Desserts can be made at home and there are some things that look great when on a budget. My tea times with guests have focused more on the menu and we just used mugs and salad plates or paper plates until I had enough tea cups with saucers. Make sure to look in the recipe section for recipes with a single dollar sign ($) on the page. This will indicate the treats that are extremely affordable and can probably be made with ingredients that are always in your kitchen.

Other foods that are tea time staples are milk, sugar, lemon slices, jam, clotted cream. If your family does not eat sugar, honey could be an alternative. If you do not live some place where clotted cream can be found in the grocery store, then you can try and buy some online or make it yourself.

Money Saving Tips
- Ask guests to bring items: scones, finger sandwiches, or mini desserts.

TASK: *Choose how many different kinds of finger sandwiches you will make. Also, choose what scones and desserts you will serve. Remember, cupcakes are not traditional if you're wanting to stay authentic to the English tea. Select the jam or curd that will be served with your scones. Recipes for what was just mentioned can be found in the recipes section of this book.*

Selecting the Tea

First you will have to choose if you are going to use loose-leaf tea or tea bags. When having guests you will want to try and have three flavors to choose from. Of course, if you only have one or two, nobody is going to drag you off to tea jail. A selection just makes sure that everyone has something they will enjoy. That being said, I have had a few tea times where I only had mint, chamomile, or sleepy time tea (a popular herbal blend in the USA) when I had a small group of young visitors. These teas are generally liked by children.

Not everyone drinks green tea and not everyone enjoys herbal teas. Some people may not drink caffeinated drinks or leaf teas for a number of reasons. So having at least one herbal tea on hand will make sure everyone is accommodated.

Some more popular tea leaf teas include green, black, earl grey, English Breakfast, oolong, and chai.
Some popular herbal teas include peppermint, echinacea, chamomile, peach, and ginger.
A couple extra fancy teas include blooming tea and jasmine tea .

TIP: *Do not buy teas that say they are "flavored." The flavor is not authentic, but synthetic.*

Making the Tea
To make loose leaf tea add 12 grams or 2.5 teaspoons of leaf tea to a teapot and then add 100ml or 4.25 cups of hot water. Steep for 3–5 minutes. Do not over steep; after 5 minutes the tea may become noticeably bitter.

With a tea bag you can put the tea bag in the individual cup and pour the hot water over it. Steep for 3–5 minutes. If you would like to pour the tea from the teapot, then add 1 tea bag for every cup or 250ml of water.

Money Saving Tip
- Use tea bags rather than loose leaf tea (now you don't have to buy the tea strainers.
- Ask each guest to bring two tea bags for a tea exchange. Place them on a platter and guests all choose one to try.

TASK: *Choose the tea you will be serving.*

Event Length
Just like any well-planned party you should have a planned ending time. Not only does that make it easier for you to plan, but it also provides a pickup time if you are inviting children over for the tea. You need to decide if this is a social gathering where guests will be socializing or if the main event is sitting down for tea and poetry.

If you are wanting just tea and poetry you can estimate that it will last about an hour and this will still leave a little time for mingling. You should have time for everyone to be served their tea, have poetry read or recited, and any leftover time for mingling.

If your plan is to have an event that is not only mind stimulating (with poetry of course), but a time to visit and catch up, then your end time should take mingling time into account.

TASK: *Pick your starting and ending time.*

Order of Events

Decide how you will run your poetry tea time. This organization will keep your tea running smoothly and you won't forget anything. Here are my two suggestions.

1. You can do the poetry and the tea time separate. This would allow poetry to be the focus and then for visiting during the tea portion of your gathering.
2. You can have everyone sit down to tea and be served and then have the poetry reading and reciting while people eat.

For younger guests I suggest you go with the second option, because eating will help keep them quiet and keep them listening to the poetry. There is just something about sipping one's tea and pondering a poem. The only reasons I would suggest the first option, is if your seating is not all in one room or if guests have worked a long time on their recitations and you would like the guests to give them their undivided attention.

Make sure you also spend a little time determining the flow. By this I mean:
- Where will your guest gather until you sit down to tea?
- Who will be reading or reciting and in what order?
- Where will the reader/reciter stand or sit while presenting?
- What will your guests do once the tea is over?

If you think of these details now, you won't be left scrambling in the moment.
If your guests are children, then having something planned before and after tea may be smart to help keep everyone occupied. Something as simple as coloring sheets or folding a tea cup out of paper will do.

TASK: *Pick the start and end times of your event and plan your flow. (Keep in mind the age of your guest.)*

Age of Guests

Time to think of the ages of your guests. Guest age can affect everything from invite design to menu.

Elementary Age

Younger children can have their challenges, but if you plan accordingly, you will be fine. If you are inviting more than six young children, you may want to have a couple more adults to help out. Maybe one adult for every three to four children. This will make serving go much quicker. Tableware can be on the less expensive side. Don't put out your finest china. Keep your menu on the "safe side" and avoid things like finger sandwiches with smoked salmon, and desserts with lavender. Now I love exposing my own children to different and exotic foods and flavors, but when you are dealing with a lot of children, *safe* is better. If the group ends up coming over once a month then go for it and make an item on the menu that will stretch their culinary experience.

As mentioned earlier, keep flow in mind and have some coloring sheets or some other simple activity for a time filler if needed. If any children get cold feet when it's their turn to recite or read, just let them wait and ask them towards the end if they would like a try. If you keep it low stress they may even ask to do it once people are leaving. Just remember, they are conquering a fear and even if they only recite in front of you, or the few guests that are left, that is a step in the right direction. You could also offer for them to stand with you after the last recitation and read it for them. So be flexible. Children will also need reminders of proper etiquette.

Middle School

This age is starting to mature some, but it's the age of wanting to look "cool" so be ready for the kids to possibly make fun of etiquette. Of course, you can insist on a certain level of decorum. This is your poetry tea time. Presentations of poems may also feel like they are lacking and not taken seriously. For the most part try to keep in mind that they are getting something out of it. This experience may help them develop skills that will help them in their teen years.

Even though they want to think of themselves as not being children any more, they are and feelings are often at the surface. Insist on respect towards others. Mocking a person's poetry choice or ability to perform should not be permitted. You may want to think twice before you take out your finest china. Some growing children are still working on coordination. Of course, if you are gathering a spectacular group of youth, and you know the kids very well, then they may be able to handle a bit more finery. Explore foods and dig a little deeper into your poetry conversation.

High School

Teens are crossing over to mini, preadults and you have the potential for a little more seriousness. They don't want to look stupid in front of their peers. At the same time, there will be the "class clown" or the desperately shy ones. Again, be firm on the standards and what the expectations are. Be patient with those who may be your shrinking violets. If you are hosting a group that will meet regularly, really make sure your standards are understood during your first tea.

You will also need to decide if your finest serving dishes and tea cups will be adorning your table. Teens love to feel more adult and if you treat them that way, often they will step up to the plate and can impress you. They are also old enough to be assigned task like making food. Assignments will also help them develop adult skills. You could also rotate which teen is the host (even if it is always at your house). They can be taught how to plan a tea and be responsible for choosing a theme, the poetry, developing the menu, and sending out the invites. Some of these skills could be started with the more mature middle school aged children.

Adults

If you want to hold a poetry tea time with adults, then go for it. This can be an opportunity to set an example to your own children. It shows them that you value good, wholesome educational activities. Children learn so much from seeing their parents do worthwhile things and investing in their own education. Make sure you have your flow planned out so your poetry tea time doesn't just turn into chatting and tea time—though it may be tempting to just be social. Have fun and make it as fancy as you want.

Adult with a Child Date

A fun way to hold a fancier tea would be to invite a parent or guardian and a single child to your tea. This way each child has an adult with them and you could fancy it up some. All ages love to act grown up and children typically love one on one time with mom, dad, or a significant adult in their life.

Mixed Age Groups
Mixed ages can work really well if your older kids are helpful, especially if they are siblings. They can help serve the younger attendees, and you could even have a special poetry session featuring poetry told by two people. An event of this sort can easily be accomplished by inviting a few families.

TASK: *Choose what ages will be attending your poetry tea time.*

Dress Code
So how fancy are you thinking? Will girls be expected in dresses and boys in slacks? This is entirely up to you. Typically, afternoon tea would be "smart casual" at the least. But it can be as nice as wearing a cocktail dress, so, you be the judge. What type of atmosphere are you trying to create? Would you rather your guests dress to match a tea time theme you picked? Make sure to include the expected dress code on the invitation. Here is a guide as to what different dress codes mean.

Casual: If you are fine with ripped jeans, T-shirts, halter tops, shorts, and flip-flops, then casual is your style. Be kind and still put on the invitations that the attire will be casual, so your guests are not left to guess how to dress.

Business Casual: This would be like what people wear to work.
Males in a polo or casual button up shirt with a pair of khakis. Dress shoes or loafers are good shoes.
Females in nice khakis and a nice top or in a casual dress or skirt.

Smart Casual: Can also be referred to as "dressing up jeans."
Males would wear dark jeans or khakis and pair it with a blazer, vest, or shirt with a tie.
Females would wear nice slacks, skirt, or dark jeans with a dressy top. Blazer and jewelry give an extra touch.

Business/Informal: Don't let this title fool you. This is yet another step dressier.
Males would wear a business suit and tie, or slacks and a sports jacket with tie, with dress shoes.
Females would wear a business suit or business style dress and heels.

Semi-Formal: This level is the fine line between informal and formal.
Males wear a dark suit with a long tie.
Females wear a classy evening dress that is about knee length. Super short dresses are not appropriate.

Formal/black tie/black tie optional: We've reached the top.

Males wear a tuxedo with vest or cummerbund, and bow tie. If black tie is optional then you can opt for a black suit and conservative colored tie. It does not have to be black. Females will wear floor length evening gowns with an up or partially up hair style and she can wear her finest jewelry.

TASK: *Choose the dress code for your poetry tea party.*

Formality

Now think about the formality of your poetry tea time. Will only one person, the "mother," be serving the tea? Will everyone be serving themselves? Remember, you're the host and you get to run your tea time the way you want to.

Be practical and keep the group size in mind. If it is an intimate gathering of two to six people, then having a "mother" serve the tea is manageable. But a group of ten would probably be a bit harder. You will need to take into account how many tea pots you have and how easy it will be for your guests to reach the other tea time goodies to eat. Why? If you have more than one teapot and the ability to put food in more than one location (either on the single table or at different tables), the serving and distribution can be shared, making it possible to keep your tea more orderly.

If formality isn't possible and you would rather be a little more casual, you could also choose to have a tea service area and a food area where people could serve themselves and then go to their seats. This could work if seating will be in a number of places.

TASK: *Decide how strictly you will be keeping to the traditional tea etiquette.*

Choosing a Theme

It can be a lot of fun to pick a theme, even though theming isn't traditional. You may just want to use tea as your theme. Themes can be concrete or abstract. Here are some ideas:

- Seasons: Spring, summer, winter, fall
- Holidays: Christmas, Easter, Halloween, Independence Day, Valentine's Day, St. Patrick's Day
- Books: Alice in Wonderland, Jane Austin, Charles Dickens, C.S. Lewis
- Nature: flower, leaves, gardening, birds, butterflies, woodland creatures, bunnies, Beatrix Potter
- Trees: pinecones, birds nests, tree blossoms, twigs
- Time: clocks, watches, numbers, hourglass
- Love: hearts, William Shakespeare, cupid, mythology, love birds, love letters
- Twisted: Edgar Allen Poe, Ravens, black lace, moon, night, candles, Mad Hatter, Cheshire Cat
- Poets: Stevenson, Dickinson, Sandburg, Frost, Angelo, Wordsworth, Longfellow, Alcott
- Victorian: hats, gloves, peonies, calligraphy, roses, lace, period clothing
- Travel: postcards, passports, suitcases, planes, trains, cars, taxis, cameras
- Musicals: My Fair Lady, Singing in the Rain, The Music Man, Hello Dolly, West Side Story
    If you're looking for something fun and different, watch the musical after your tea time.
- Paris: Eiffel Tower, croissants, quince, escargot, creme brulee, macaron, poodles, beret, crepes

With a theme, there will come decorations. Some simple things you can add are white, Christmas or fairy lights, flowers, themed centerpieces, napkin rings, and a whole host of other purchased or homemade decor. And don't forget, music is great for setting the mood whether you have a theme or not.

Money Saving Tips

- Pick a theme and use items you already own, like books, vases, faux flowers, branches you could paint, rose petals, Christmas lights, clocks, etc.
- Pick wild flowers to put in small vases for décor.
- Make some of your decorations, like napkin rings and center pieces that will bring your theme together.
- Have a "Favorite Tea" theme and ask everyone to bring a box of their favorite tea. Now you don't have to buy tea.
- Have guests bring an item of decor (center piece, wall hanging, piece of art) for the party that they either purchased or made. Then have a raffle or draw numbers and each person gets to go home with a cute decoration for their own home.

TASK: *Decide if you will have a theme, what colors you will use, and what you will need to get.*

To Recite, or Not to Recite

When you hold your poetry tea time you will have to decide how the poetry will be enjoyed:

1. You, the host, can read a selection of poetry out loud.
2. You have yourself and children memorize poetry to recite from memory.
3. You invite each guest to come prepared to share one to three poems, either memorized or read.
4. You invite everyone to share one to three poems.
5. You invite everyone to come prepared to share a poem from the same poet. You could even include a poem with their invitation so you don't have any repeats.

Make sure to make any assignment well in advance—probably a month in advance if you are hoping for people to recite from memory. If you are asking people to just read, then you should give them two weeks to a month advanced notice. Remember, for some people, it's easy to stand in front of others and talk, others need more time to prepare and be comfortable with the idea.

TASK: *Decide how poetry will be shared, select performers, and notify them in advance.*

Invitations

Times are changing and there is more than one way you can invite your guests to your poetry tea time.

Physical invitations are always nice and very classy. You can mail them or hand deliver. If you see your guests often, then giving them their invite in person will save you a little money and you will know that they received the invite. On the other hand, if you feel uncomfortable giving an invite in front of others who are not being invited, then go with the mail.

Handmade Invitations

Remember, mailing costs more to deliver if the invite has any embellishments like bows and buttons. So if you do anything extra cute like a tea bag in your invite I would suggest taking it straight to the post office so you can pay the exact extra postage. If making them by hand sounds like your style, then you should check out the *A Year of Poetry Tea Time* Pinterest page for some great invitation ideas.

Printed Invitations

Printed invitations can be made right on your computer or ordered. Either download an invitation template or take a look at some different examples online and create your own. You could use Canva.com to create your invites and they have a ton of different templates. It has a free level so you don't ever have to pay. If you want to order printed invites, then check out companies like Smilebox, Shutterfly, Greetings Island, and Zazzle.

Evites

If you are the environmentally continuous type, then evites may be for you. This method is also a great way to cut costs. Try visiting punchbowl.com and search for "tea party." There are at least ten tea-themed invites to choose from and many other beautiful designs to choose from. You design your invite, enter your guests emails or phone numbers and their invites are delivered. This is a paid service but it does have a free trial you could use. You may want to send a reminder about five days before the party. Another company is Greeting Island (lots of tea designs), Paperless Post, and Evite.

Through Social Media

Invite your friends through your social media. Create an event and invite your friends to the event. People can mark if they are coming, not going, or maybe. This also gives you a place to keep people up to date.

Call or Text

Maybe you want to keep it simple and would just like to pick up the phone or send a text to invite your guests. That is fine, but make sure to send a follow up reminder at least five days in advance to make sure your guests remember since they don't have a physical invite to remind them of the tea.

What to Include on the Invitation

Don't forget to include all of the important information on your invitations:
- What the party is for, such as a poetry tea party
- Date
- Location
- How and by when to RSVP
- Dress Code
- If you are allowing a Plus One (permitting your guest to bring an extra person with them)
- Any other special instructions for the event

TASK: *Decide how you would like to invite your guests.*

Party favors

Party favors are 100% optional. For more fancy or formal gatherings, party favors push the event to the next level. It is a nice gesture, especially if you have asked guests to bring a food item or to recite poetry. This can be as simple as a tea bag in an envelope with instructions on how to make a perfect cup of tea. It could be a honey stick with a little thank you tag, a nicely wrapped petit four, a homemade truffle, a flower, a packet of seeds, a poem quote made into a magnet, and so on.

TASK: *Decide if you will be having a party favors and, if so, what it will be.*

Food Allergies

As a good host, you will want to check with your guests and see if anyone has allergies.
1. You don't want a guest unable to eat anything.

2. You don't want someone leaving with an upset tummy, or worse.

In the recipe section you will find foods that are naturally, or can be altered to be made, gluten free, egg free, dairy free and/or nut free.

TASK: *Contact your guest list and ask if they have any food allergies.*

How do you get it done?

Now you have all of your tasks done. If you haven't yet, go to www.ayearofpoetryteatime.com and download your Tea Time Planner guide. It has a printable version of what you see below with even more details and to help keep your poetry tea time organized.

Two Months Before
- Set a budget.
- Pick a date.
- Create your guest list.
- Choose a theme.
- Secure a location to hold your tea time (if you're not doing it at home).

One Month Before
- Create and send your invitations.
- Plan any games or activities you may be doing.
- Create your menu.
- Shop for any supplies you need.
- Gather and plan decorations.
- Make any poetry or food assignments.

Two Weeks Before
- Choose music.
- Complete any unfinished decoration prep.

One Week Before
- Contact guests that have not RSVPed.
- Create your tea time flow.
- Confirm your venue location.
- Make party favors.

Two Days Before
- Purchase any food needed.
- Remind people of their responsibilities if assignments were made to guests.

One Day Before
- Prepare any food that can be made a day in advance.
- Set up any decorations that can be done a day in advance.
- Pick up flowers and place them in vases/arrangements.

Poetry Tea Time Day
- Prepare food.
- Set the table(s).
- Set up music and activities.
- Finish decorating.

Bring Poetry to Life

Bringing Poetry to Life

I believe that learning can be done just about any place, and that there is more to learning than just reading, writing, and arithmetic. Getting out and experiencing life, exploring the world around us and touching the lives of others is part of what makes each individual a unique person. The experiences we share and knowledge we gain by stepping out of our personal bubble is what makes us grow.

Hosting a tea is social and makes the poetry experience fun, but that isn't the end-all. Reading poetry transports us into another's mind and heat, and we experience something new every time. We see and feel what another person has experienced and learn empathy. We experience joy, laughter, peace, and pain. Poetry is a form of literature that all ages can enjoy together. Don't limit your experience to your dining room table. Get out there and bring poetry to life.

Poetry and Gardens

One of my favorite things to do is read in a garden. It might seem silly, but when you're reading something that highlights or brings attention to your surroundings it creates a memory. For instance, I once took my children to the Chicago Botanical Garden where we only had a few chapters left of *The Secret Garden*. We took a picnic lunch and read for a while on a blanket before going in. Then we went into the English walled garden and read for a while, ending our reading next to a pond. To this day my children will say that has been their favorite reading experience.

This can be done with even more ease when it comes to poetry. You can read maritime themed poetry at the beach, visit a zoo and read poems at the different animal enclosures. Take a walk around a lake and read poems by Henry David Thoreau. Visit a farm and read poems about farm animals, hard work, and life. The possibilities are endless.

Poetry and Service

Retirement and nursing homes are often looking for new things to add to their programming.
There are also many seniors who are rarely visited by family and miss seeing the life and excitement of children. Work on memorizing a poem or reading some poems with great expression. Reach out to a local community home and ask to set up a time to come and perform. If that doesn't work with their schedule you could see if going room to room is a possibility. Do this with just your children or with a poetry-tea-time group. As a confidence building experience, it helps the children learn to speak in front of groups and help children to look past their own needs and see the needs of others. All ages can participate—get some parents involved too.

Poetry and Preschool

What better way to spread the love of poetry than to teach the youngest of minds? Reach out to someone who owns a preschool and set up a time for your kids or group to come by and share poetry. Some possible activities:

- Teach poems with hand actions.
- Teach simple Mother Goose rhymes.
- Memorize a few lines of a longer poem each time you go.
- Choose a different animal poem each time and learn about the animal.

These are all things that little kids will enjoy. Just keep it simple and focus on memorization and making it an active experience – act like the animal, sound like the animal, color a picture of the animal with the poem on the paper and so on.

Get Out and Learn
Check into your local area and find libraries, museums, and historical sites that are dedicated to a poet. One summer we were staying in North Carolina for a while and our friend Michael Jordan (an English Professor at Hillsdale College) asked us if we were planning on visiting the Carl Sandburg house. Sadly, we had never heard of this person who was considered one of the greatest American poets.

We decided to jump at the chance to learn something new. We looked up his poetry and found one poem that was nice and short entitled: "Fog." We worked on memorizing it for a couple days. We made the pilgrimage out to the house on the day they held their bluegrass music festival. We enjoyed music, took the tour, petted the sheep, and then recorded all of the children reciting the poem in front of Sandburg's house. The kids still know the poem to this day, years later.

Poetry Rabbit Trails

Below are hands on activities and learning experiences inspired by the poetry in this book. You will find the poem and poet underlined for each activity. Feel free to do the activity as described or put your own twist on it. The most important thing is that you and your children are enjoying the poetry and that it sparks their love of learning. Learn more about creating an awesome homeschooling environment and learning through classic literature. Learn this and more in my book *Relaxed Homeschooling or visit LittleRabbitTrails.com.*

January
- Make Bag Pudding on page 281. "Good King Arthur" (anonymous) p27
- Memorize the poem "New Year" by Emily Mary Barton. Write down one goal you want to accomplish this year.
- Learn where Saltzburg, Austria is (Mozart's birthplace) and listen to Mozart's Minuet in G, K1. This was the very first piece of music he wrote at the age of 5. Draw a picture of what the music makes you think of. "A Minuet of Mozart" by Sara Teasdale p22
- It's time to turn your room, living room, or play room into a magical place. Use sheets, blankets, chairs and anything else you have to create the best fort or magical land ever. Maybe you can even sleep in it.
- "Block City" by Robert Louis Stevenson p32

February
- Learn about purpose of white blood cells and draw a white blood cell and label its parts. "The Land of Counterpane" by Robert Louis Stevenson p47
- Pick one trait or bad habit you would like to improve on. Maybe being nicer to a sibling, following through with commitments, keeping your room clean, thinking positive thoughts. Write this on a piece of paper and post it in your room where you will see it over and over. "Faults" by Sara Teasdale p48
- Learn the myth of Cupid and Psyche. Create a comic or stick puppet show to recreate the story. "Cupid" by Ben Jonson p50
- Give a short presentation about Frederick Douglas after learning about him. "Frederick Douglass" by Paul Laurence Dunbar p42
- Paint or draw your own topsy turvey world. "Topsy Turvey World" by Willim Brightly Rands p40

March

- Learn about the Moua Museum of Underwater Art in the Great Barrier Reef of Australia. Use clay or playdough and make a sculpture that you think would be really cool in an underwater art museum. "Our Australian Land" by J. Sheridan Moore p63

- Learn how to locate the northern star (in the northern hemisphere) or the Southern Cross (in the southern hemisphere). How did these stars help sea navigation? "Speak of the North! A Lonely Moor" by Charlotte Brontë p59
- Write your own story or poem about a unicorn. Turn it into a play and perform it. "The Lion and the Unicorn" (anonymous) p59
- Learn about how bells make their sounds. Try hitting things around your home and see how their vibrations sound different. "Song of the Bell" by William Henry Giles Kingston p54
- Learn the call of two or three birds that live in your area. Sit outside and try to identify a bird just by hearing it. "A Minor Bird" by Robert Frost p56

April

- Write a letter to a relative or to an elderly person who lives on your street. "The Weekly Mail" by Emily Mary Barton p87
- Learn about the mythological Greek God, Pan, and his musical duel with Apollo. Learn where Greece is on the globe and listen to pan flute music. "A Musical Instrument" by Elizabeth Barrett Browning p80
- Learn about two types of cloud formations that you see in the sky often, what causes them, and what they tell you about the weather. "I Wandered Lonely as a Cloud" by William Wordsworth p76
- Learn about the life cycle of the caterpillar, visit a butterfly house, order caterpillars and watch them change into butterflies, or do a butterfly squish painting. "The Caterpillar" by Robert Graves p73
- Its Earth day on April 22nd. See if there are any Earth Day events happening in your area or go out and pick-up trash in some of your favorite parks. "Earth" by Joseph B. Soldano p72

May

- Make a fairy garden in your yard using only natural things like rocks, sticks, leaves, moss, etc. Include things like a little house, walking math, privy, or whatever you like. "The Fairies" by William Allingham p90
- Learn about May Day. Then either pick a few small bunches of flowers or purchase a bouquet of flowers you can split into a few tiny bouquets. Make paper cones and place a mini bouquet in it. Leave it on a persons doorstep, knock and yell May basket and then run away. "The First of May" by Caroline W. Leakey p91
- Plant a garden in the ground or plant some seeds in a few pots. "We Have a Little Garden" by Beatrix Potter p91 or "A Seed I Sow by Cayden Shepherd p92
- Paint an apple blossom tree. With a black pen or brown paint draw a tree trunk and some branches. With a Q-tip cotton swab, and 2-3 different shades of pink, dab pink dots to create the tree blossoms. "Apple Blossom" by Horatio Algar Jr. p94
- Learn how a lunar eclipse works. "At a Lunar Eclipse" by Thomas Hardy p99
- Learn how to tell the age of a tree. "Trees" by Sara Coldridge p93

June

- o Write a poem for your father or other important male figure in your life. "Only a Dad" by Edgar Guest p123 or Father by Edgar Guest p121
- o Learn about the Jelly fish and visit a local aquarium. If you don't have an aquarium nearby then learn how to make an origami jelly fish. "A Jelly Fish" by Marianna Morre p113
- o Learn about Iambic Pentameter and practice using it while reading. "Sonnet 18" by William Shakespeare p108
- o Learn about the biology of the mosquito and how it eats. "A Skeeter Conversion" by Forrest Lybrand p110
- o Visit a zoo or local petting zoo and observe an animal. Draw it and write down a list of behaviors you see it do. At the Zoo by A.A. Milne p111 or Our Crazy and Wonderful Zoo by Nicholas C.A. Sparkman p112
- o Write your own abecedarius poem with any theme you would like. "Seaside ABC's" by Cambry Glassett p114

July

- o Go to a minor or major league baseball game "Casey at the Bat" by Ernest L. Thayer p143
- o Learn how to make your own bubble solution and giant bubble makers with string and straws. Then make giant bubbles and have someone take pictures of them. How long does it take big bubble to form into a circle? What colors do you see on the bubble. Why do bubbles pop? "The Bubble" by William Allingham p142
- o Learn about the Limerick and try to write your own. "Book of Nonsense Limerick 31 by Edward Lear p142
- o Learn why the moon gives off light or learn about the cycle of the moon. The Moon" by Robert Louis Stevenson p139
- o Go on a hike to a waterfall and take a towel so you can dry off after playing in the water. "In the Wood" by Sara Teasdale p134

August

- o Learn about 2-3 different star constellations that can be seen in your local sky. Then go outside after it is dark and try to find them. Evening Star by Edgar Allen Poe p147
- o What is a dirge? Learn what it is and then listen to the song Saint James Infirmary performed by Cab Calloway. This blues song is a dirge that would be played at a funeral. "A Dirge" by Percy Bysshe Shelley p149
- o Go swimming in a natural body of water rather than a pool. "The Day When We Went Swimming" by Henry Lawson
- o Learn about the life cycle of the cicada. "The Cry of the Cicada" by Matsuo Basho p159
- o Learn how to draw your favorite dinosaur. "The Best of the Best" by Max Lawrie p160
- o

September

- o Memorize the poem "Fog" by Carl Sandburg p179 and discus imagery.
- o Read "The Banjo Player" by Fenton Johnson p177 and then play some banjo music and dance to it.

- o Go on a late evening walk and talk about how it is different from going on a walk in the middle of the day. If you don't take walks often, then take a walk during the day and then take your evening walk later that day.
  "A Late Walk" by Robert Frost p174
- o Go apple picking and then make an apple pie, apple cider, or just enjoy eating the apples. "September" by Helen Hunt Jackson p175
- o Go on a day trip to go fishing. If you don't know how to fish, find someone who is willing to teach you. "Wynken, Blynken, and Nod" by Eugene Field p171

October
- o Roast Pumpkin Seeds after reading "Theme in Yellow" by Carl Sandburg p188
- o Learn how to draw a raven "Raven" by Edgar Allen Poe
- o Memorize the poem "Double, Double, Toil and Trouble" p199 and learn who Shakespeare is.
- o Pull out some art supplies and read the poem "Jabberwocky" by Lewis Carroll p194 and have each person draw what they think it would look like. You could also do this with the poem "The Kraken." By Alfred Lord Tennyson p187
- o Read the poem "Autumn Dusk" by Sara Teasdale p185 and try to write a short poem like it on any subject.
- o Memorize the poem "The Road Not Taken" by Robert Frost p182
- o Go for a nature walk and collect fallen leaves. Take them home and make leave rubbings. Look closely and find all of the leaf's details. Learn about the parts of a leaf.

November
- o Make a pumpkin pie OR Learn how to make a pumpkin pie like a pilgrim. "Pilgrims" by Henry David Thoreau p215
- o Memorize the last stanza of "Thanksgiving" by Edgar Guest's p216
- o Rake together a giant pile of leaves and jump around in it. "Gathering Leaves" By Robert Frost p209 OR Fall, Leaves, Fall by Emily Brontë p212
- o Learn about the Navajo Indians. "A Song of the Navajo Weaver" by Bertrand N. O. Walker p214
- o Paint a picture inspired by the poem "Symphony in Yellow" by Oscar Wilde p211 and talk about primary colors. Look for things in your house or in nature that are yellow.
- o Make custard with the recipe on page 281 inspired by the poem "The Custard" by Robert Herrick p208

December
- o Make paper snowflakes and hang them from the ceiling with thread. "Winter" by Jordan Henrie p222
- o Roll up paper into balls and have a snowball fight indoors "Stopping by Woods on a Snowy Evening" by Robert Frost p224
- o Learn about Wilson Bentley, the first snowflake photographer. Now give it a try yourself and try to take pictures of snowflakes. "Snowflakes" by Henry Wadsworth Longfellow p225
- o Learn about fractals, then look for them in nature or in snowflake photography "Snowflakes" by Henry Wadsworth Longfellow p225

- o   Make Gingerbread cookies after reading <u>"Gingerbread by Louisa May Alcott</u>. P232
- o   Go caroling to your neighbors. <u>"Carol" by Kenneth Grahame</u> p234

Poetry Field Trips

Here are some great places you can visit to learn about poets. Even if you don't live close to any of these locations, try looking up historical sites or poets who came from your area. Also, remember to check for poets in any area where you might be visiting.

International

Poetry Jukebox
The poetry jukebox can be found in eleven locations around the world. Each one is in a prominent public space and features about twenty themed poems. Locations include, Belfast, North Ireland; Edinburgh, Scotland; New York City, USA; and several other locations in Europe.

Visit thepoetryjukebox.com to see all of the locations.

Australia

Australia Poetry Hall Of Fame
This place is dedicated to preserving the poetry, song lines, and language.
144 Bradley Street Guyra NSW 2365 Australia
Phone# +61 0423 478 656

Henry Lawson Centre Gulgong
A museum dedicated to teaching people about the life and works of Lawson. They have pictures, paintings, original works and more.
147 Mayne Street, Gulgong NSW 2852
Phone# +61-02 6374 2049

Canada

Shevchenko Museum
An entire museum dedicated to the Kobzar (poetry) of Tars Shevchenko, a Ukrainian poet. It has four galleries, a library, several offices, and a studio space where art classes are held. It was moved to a brand-new location and reopened in 2020.
1604 Bloor Street West Toronto, Canada
Phone# +1 (416) 534-8662

Great Britain

Beatrix Potter: Hill Top
Who wouldn't want to visit the home of the lady who revolutionized the children's picture book? Creative from a young age she drew and wrote. She purchased this house with the money made from her first book *The Tale of Peter Rabbit*. When you visit her house it's like stepping in to find that your friend Beatrix had just stepped out. It has been set up as if she is still living there.
Near Sawrey, Hawkshead, Ambleside, Cumbria, LA22 0LF
Phone# +44 (0)15394 36269

The Brontë Parsonage Museum
I can say that I have stood out in front of this building and dreamed of going inside. Tour the home, view the world's most comprehensive collection of Brontë writings. Also see a collection of portraits and iems owned by the Brontë family.
Church Street,Haworth,Keighley,West Yorkshire BD22 8DR
https://www.bronte.org.uk

The Globe Theater
Take a tour of the Old Globe theater where Shakespeare entertained countless people during his time. See how people experienced outdoor theater. You can even see one of his plays here.
21 New Globe Walk, London SE1 9DT.
https://www.shakespearesglobe.com

Robert Burns Birthplace Museum
Visit the birthplace of Scotland's National bard. This is the best place to get to know this world famous poet and songwriter. He was a literary rockstar at the young age of 27.
Murdoch's Lone, Alloway, Ayr KA7 4PQ, United Kingdom
Phone# **+44 1292 443700**

Rudyard Kipling's Batemans, East Sussex
Here is a chance to visit a real manor and explore the life of a writer and poet. His study has been left just the way he likes it. You can see his Nobel Prize, art from his books, and other belongings. He also wrote the poem "If" at this house.
Bateman's Lane, Burwash, East Sussex, TN19 7DS
Phone# **+44** (0)14358 82302

Thomas Hardy: Max Gate and Hardy's Cottage
Visit the cottage he grew up in and the house he designed himself and lived in from 1885–1928. Both locations created inspiration for his writing.
Max Gate: Alington Avenue, Dorchester, Dorset, DT1 2AJ
Phone# +44 01305262538
Hardy's Cottage: Higher Bockhampton, near Dorchester, Dorset, DT2 8QJ
Phone# +44 (0)13052 62366

Wordsworth: Dove Cottage

Home of William Wordsworth, the Romantic English poet who lived here 1799–1807. It was here that he wrote the poem "I Wandered Lonely as a Cloud." Transport yourself back in time to experience a simpler time.

Dove Cottage, Grasmere,Cumbria, LA22 9SH

Phone# +44 (0)15394 35544

Ireland

Dublin Writers Museum

At this museum you will learn about many different Irish writers, including the likes of Yeats, Wilde, and Swift.

18 Parnell Square Dublin, Ireland

Phone# +353 (0)18722077

Poetry Ireland Center (COMING SOON)

The Poetry Ireland and the Ireland Heritage Trust are working together to create a center that is "dedicated to the celebrating, supporting and promoting poetry, poets and writers." It will be in Dublin Ireland at No. 11Parnell Square in a four-story, 250-year-old, Georgian historical home. They launched their last major fundraiser in February of 2020.

United States of America

American Poetry Museum

The mission of the American Poetry Museum is "dedicated to celebrating poetry, promoting literacy, fostering meaningful dialogue, encouraging an appreciation for the diversity of the American experience, and educating local, national, and international audiences through the presentation, preservation and interpretation of American poetry."

716 Monroe St NE #25th, Washington, DC 20017

Phone# +1 **(202) 670-6252**

American Shakespeare Center's Blackfriars Playhouse

Did you know that the world's only re-creation of the Blackfriars Theater is in Virginia? Shakespeare's play company started performing at the original location in England in 1608. That's right! You can go and boo, cheer, and hiss at the performers while sitting on wood benches (cushions for rent). They do have suggested age minimums so call in advance. They also host more than just Shakespeare plays.

10 S Market St, Staunton, VA 24401

Phone# +1 **(877) 682-4236**

The Carl Sandburg House

Carl Sandburg is known as, "The Poet of the People." When his house was donated to the National Park Service it was handed over as it was when he lived there, furniture and all. Nothing changed. It is like stepping back in time. His wife was a sheep herder and her sheep line lives there to this day and you can mingle among them. They also hold a wonderful bluegrass music festival once a year during the summer. There is no fee to hike the small trails or to walk the grounds and see the sheep. To take the house tour there is a fee, but children fifteen and under and seniors are free.

81 Carl Sandburg Lane, Flat Rock, NC 28731

Phone# +1 (828) 693-4178

Chicago Shakespeare in the Park

There is nothing cooler than watching experienced performers bring Shakespeare to life in an outdoor setting. Chicago's Shakespeare in the Park is a great casual way to experience Shakespeare where your children don't have to sit in absolute silence. They perform in a different Chicago park every weekend. Just get there early to save yourself a piece of grass, lay out a big blanket and bring food and drinks to keep everyone happy. The best part is that it is totally free.

chicagoshakes.com/parks

Dr Seuss Museum

This museum has a wonderful garden out front with many of the iconic Dr Seuss characters in life size. You can even see Theodor Geisel himself hanging out with the Cat and the Hat. Inside the museum any child, or adult, would be excited by all the color and whimsical art and displays. Full of hands-on exhibits, your children will experience art and words in a whole new way.

21 Edwards Street, Springfield, MA 01103

Phone# +1 (413) 263-6800

Emily Dickinson Museum

You can visit two different houses. The house she was born in, spent her life in, and where her poems were discovered after her death. You can also visit her brother's home. Tours are held March–December and grounds, gardens, and exhibits are free. House tours do have a fee and are first come first serve.

280 Main St, Amherst, MA 01002

Phone# +1 (413) 542-8161

Louisa May Alcott Orchard House

The house was the home of the Alcott family, where Louisa May Alcott wrote her book Little Women, and the setting for the aforementioned book. The house has been taken care of so well that a visit is like walking through the book of Little Women. Open April-October

399 Lexington Road, Concord, Massachusetts 01742, United States

Phone# +1 (978) 369-4118

The Montford Park Player

Experience Shakespeare the way it is meant to be experienced: Outdoors, no microphones and plenty of space. Bring your own chairs and you can bring your own snacks. They have an intermission where they sell refreshments. Great performers and a theater experience you will never forget.
92 Gay St, Asheville, NC 28801
Phone# +1 **(828) 254-5146**

The Ralph Waldo Emerson Memorial House

Would you believe that Emerson purchased this house because it was "the only good cellar built in Concord?" You can tour the house with all original furnishings and some of his personal effects. There is a fee and size limitations. A bonus is that there are multiple authors from Concord and there is a lot to see. RV parking is not available anyplace in Concord.
28 Cambridge Turnpike
Concord, Massachusetts 01742
Phone# +1 (978) 369-2236

The Robert Frost Stone House Museum

The stone house sits on 7 acres and was Frost's home from 1920-1929. During that time he wrote his iconic poem "Stopping by Woods on a Snowy Evening" and won his first Pulitzer Prize. They hold workshops and other fun events throughout the year.
121 Historic Route 7A, Shaftsbury, Vermont 05262
Phone# +1 (802) 447-6200

Robert Louis Stevenson Museum

This poet is from Scotland, but this museum is in California, USA. It was created by a fan of Stevenson, and one of America's leading bibliophiles, Norman H. Strouse. See items that belonged to Stevenson and collections of his writing and learn about his life.
1490 Library Lane St. Helena, CA 94574
Phone# +1 (707) 963-3757

The Wadsworth–Longfellow House

Here you can visit Henry Wadsworth Longfellow's boyhood home where he was born and raised. Three generations of Longfellow's lived in the house. The last person to live there was Anne, Longfellow's youngest sister, and she handed the house over to the Maine Historical Society. Because of this the house is virtually untouched. Download the Wadsworth Longfellow House App to make your visit a more complete experience. Tours are available May-October.
489 Congress Street, Portland, ME 04101
Phone# +1 (207) 774-1822

Poet Quotes

Here is a fabulous collection of quotes from poets through the ages. These, in addition to the quotes, included at the beginning of each month's chapter, provide a total of fifty-six quotes. These quotes could be used for weekly memorization, copywork, discussion, morning inspiration, on a changeable letter board, and more. Use them any way you like.

"For last year's words belong to last year's language And next year's words await another voice."

—T. S. Eliot

"Words are, of course, the most powerful drug used by mankind."
Rudyard Kipling

"The great art of life is sensation, to feel that we exist, even in pain."
—Lord Byron

"Fill your paper with the breathings of your heart."
—William Wordsworth

"I become insane, with long intervals of horrible sanity."
—Edgar Allen Poe

"War is what happens when language fails."
—Margaret Atwod

"To see a World in a Grain of Sand And a Heaven in a Wild Flower, Hold infinity in the palm of your hand And Eternity in an hour."
—William Blake

"My course is set for an uncharted sea."
—Dante Alighieri

"Follow your inner moonlight; don't hide the madness."
—Allen Ginsberg

"One day I will find the right words, and they will be simple."
—Jack Kerouac

"Failure is not fatal until we surrender trying again is the key of glorious victory."
—Muhammad Iqbal

"Patience is a conquering virtue."

—Geoffrey Chaucer

"Never be afraid to raise your voice for honesty and truth and compassion against injustice and lying and greed. If people all over the world...would do this, it would change the earth."

—William Faulkner

"In three words I can sum up everything I've learned about life: it goes on."

—Robert Frost

"Don't judge each day by the harvest you reap but by the seeds that you plant."

—Robert Louis Stevenson

"One must dare to be happy."

—Gertrude Stein

"I have always imagined that Paradise will be a kind of library."

—Jorge Luis Borges

"Perhaps it's impossible to wear on identity without becoming what you pretend to be."

—Orson Scott Card

"May you live every day of your life."

—Jonathan Swift

"Genius is the recovery of childhood at will."

—Arthur Rimbaud

"Always be a poet, even in prose."

—Charles Baudelaire

"It takes courage to grow up and become who you really are."

—E. E. Cummings

"The earth has music for those who listen."

—George Santayana

"That man is best who sees the truth himself. Good too is he who listens to wise counsel. But who is neither wise himself nor willing to ponder wisdom is not worth a straw."

—Hesiod

"As you move toward a dream, the dream moves towards you."

—Julia Cameron

"Worse than not realizing the dreams of your youth would be to have been young and never dreamed at all."

—Jean Genet

"There must be those among whom we can sit down and weep and still be counted as warriors."

—Adrienne Rich

"It is only through mystery and Madness that the soul is revealed."

—Thomas Moore

"Sweet words are like honey, a little may refresh, but too much gluts the stomach."

—Anne Bradstreet

"Our greatest glory is not in never falling, but in rising every time we fall."

—Oliver Goldsmith

"Reading is to the mind what exercise is to the body."

—Joseph Addison

"A person often meets his destiny on the road he took to avoid it."

—Jean de La Fontaine

"Sh, child and youth, if you know the bliss which resides in the taste of knowledge, and the evil and ugliness that lies in ignorance, how well you are advised to not complain of the pain and labor of learning."

—Christine de Pizan

"Of all sad words of tongue or pen, the saddest are these, 'It might have been."

—John Greenleaf Whittier

"Poetry heals the wounds inflicted by reason."

—Novalis

"You shall create beauty not to excite the senses but to give sustenance to the soul."

—Gabriela Mistral

"Truth crushed to earth shall rise again."

—William Cullen Bryant

"Never say more than is necessary."

—Richard Brinsley Sheridan

"Suffering is not good for the soul, unless it teaches you how to stop suffering. That is its purpose."

—Jane Roberts

"It takes a long time to bring excellence to maturity."

—Publilius Syrus

"Well-timed silence hath more eloquence than speech."

—Martin Farquhar Tupper

"I don't want to get to the end of my life and find that I have just lived the length of it. I want to have lived the width of it as well."
—Diane Ackerman

"Time is Too Slow for those who Wait, Too Swift for those with Fear, Too Long for those who Grieve, Too Short for those who Rejoice; But for those who Love, Time is not."
—Henry Van Dyke

"Reason respects the differences, and imagination the similitudes of things."
—P. B. Shelly

Mini Poet Bios

Adams, Francis William Lauderdale – 1862–1893 – Malta
In 1884 Adams was published in Australia where he lived. Later he moved to England. He continued to be published in both Australia and England. His most popular work was *Songs of the Army of the Night* in 1887.

Alcott, Louisa May – 1832–1888 – Massachusetts, USA
Best known as the author of *Little Women* and *Little Men*, Alcott also wrote short stories and poetry. She was a nurse during the Civil War for six weeks. Her first publication was *Flower Fable* in 1854.

Alger Jr., Horatio – 1823–1899 – Massachusetts, USA
Alger, an American novelist, is known for writing rags-to-riches stories about boys who worked their way up to the middle class. He emphasized ideals of hard work, courage, and determination. He gained popularity with his book *Ragged Dick*. His novel themes were known as a "Horatio Alger myth."

Allingham, William – 1824–1889 – Ireland
Allingham was a poet, editor, and a diarist. His most popular poem is "The Fairie," published in 1850. He is also well known for his work titled *A Diary*, published posthumously.

Amans-Lucas, Elaena – b. 2007 – Virginia, USA
Amans-Lucas is an artist, writer of stories, and poems.

Arnold, Matthew – 1822–1888 – England
His writing addressed contemporary and social issues and chastised the reader. Some refer to Arnold as a sage writer because of this technique. In 1849 he published his first book of poetry *The Strayed Reveller and Other Poems*. He became professor of poetry at Oxford in 1857.

Bai Juyi – 772–846 – China
Bai Juyi was a Tang dynasty government official and an eminent Chinese poet. His poetry actually led to his exile of about four years. Most of his poetry comes from his observations of life and his career.

Baring-Gould, Sabine – 1834–1924 – England
From Lew Trenchard, Devon, England, Baring-Gould was an Anglican priest, scholar, antiquarian, hagiographer, novelist, and folk song collector. He is best known for hymns such as "Onward Christian Soldiers" and "Now the Day Is Over."

Barton, Emily Mary – 1817–1909 – England
Barton was born in England and had a classical education. She was fluent in French and Italian, knew Latin, and some Greek and German. She met her husband when on a voyage to Australia. She was known as a painter and a poet. Her poetry was used in the Sydney news and in letters. She passed away in Australia.

Blake, William – 1754–1827 – England
Blake was born in Soho, London. He grew up to be an English poet, printmaker, and painter. He attended school long enough to learn to read and write. After that, he learned at home, read books of his choosing, and at this point he became interested in poetry. He attended a drawing school at age ten.

Bowditch, Nathaniel Ingersoll – 1773–1838 – Massachusetts, USA
Bowditch was born in Salem, Massachusetts. He was a natural at math at a young age and, as an autodidact, taught himself algebra at age fourteen and later calculus, as well as Latin and French. He is known for writing the maritime navigation book American Practical Navigator that is still used on ships today.

Bowles, William Lisle – 1762–1850 – England
Bowles was born in England and attended Winchester College at age fourteen. He was a clergyman for the Church of England. He was also a poet and critic. He and Charlotte Turner Smith were credited with the revival of the sonnet in their time.

Bridges, Robert – 1844–1930 – England
Bridges studied Medicine and was a doctor by trade. In 1882 he retired due to lung disease and devoted all of his time to poetry. His faith had a great influence on his writing.

Brontë, Anne – 1820–1849 – England
Brontë was a poet and novelist. At age nineteen she was a governess for six years and then returned home. After leaving her teaching job, she published her first volume of poetry with her sisters. She also wrote two novels *Agnes Grey* and *The Tenant of Wildfell Hall* all under the pen name Acton Bell.

Brontë, Charlotte – 1816–1855 – England
At age fourteen, Brontë attended school and returned home the year after to teach her own sisters. She worked as a governess briefly. The sisters worked together to publish a book of poetry in 1846 using the pen name Currer Bell. Her first published novel was *Jane Eyre* in 1847.

Brontë, Emily – 1818–1848 – England
Brontë is a poet and novelist, best known for her novel *Wuthering Heights*. She also collaborated with her sister in publishing the book *Poems by Currer, Ellis, and Acton Bell*, her pen name being Ellis Bell. People found her poetry to be "poetic genius." The sisters grew up in Haworth, England.

Brown, Sarah Janisse – b 1976 – Hawaii, USA
Brown and her husband are the founders of Thinking Tree Publishing and creator of Dyslexia Games Therapy. Her family served a mission in Ukraine where they adopted five of their fifteen children and counting.

Browning, Elizabeth Barrett – 1806–1861 – England
Browning was a Victorian-era poet and was popular in both the US and England. She started writing poetry at eleven years old. Her childhood collection of poetry is one of the largest juvenile collections in England. As an adult, her first collection of poetry was published in 1838. She is interred in Italy.

Bryant, William Cullen – 1794–1878 – Massachusetts, USA
Bryant was born in a cabin in Massachusetts and was interested in poetry at a young age. Later he went to school for law and became a lawyer. During one of his seven-mile walks to work, he saw a bird flying and was inspired to write *To a Waterfowl*. He was an American romantic poet, journalist, and editor.

Burns, Robert – 1759–1796 – Scotland
A poet and lyricist who wrote in both English and Scots dialect. Burns is still very popular in Scotland, and in 2009, a public vote won him the title of "Greatest Scot." He was a collector of folk songs. His poem turned song "Auld Lang Syne" is popular around the world.

Campbell, Thomas – 1777–1844 – Scotland
Campbell was the first president and founder of the Clarence Club and helped to establish the University College London. He is known for didactic poetry and patriotic war songs, including "Battle of the Baltic" and "The Soldier's Dream".

Cambridge, Ada – 1844–1926 – Australia
Born in England, Cambridge was educated by a governess (she did not like it). She was a poet, novelist, and journalist for an Australian newspaper, and the wife of a clergyman. She published three volumes of poetry and over twenty-five fiction novels. There are four literary prizes named after her.

Carroll, Lewis (born as Charles Lutwidge Dodgson) – 1832–1898 – England
Best known for his book *Alice in Wonderland* (published in 1856), Carroll was also a poet-mathematician, photographer, illustrator, teacher, inventor, and an Anglican deacon. He was educated at home until the age of twelve. From a young age he wrote poetry and short stories. He first used his pen name in 1856 with the romantic poem, "Solitude."

Cawein, Madison Julius – 1865–1914 – Kentucky, USA
After graduating high school, Cawein worked at a pool hall for six years to save enough money to return home and write. He wrote a total of 1,500 poems and 36 books. His first publication was a collection of poems titled *Blooms of the Berry* in 1887.

Clare, John – 1793–1864 – Englnd
As a child, Clare was an agricultural worker and went to school until he was twelve. Known as the "peasant poet," he tried many styles of living, including living with gypsies. His first poetry collection published was *Descriptive of Rural Life* in 1820 followed by *Village Minstrel and Other Poems* in 1821.

Coleridge, Samuel Taylor – 1772–1834 – England
As a child, Coleridge loved to read books and enjoyed playing on his own. After his father's death, he was sent to a school for the rest of his childhood where he studied and wrote poetry. Known for the poems *Kubla Khan* and *The Rim of the Ancient Mariner* and was a founder of the Romantic movement.

Cowper, William –1731–1800 – Hertfordshire, England
Cowper was one of the forerunners of Romantic poetry. His poetry introduced the phrase "God moves in a mysterious way" to the English language. Notable works are *The Negro Complaint*, *Yardley-Oak*, and the *Olney Hymns*. He was a very popular poet and hymnodist.

Crowther, Melissa – b. 1981 – Utah, USA
Crowther is a cellist and loves to play music with her family and local chamber orchestra. She enjoys gardening, hiking, and reading poetry while having tea.

Cutler, Elena Tatiana – b. 2006 – Utah, USA
Cutler enjoys reading, writing, musicals, singing, baking, photography, hiking, and her dogs Pippi and Pidge. She loves to help others and is an aspiring teacher.

Daley, Victor James – 1858–1905 – Australia
Daley was born in Armagh, Ireland. He received his education in England. In 1878 he immigrated to Australia and became a freelance journalist and writer. He helped establish clubs for poets and writers. He also used the pseudonym Creeve Roe (Red Branch in Irish). Best known poem is "A Sunset Fantasy."

Dickinson, Emily – 1830–1886 – Massachusetts, USA
Dickinson's father wanted his children to have a very good education and she was considered a well behaved child. She had a formal education, and in 1840 she attended Amherst College. She preferred being alone and she wrote over 1800 poems of which only about ten were published while she was alive.

Dregge, Reagan – b. 1984 – Minnesota, USA
Dregge studied creative writing and theatre arts. Today she writes letters by hand and writes about her life in her little prairie house with her husband and daughter on her blog, thegracebook.wordpress.com

Dunbar, Paul Laurence – 1872–1906 – Ohio, USA
Dunbar's first poem was written at age six, first recital at nine, and published in Dayton's *The Herold* at age sixteen. In 1892 he published a collection of poems titled *Oak and Ivy*. He then wrote a total of twelve books of poetry, four novels, four books of short stories, a play, and lyrics for a musical. Writing in both English and in "negro dialect", he was one of the first internationally known African-American writers.

Doyle, Sir Arthur Conan – 1859–1930 – Scotland
Doyle started writing short stories while attending medical school. In 1879 his first published short story was titled *The Mystery of Sasassa Valley*. He was a practicing doctor on ships such as the Greenland whaler *Hope of Peterhead* and eventually opened his own practice. At age twenty-seven, his first Sherlock Holmes story was published.

Du Mu – 803–852 – China
Popular during the Late Tang Dynasty Du Mu was known for his romantic and lyrical quatrain poetry. He was an expert at lyrical quatrains with historical or romantic themes. There is a twenty-book volume of his prose still around. In addition to prose he is also a master of Shi and Fu.

Emerson, Ralph Waldo – 1803–1882 – Massachusetts, USA
Known as a philosopher, Emerson was also a poet, essayist, and lecturer who led the transcendentalist movement. At age nine he attended Latin school and at fourteen he attended Harvard. He was class poet of Harvard's 1821 graduating class.

Field, Eugene – 1850–1895 – Missouri, USA
Field was a journalist and poet. He was known for his humorous writing and children's poetry. He first started publishing his poetry in 1879 with his poem "Christmas treasures." His most famous children's poem is "Wynken, Blynken, and Nod."

Field, Thelma Arlene (Walters) DeGroff – 1917 –1998– New York, USA
She was born to the Walters family in Caro, Michigan and adopted at age 3 to the DeGroff family in Bath, New York. She grew up on a farm and attended school through grade nine. She began writing poetry when she was 12. While in the eighth grade she was given the assignment to memorize a large portion of Longfellow's Epic Poem *The Song of Hiawatha* which she was able to recite the remainder of her life. Thelma wrote poetry mainly for those she loved. She raised a family of 5 children and wrote poetry well into her 80's.

Fairs-Billam, Isla – b. 2008 – Zambia
Fairs-Billam was born in England but moved to Zambia in 2012. She enjoys poetry and is currently working on a book. She excels in areas of art and literature.

Foott, Mary Hannay – 1846–1918 – Australia
Foott was born in Glasgow, Scotland, but then moved to Australia with her parents. She published her first volume of poetry in 1885 titled *Pelican Builds and Other Poems*. She also became a journalist.

Freeman, John Frederick – 1880–1929 – England
Freeman was a poet and essayist who was featured in the *Georgian Poetry*. He also won the Hawthornden Prize.

Frost, Robert – 1874–1963 – Massachusetts, USA
Frost was born in San Francisco, California, but moved after his father's death. His first poem was published in his high school's magazine. He did many kinds of jobs as an adult, but felt his true calling was poetry. He sold his first poem: "My Butterfly. An Elegy." His first book of poetry was published in England in 1913 titled *A Boy's Will*. He won many Pulitzer prizes and was presented with the Congressional Gold Medal. He was known for his ability to use American Colloquialism and capturing rural life.

Gagnon, Caden R. – b. 2007 – South Korea
Born in San Diego, California, Gagnon loves to write stories, poems, draw and spends lots of time reading books. She currently lives in South Korea.

Glassett, Cambry – b. 2007 – Virginia, USA
Glassett likes to go on walks and runs on the paths and trails around her house. Her other interests include: sewing, drawing, playing the piano, being in nature, reading, and playing outside with her siblings and friends.

Goethe, Johann Wolfgang von – 1749–1832 – Germany
Goethe was multitalented in writing both epic and lyrical poetry. During law school he preferred to learn about poetry rather than law. He was well known by age twenty-five after the success of his book *The Sorrow of Young Werther*. He sat on a council under the Duke of Saxe-Weimar, Karl August, who ennobled him. As the modern era's literary genius, he not only wrote poetry, but also worked in science and politics and wrote novels, and dramas, including his play *Faust*.

Grahame, Kenneth 1859–1932 Scotland
Born in Edinburgh, Scotland, Grahame later lived with his grandmother in the village of Cookham. As an adult he worked in banks. He is best known for his book *The Wind in the Willows* and *The Reluctant Dragon*.

Graves, Robert – 1895–1985 – England
Graves was the son of Charles Graves, an Irish poet, who wrote the song "Father O'Flynn." During school he was good at boxing and began to write poetry. During WWI he wrote even more poetry while in the British Army and he came to be known as the war poet.

Greenaway, Kate – 1846–1901 – England
As a child Greenaway was taught at home and she loved to read. She attended school to learn art and in 1879 her first book, *Under the Window*, was published. It was a collection of children's verses with her own illustrations.

Guest, Edgar – 1881–1959 – Michigan, USA
Born in England, but his family immigrated to the US shortly after. Guest's first poem was published in 1898. He was known for his optimistic poetry and was called the "people's poet." He wrote about 11,000 poems and many were published in various publications to include *A Heap o'Livin* (1916) and *Just Folks* (1917).

Han Yu – 768–824 – China
Han Yu was also a writer and government official during the Tang Dynasty. He is compared to other pivotal poets like Shakespeare, Goethe, and Dante. Throughout his life, he experienced hardships including exiles and attempted executions. He also had success in the imperial war office and led a university.

Hardy, Thomas – 1840–1928 – England
Influenced by romanticism and his dislike of social classes Hardy left his career as an architect to pursue writing. From 1912–1913 his poetry was strongly influenced by the death of his first wife. He was nominated for the Nobel Prize twice during his lifetime.

Harper, Charles – 1863–1943 – England
In addition to poetry, Harper was an author of many travel books that he illustrated himself. He also wrote some books on drawing technique.

Henrie, Jordan Elizabeth – b. 2010 – Colorado, USA
Henrie is the middlest [*sic*] of 3 sisters. She loves people, dragons, and poetry.

Henley, William Ernest – 1849–1903 – England
As a young man, Henley suffered from tuberculosis of the bone, leading to half of his left leg being amputated. As an adult he moved to London to become a journalist, but spent three years in hospital because of illness (1873–1875) and he wrote a collection of poems called *In Hospital*. He is best known for his poem "Invictus." Fun fact: He was Robert Louis Stevenson's inspiration for the character Long John Silver in *Treasure Island*.

Herrick, Robert – 1591–1674 – England
Herrick was a cleric and lyric poet of the 17th century. He is best known for his collection of poems titled *Hesperides*. About half of his 2,500 poems written were included in the aforementioned book. His first book *Noble Numbers* was published in 1648.

Hiller, Juliette – b. 1983 – Washington, USA
Hiller currently lives with her husband and seven children. After college and a year in Scotland, she served in the United States Army as a medic. In addition to her family, she enjoys ballet and writing.

Holmes Sr, Oliver Wendell – 1809–1894 – Massachusetts, USA
Holmes grew up with asthma. His first recorded poem was written down by his father at age thirteen. Not only was he a poet, but also a physician and a member of the Fireside Poets. His most popular work was a collection of prose titled *Breakfast-Table*. His most famous poem is "Old Ironsides."

Hood, Thomas – 1799–1845 – England
Hood is a poet who used humor and is best known for the poems "The Song of the Shirt" and "The Bridge of Sighs." He also learned how to do engraving which gave him the ability to illustrate his own works. He even had a publication, *Comic Annual*, where he would create caricatures of current events and used lots of puns.

Hopkins, Gerard Manley – 1844–1889 – England
Hopkins was a poet and Jesuit priest. He used his poetry to show praise to God and created a concept called sprung rhyme by manipulating the meter (metre in Britain). He became famous posthumously and became one of the most popular Victorian poets.

Ish-Kishor, Judith – 1896–1977 – New York, USA
Ish-Kishor was born in England and is of Jewish heritage. She started writing poetry at age five and some of her poetry was published by age ten. At thirteen her family moved to New York City. She was published in multiple popular magazines. Her father was a popular author of children's literature for Jewish children.

Jackson, Helen Hunt – 1830–1885 – Massachusetts, USA
At seventeen, Jackson attended the Ipswich Female Seminary where Emily Dickinson was her classmate. Her writing career didn't start until later in life. Her first successful poem was "Coronation." Her early work was published under the name H.H. and her poetry was admired by Ralph Waldo Emerson. She was an activist for the Native Americans.

Jennings, Elizabeth – 1926–2001 – England
Jennings' early poetry was published in many publications, but her first book was published when she was twenty-seven. Her second book, *A Way of Looking,* won the Somerset Maugham award. She was more traditional in her writing, and her rhyme and meter were simple. Catholicism was an influence on her poetry.

Johnson, Fenton – 1888–1958 – Illinois, USA
Johnson grew up in Chicago and later taught English at a private, black, Baptist University in Kentucky for 1 year. He published his first volume of poetry, *A Little Dreaming*, in 1913. One of his most famous poems, "Tired," was published in 1919 in *Others* and in the *Book of Negro Poetry* in 1922. Besides poetry he edited and wrote essays and plays.

Jonson, Ben – 1572–1637 – England
Jonson was classically educated and well read. He popularized stage comedy and was also known for his lyric poetry during the English Renaissance. His plays were second only to William Shakespeare. He was a great influence on playwrights and poets of the Jacobean and Caroline eras. One of his famous poems is "To Celia."

Keats, John – 1795–1821 – England
A romantic-period poet who died at the young age of twenty-five. He did not become popular until the end of the 19th century. Through the use of imagery, he would display great emotion. Some of his most famous poems are "Ode to a Nightingale", "Sleep and Poetry", and his sonnet "On First Looking into Chapman's Homer."

Kingston, William Henry Giles – 1814–1880 – England
Kingston is known for his adventure stories written for boys. His first book was *The Circassian Chief* in 1844. He wrote over 100 stories.

Kipling, Rudyard – 1865–1936 – England
Kipling is easily one of England's most popular writers. Not only did he write the famous books *The Jungle Book* and *The Just So Stories,* he was also a poet, and journalist. His being born in British India had a great influence on his writing.

Kwok, Grace – b. 2006 – Nevada, USA
Kwok has won writing awards from the PBS Kids Writers Contest and American Chemical Society Illustrated Poem Contest. She hopes to publish her fiction stories. Her completed literary works are dedicated to *Ad majorem Dei gloriam.*

Lanier, Sidney – 1842–1881 – Georgia, USA
Lanier was a poet, musician, and writer. He was known for using different dialects in his poetry and it could be considered a heightened, archaic American English. He's known for writing his poetry in a musical meter. You can see this in his poems "Sunrise" and "The Marshes of Glynn." In the Southern United States, he is known as the "poet of the Confederacy."

Law, Steven Wesley – b. 1969 – Arizona, USA
In addition to writing poetry, Law is an award-winning essayist, travel writer, and journalist. He lives in northern Arizona with his wife and two children. He is the author of *Polished.*

Lawson, Henry – 1867–1922 – Australia
At age ten, an ear infection left him partially deaf. He was totally deaf by fourteen. His school teacher taught him all he could about poetry and later became one of Australia's best-known poets and short story writers. His first poem published was "A Song of the Republic" in 1887. His mother Louisa Lawson, also a poet, published his first collection of poems in 1904. He focused most of his poetry on the Australian bush and aimed for realism in his writing.

Lawrie, Max Edward – b. 2014 – Australia
Lawrie lives with his parents and two younger siblings. He plans to be a paleontologist. He is a prolific storyteller and has created many dinosaur-related narratives.

Lazarus, Emma – 1849–1887 – New York, USA
Lazarus is best known for her poem "The New Colossus" written in 1883. It was so popular, it was engraved on the Statue of Liberty. It also inspired the song "Give Me Your Tired" by Irving Berlin, and a 1985 song, "The Lady of the Harbor." She also wrote translations and prose. She was an activist for the Jewish people. She was educated at home and started writing poetry at age eleven and learned German, French, and Italian.

Leakey, Caroline W – 1827–1881 – England (popular in Australia)
Born in England, Leakey dealt with childhood illness that prevented her from formal schooling, but she loved to read, especially poetry. She traveled to Tasmania to visit her sister and became very ill and stayed there for five years. Her last year there, she began to write poetry again. In 1853 she returned to England and in 1854 a collection of poetry, "Lyra Australis (Attempts to Sing in a Strange Land)," was published. She also wrote the book *The Broad Arrow*. She used the pseudonym Oline Kleese.

Lear, Edward – 1812–1888 – England
From the age of six Lear suffered from grand mal seizures, asthma, and bronchitis. Later in life he even became partially blind. Known for his Limericks, prose and nonsensical poetry. Limericks became popular through his pen. He was a man of many talents including music (played multiple instruments), illustrating, writing, and art.

Li Shen – d. 846 – China
Alive during the Tang Dynasty, Li Shen held different positions under six different emperors. Under Wuzung he was a Chancellor. While working within the government he gained notoriety as a poet.

Liu, Kylie – b. 2008 – Texas, USA
Kylie is an avid reader and writer. When she's not typing on her computer or scribbling down
ideas for her next poem or story, she can be found swimming, dancing, singing, or drawing.

Longfellow, Henry Wadsworth – 1807–1882 – Massachusetts, USA
As a young child, Longfellow was bright and studious and learned Latin. In his lifetime he studied many languages. He is most popular for his poems "Paul Revere's Ride" and "The Song of Hiawatha," and was the first to translate *Dante's Divine Comedy*. In 1820 his first poem, "The Battle of Lovell's Pond,"
was published.

Lybrand, Forrest – b. 1991 – Texas, USA
Lybrand has been writing stories and poems since he can remember. He attended the University of Texas at Austin where he earned his BA in English. He has self-published *Trixie & Roy*, *The Sassafras Three*, and *Twigchap*. Each book is illustrated by the author.

Martinez, Lily – b. 2002 - Louisiana, USA
Lily serves as the violinist in two local choirs and an active member in 4-H. She enjoys both writing and theater and she plans on attending college.

Matsuo Basho – 1644–1694 – Japan
Matsuo Basho was born in Japan and introduced to poetry at a young age. He was the most famous poet during Japan's Edo period. He wrote in a special form of poetry named haiku (hokku). He was considered the master of haiku, but he felt that his true genius lay in another poetry form called renku.

Mei Yaochen – 1002–1060 – China
Mei Yaochen was a poet during the Song dynasty and one of the inventors of the "new subjective" poetry that came to be known as Song Poetry. He has written about 3000 poems, most of which are written in the Shi style even though its content is less restrictive. He focused on things like lack of ambition, being critical of society and Neo-Confucian philosophy.

Mellor, Kathy – b.1962 – California, USA
Mellor has degrees from BYU and SDSU but considers her real education to have begun when she picked up her first Shakespeare play. Her heart is firmly planted at the beach in Southern California. Life for her can be boiled down to avocados=good and eggplant=bad. She has mentored thousands in public speaking, writing, liberal arts, and entrepreneurship.

Melville, Herman – 1819–1891 – New York, USA
At the age of 20, Melville became a sailor after his father's death. From his experiences at sea, he wrote "Typee" and "Omoo" which were quite successful. During the American Renaissance he published his book *Moby Dick* in 1851, but it's popularity was short-lived. Not until 1919 (well after his death) did *Moby Dick* reach its height of fame. Later in life he spent twenty-five years writing poetry. His collections include *Battle-Pieces* and *Aspects of the War* and the epic poem *Clarel: A Poem and Pilgrimage in the Holy Land* in 1876.

Millay, Edna St. Vincent – 1892–1950 – Maine, USA
When Millay was twelve her divorced mother moved her impoverished family from place to place. Every time they moved her mother took a trunk full of classic literature. Her mother read Shakespeare, Milton, and other great literature to her and her sisters. They settled in Maine where she would write her first poems which were published when she was fifteen. She won the Pulitzer Prize for poetry in 1923 for "The Ballad of the Harp-Weaver."

Miller, William – 1810–1872 – Scotland
Miller was a woodturner and cabinet maker. He also wrote children's rhymes and poetry, mostly using Scots. His poetry was published in different publications including the 1842 publication of *Whistle-binkie* books which included his poem "Wee Willie Winkie." It was translated into many languages and made Miller famous for a short time.

Milne, A. A. – 1882–1956 – England
Well known for his beloved children's book *Winnie the Pooh* (1926). In 1903, Milne graduated from Cambridge with a mathematics degree. He served in both the First and Second World Wars. He wrote for *Punch* magazine and wrote eighteen plays and three books, one being *The Red House Mystery*. In 1924, two years after his son was born he wrote a collection of poetry titled *When We Were Very Young*. His second collection of poetry, *Now We Are Six* was published in 1927.

Milton, John – 1608–1674 – England
Milton was formally educated with a B.A. earned in 1629 and a M.A. in 1632 and an additional six years of self study. He learned seven languages, including Old English. He also traveled all over Europe. He is considered to be one of the most educated poets. He is best known for his epic poem "Paradise Lost" (1667) written in blank verse.

Moore, Clement Clarke – 1779-1863 – New York, USA
Moore was a professor of Biblical learning, Divinity, and of Oriental and Greek literature. His biggest claim to fame is his poem "A Visit from St. Nicolas" now referred to as "Twas the Night Before Christmas." He wrote the poem for his children and published it anonymously in 1823. He originally did not want to be known as the author because of his position as a religious and literature professor.

Moore, J. Sheridan – 1828–1891 – Australia
Born in Dublin Ireland, Moore was educated by the Jesuits, was a religious man, and became a teacher. He immigrated to Australia in 1847. He was also a lecturer, writer, and poet. He published a collection of poetry in 1864.

Moore, Marianne – 1887–1972 – New York, USA
Moore's first poem was published in 1915 and her first book of poetry titled *Poetry* was published in 1921, without her permission. In 1924 her second book *Observations* won the Dial award. Her poetry also won the Pulitzer Prize.

Nielson, Kathryn – b. 2011 – Arkansas, USA
She loves art, poetry, and science. She enjoys music, especially piano and guitar.

Owens, Christine – b. 1976 – California, USA
Born Christine Lynn Faulkner and raised in San Diego, California, Owens has enjoyed writing and drawing from a young age. She was married and traveled to twenty countries before having her four children. She draws inspiration from her life experiences and people she has met. She is the author of the books *Relaxed Homeschooling* and *A Year of Poetry Tea Time* and owner of Little Rabbit Trails.

Parkes, Henry – 1815-1896 – Australia
Parkes was born in England. In 1839 he and his wife immigrated to Australia. He had little education as a child and started working at a very young age as a ropewalk. As a young adult he educated himself purely by reading books. During this period of reading, he became very interested in poetry. While working a government job, he continued to write. His first collection of poetry published was titled *Stolen Moments* in 1842.

Perrine, Niccole – b. 1983 – Idaho, USA
Perrine was born in Upstate New York, raised in Southern California and Southcentral Alaska. She made her home in Southwestern Idaho and is the mother of five and author of *The Joy Series*.

Prior, Mathew – 1664–1721 – England
Prior used levity and lyricism in his poetry. He was a well-known poet of his time. He attended Cambridge to study logic and divinity. The first publication that gave him success was "The Hind and the Panther Transvers'd" a satire of a publication of Dryden's.

Poe, Edgar Allen – 1809–1849 – Virginia, USA
Poe was born in Boston, Massachusetts, and then after his father left and mother died he moved to Virginia with the Allen family. He released his first forty-page book of poetry at age eighteen titled, *Tamerlane and other Poems*. He was a poet, writer, editor, and a literary critic. He is most famous for his poem "The Raven" and he is said to be the originator of the detective story. His poetry is known for being dark and strange.

Posey, Alexander – 1873–1908 – Oklahoma, USA
Born in the Eufaula, Creek Nation, Indian Territory, and in 1901 he started the very first newspapers for Native Americans in 1901. Henry David Thoreau was one of his major influences. He wrote poetry for the newspaper. He also used the pen name Fus Fixico to write political commentary.

Potter, Beatrix – 1866–1943 – England
Best known for her story of *Peter Rabbit* (1902), Potter also wrote poetry which you can read in *Cecily Parsley's Nursery Rhymes* (1922). Growing up and being educated at home, she also had a lot of animals as pets that inspired her. She wrote a total of thirty books. She enjoyed learning about the world, especially botany. As a child, she also loved art and she made a little business with her brother to sell hand drawn cards.

Rands, William Brighty – 1823–1882 – England
Rands did attend school from ages eight to thirteen, but he was mostly self taught. He loved languages and, in his lifetime,, he mastered Latin and Greek and also learned Spanish, French and Chinese. He started to work as a reporter in 1857 and would write children's literature when he was not busy.

Riley, James Whitecomb – 1849–1916 – Indiana, USA
Riley started out by submitting poems to newspapers. He eventually became more popular with a little help from Henry Wadsworth Longfellow. He did poetry reading tours. He was known as a best-selling author by the 1890s. His most famous publication was a collection of children's poetry titled *Rhymes of Childhood* and it was illustrated by Howard Chandler Christy.

Rilke, Rainer Maria – 1875–1875 – Austria-Hungary (modern Czech Republic)
Rilke traveled throughout Europe and this traveling inspired many of his poems. He wrote a novel and many collections of poems. He is best known for his poetry written in German, but he had written over 400 poems in French as well. His most famous collection translated into English is *Duino Elegies*.

Rossetti, Christina – 1830–1894 – England
Rossetti was of Italian descent and came from a family of writers and grew up to be a writer and poet herself. She was educated by her parents at home and was well versed in fairy tales, classics, and religious works. Her most famous collection of poems is titled *Goblin Market and Other Poems*. There are also two Christmas songs that are well known in England for which she wrote the text –"Love Came Down at Christmas" and "In the Bleak Midwinter."

Sandburg, Carl – 1878–1967 – Illinois, USA
Sandburg left school at the age of thirteen and did many different jobs. Later he became a journalist in Chicago. His time in Chicago would influence much of his writing. He won three Pulitzer Prizes, two for poetry collections and one for his biography of Abraham Lincoln. He is also famous for his *Rootabaga Stories* written for children.

Service, Robert W. – 1874–1958 – England
Service is known as the "Bard of the Yukon." This poet of Scottish descent was a banker but later traveled to the United States and Canada. His first poems were inspired by the Klondike Gold Rush and became popular. He continued to write poetry and published a collection titled *Songs of Sourdough*.

Shakespeare, William – c. 1564–1616 – England
Shakespeare was a poet, playwright, and actor who wrote thirty-nine plays, 154 sonnets, and other works. He is known as "The Bard," and his plays are known all over the world. He is the creator of the Globe Theater and the master at both tragedy and comedy. He also created historical plays. He created about 1700 new words to the English language like *zany* and *jaded*.

Shelley, Percy Bysshe – 1792–1822 – England
Shelley is an English, Romantic poet who was known for his radical views both in his poetry and life. In the English language he is believed to be one of the best philosophical and lyrical poets. Some of the best-known poems are "Ozymandias", "The Skylark," and "The Cloud." He received his early education at home.

Shults, George Francis – b. Unknown – Unknown
Shults is only known for writing the poem "Under the Mistletoe."

Shepherd, Cayden – b. 2010 – Indiana, USA
He is a creative soul with a brilliant mind. He lives with his parents and two younger siblings. He loves drawing, designing, music, the piano and the outdoors.

Smith, Clark Ashton – 1893–1961 – California, USA
Smith attended grammar school, but rather than attend high school, he studied at home. He loved reading generally and he even read from the dictionary. He was noted for his powerful imagery and his odd subject matter. Until he married, he stayed mainly in Auburn, California, though he did not care for the small-town life.

Soldano, Joseph B. – b. 1928– New York, USA
Born in Utica, New York, Soldano comes from a strong Italian heritage. He was a printer and plays the piano and electric organ. He was in a few bands and played music for dancing and listening. Not only does he love music, but he enjoyed writing poetry and bodybuilding.

Sparkman, Nicholas C.A. – b. 1995 – Arizona, USA
Sparkman has a published book of poetry titled *Fractures in a Glass Mind: A Collection of Poetry and Songs* and also has a poem in an anthology titled *Upon Arrival*. He is married and is a proud father in Bremerton, Washington.

Squire, Sir John Collings – 1884–1958 – England
Squire was a writer, editor and poet. He did editing for a newspaper and his poetry was published over a span of fifty years. He wrote in the Georgian style and from 1919–1934 he was an editor for the *London Mercury* which featured this style of poetry. He was knighted in 1933.

Stevenson, Robert Louis – 1850–1894 – Scotland
Even though Stevenson had bronchial troubles his entire life, he enjoyed traveling. He wrote continually. Not only is he known for his novels, *Treasure Island*, *Kidnapped*, *Strange Case of Dr. Jekyll and Mr. Hyde*, he is also very well known for his collection of children's poems titled *A Child's Garden of Verses*.

Swift, Jonathan – 1667–1745 – Ireland
At age six Swift's uncle sent him to school. In 1682, he went to Dublin University (Trinity College). He enjoyed writing satire in different forms such as poetry and essays. He was great at using both Hostian and Juvenalian satires in his poetry, essays, and stories.

Taylor, Jane – 1782–1824 – England
Taylor grew up in a family of writers and in 1804 a collection of poems titled *Original Poems for Infant Minds* was published of which she and other family members had contributed. In 1805, another volume was published because of the success of the first one. These were published as anonymous works. Jane and her sister Ann created *Rhymes for the Nursery* in 1806 and *Hymns for Infant Minds* in 1810. Her most famous poem is still known today: "Twinkle, Twinkle, Little Star."

Teasdale, Sara – 1884–1933 – Missouri, USA
Teasdale was plagued with poor health during her young childhood so she was educated at home until age nine. When she was about twenty, she was part of a group of older teens and young women who called themselves the Potters. They published their own magazine full of art and literature. Her first poem was published in 1907 and her most popular collection of poetry, *Rivers to the Sea* in 1915. She won a Pulitzer Prize for her 1917 collection *Love Songs*. Her Lyrical poetry was loved by many.

Tennyson, Alfred Lord – 1850–1892 – England
During the reign of Queen Victoria he was the Poet Laureate of England and earned the Chancellor's Gold Medal for the poem "Timbuktu." Classic mythological themes show up in much of his poetry. He wrote in the lyrical and blank verse styles and tried his hand at being a playwright, but that was not as successful. Many of his writings have held strong within the English language like "Tis better to have loved and lost, than never to have loved at all."

Thayer, Ernest L. – 1863–1940 – Massachusetts, USA
Thayer graduated from Harvard in 1885 where he was an editor for the school's *Havard Lampoon*. He is best known for writing the poem "Casey," the most famous poem about baseball. DeWolf Hopper is famous for reciting it.

Thomas, Adison – b. 2006 – Utah, USA
Thomas enjoys the outdoors and loves the ocean, books, and animals.

Thoreau, Henry David – 1817–1862 – Massachusetts, USA
Thoreau was an important figure in the Transcendentalist movement. He is well known for his authorship of both *Walden* (1954) and *The Maine Woods* (1864). In 1895 he published *Poems of Nature*. He is considered to be one of America's top writers for both his philosophical ideas and for his prose.

Walker, Bertrand N.O. – 1870–1927 – Kansas, USA
Walker was a Native American poet who is a descendant of the Wyandotte Nation that originated in Oklahoma. He published under his Wyandotte name Hen-toh. His collection of poetry is titled *Yon-Doo-Shah-We-Ah* (1924) and a collection of animal stories titled *Tales of the Bark Lodges* (1927).

Wang Zhihuan –688–742 – China
A poet during the Tang dynasty, Wang Zhihuan was famous for his poem "Beyond the Border." Other well-known poets of the time went to a poetry reciting performance and wagered whose poem would be heard. All the poets ended up hearing variations of their work, including Wang Zhihuan's work "Beyond the Border."

Watson, Sarah Beth – b. 1977 – California, USA
Watson has enjoyed writing poetry since she was a young child. At age sixteen she learned guitar which led to her writing music lyrics. As a mother, she lives on a homestead and homeschools her five children. She is a songwriter, blogger and homeschool community leader. Through her Christian faith and leadership skills, she encourages others using music.

Wheatley, Phillis – 1753–1784 – West Africa (most likely Gambia or Senegal)
Born in West Africa and sold into slavery at age seven or eight, Wheatley was purchased
by the Wheatley family who named her after the slave ship that brought her to America,
The Phillis. The Wheatley family members taught her how to read and write and by age
twelve she could read classics in both Greek and Latin. Her level of education was
considered untraditional for a female, let alone a slave. She wrote her first poem at age
fourteen. After her book of poetry was published in 1773 the Wheatleys emancipated
Phillis. She was the first African-American woman recorded to publish a book of poetry.

Whitman, Walt – 1819–1892 – New York, USA
Whitman had to leave his formal education at age eleven to work, but later on in life he
became a journalist, essayist, and poet. He combined the ideas of both Transcendentalism
and realism in his literature. He is well known for his poem "O Captain! My Captain!"
(written after the death of Abraham Lincoln) and his poetry collection *Leaves of Grass*,
published in 1855.

Whittier, John Greenleaf – 1807–1892 – Massachusetts, USA
Whittier was a quaker and strongly opposed slavery. He had almost no formal education,
but he loved to read and reread the six books his family had on Quakerism over and over.
His first published poem was "Exile's Departure" in 1826, because his sister sent it into a
newspaper. To complete his high school education, he worked as a shoemaker and teacher
to pay for tuition. He is known for his poems "The Barefoot Boy," "Snow-Bound," and
"Maud Miller."

Wilde, Oscar – 1854–1900 – Ireland
Wilde was educated at home as a young child and also learned French and German from a
nursemaid and governess. He joined his brother at school where he excelled academically.
In 1881 a collection of sixty-one of his poems were published in a book: *Poems*. He wrote
poetry and is known for his *The Picture of Dorian Grey*, *The Happy Prince and Other
Tales*, and his play *The Importance of Being Earnest*.

Wordsworth, William – 1770–1850 – England
Wordsworth's mother taught him how to read. His first published work was a sonnet in
1787 in the *European Magazine*. He attended Cambridge to continue his education and
enjoyed doing "walking tours" of many European countries. In 1793 his first collection of
poems, *An Evening Walk and Descriptive Sketches*, was published. In 1798 he collaborated
with Coleridge and created *Lyrical Ballads* which included Wordsworth's famous poem
"Tintern Abbey."

Yeats, W.B. –1865–1939 – Ireland
Yeats studied poetry from a young age. He received the Nobel Prize in Literature in 1923.
He also wrote plays like *The Player Queen* and *On Baile's Strand*. Another notable poem is
"The Wild Swans at Coole." He was also an active participant in Irish politics.

Glossary

Poetry is a superb way to expand one's vocabulary. Here, I have included a glossary of words that you or your children may not know the meaning of. Some words are included because they may have had a different meaning when the poem was written. The definitions included here pertain to the poems included in this book. If you believe that a word has another meaning that could very well be, but I included the definitions that were pertinent to the poetry. If the word was used in more than one poem and their meanings are different, both definitions are included. Following the vocabulary word and definition you will see in which poem(s) the word is used and month.

abysmal—extremely deep, appalling
      The Kraken (OCT) 187

aegean—a geographical area comprised of the Aegean Sea and surrounding islands and shores
      Dover Beach (JULY) 131

aerial—having to do with, being in, or created in the air
      Hope (AUG) 145

Aidenn—the Arabic word for 'paradise'
      The Raven (OCT) 200

ale—an alcoholic drink similar to beer
      Cecily Parsley (APR) 83

anarchies—when there is no law or government in power
      Sonnet To Liberty (JULY) 129

anon—shortly or soon
      Carol (DEC) 235

ape—to mimic or imitate something
      The Yellow Violet (APR) 74

arabesque—referring to Arabia
      My Cathedral (JUNE) 107

argosy—large merchant ship
      My Voice (AUG) 150

astride—to be stretched out from side to side
The New Colossus (JULY) 125

aswoon—to swoon, to sink into a faint
In the Heart of June (JUNE) 109

Athabasca—a river in Alberta, Canada
The Two Streams (OCT) 186

aureate—having the appearance of gold, made of or having gold
Autumn's Pall (NOV) 218

austere—rigid, strict in attitude and appearance
The Little Ghost (OCT) 197

auspicious—to be favorable, having promise, prosperous, signs of success
Our Australian Land (MAR) 63

azure—the color of a blue sky, resembling the color of the sky
A Baby (JULY) 140
The Eagle (JULY) 139
Hope (AUG) 145
In the Wood (JULY) 134

bade—to ask or order someone, the past tense of bid
Casey at the Bat (JULY) 143
The Yellow Violet (APR) 74

bard—ancient Celtic singer and storyteller of epic tales, poet
A Blown Rose (MAY) 100

battening—becoming fatter
The Kraken (OCT) 187
Forgotten (JULY) 127

beacon—a light that is positioned up high that can be seen from afar like from a lighthouse
"The New Colossus" (JULY) 125

beechen—something belonging to the beech tree
The Yellow Violet (APR) 74

bedight—adorned or decorated in dress
El Dorado (MAY) 104

befalls—occurs, happens
If You were Coming in the Fall (SEP) 166
bellow—a tool for stoking a fire
The Village Blacksmith (MAY) 101

348

beneficent—doing a good deed
Miss Molly and the Little Fishes (AUG) 157

benight—to shroud in darkness
Ae Fond Kiss (FEB) 41

benign—kind and gentle disposition
To Sleep (OCT) 192

benison—blessing
Carol (DEC) 235

bespeak—to speak of before; foretell
Upon the Swallow (MAY) 98

bivouac—to camp without any tents or coverings, most often referring to soldiers or those surviving in the mountains
Bivouac On a Mountain Side (JULY) 128

blanched—whitened
Dover Beach (JULY) 131

blighted—disease happening to a plant, to stop growth, to frustrate, to be blasted
Autumn Thoughts (OCT) 184
We Have a Little Garden (MAY) 91

blithesome—gay and cheerful like the song of a bird
Sanctuary (JULY) 135

bobolink—a small black and white bird with half of its head being yellow, also referred to as the "rice bird" and is found in North and Central America
A Day (MAR) 60

boon—can mean a gift or present, a prayer, or can also mean kind
Our Australian Land (MAR) 63

boughs—branches of a tree (but not shoots of a tree)
Apple Blossoms (MAY) 94
Spellbound (DEC) 222

bowers—shaded covering under a tree caused by branches
Autumn Thoughts (OCT) 184
The First of May (MAY) 91
A Southern Girl (JULY) 141
June (JUNE) 108
brawny—bulky, strong, and muscled
The Village Blacksmith (MAY) 101

bulwark—an earthen wall, rampart, or fortification that is able to withstand cannon fire or stand up to enemy attack
    Our Australian Land (MAR) 63

buoyant—floating or able to float
    Life (NOV) 206

cadence—music term meaning the rhythm or a fluctuation in a voice
    Dover Beach (JULY) 131

cannonades—continuous gun fire
    Sonnet to Liberty (JULY) 129

canting—speaking with a whiny voice
    The Good, Great Man (JUNE) 124

certitude—certain or sure
    Dover Beach (JULY) 131

cerulean—a deep blue colored sky
    Alma Mater (APR) 82

chaff—the husk left over after corn is threshed
    The Village Blacksmith (MAY) 101

chanticleer—rooster
    Daybreak (SEPT) 170

cheese-mites—mites (arachnids) that are used in the production of certain cheeses such as Mimolette
    A Parable (MAY) 106

cinderous—another word used to refer to a hot coal or cinder
    A Martyr Tree (MAR) 58

clowd—another spelling of cloud
    Autumn Birds (NOV) 211

cock—rooster
    Willie Winkie (APR) 85

conversion—a change of disposition
    A Skeeter Conversion (JUNE) 110

corses—corpses, dead bodies
    The Good, Great Man (JUNE) 124

cot—a small house or hut
    Late Autumn (OCT) 181

countenance—the expression on a person's face
    Snowflakes (DEC) 225

coxcomb—a person who is cocky and vein; a person who exaggerates his/her accomplishments
    Epitaph (JAN) 28

crag—a rough jagged rock
    The Eagle (JULY) 139

craven—scared, not having courage
    Still Will I Harvest Beauty Where It Grows (AUG) 159

croon—to sing, say or hum something in a low soft voice
    In April (APR) 71

darkling—dark or void of light
    Dover Beach (JULY) 131

dauntless—to have no fear, nothing holds you back, unstoppable
    Bond and Free (FEB) 39

decorum—how one speaks or behaves
    The Raven (OCT) 200

deftly—to work in neat and skillful way with great dexterity
    A Song of a Navajo Weaver (NOV) 214
    To Sleep (OCT) 192

delude—to trick, deceive or beguile someone
    The Captive Dove (JAN) 24

democracies—government run by the people
    Sonnet to Liberty (JULY) 129

derides—express contempt or ridiculing something or someone
    Haste Thee, Nymph (JUNE) 116

devious—wandering off the common or more direct path
    A Song of the Navajo Weaver (NOV) 214

din—loud noise
    Nature (MAY) 95

disposition—one's temperament
    A Skeeter Conversion (JUNE) 110

diverged—two lines that are not parallel, to proceed in two different directions
    The Road Not Taken (OCT) 182

doffed—to be removed
    The Feast of Lights (DEC) 221

dominie—in Scotland it means schoolmaster and, in the USA,, it means clergyman
    A Day (MAR) 60

drear—dreary and dismal
    Dover Beach (JULY) 131

ductile—in Latin it means to lead, can also mean flexible
    A Noiseless Patient Spider (OCT) 188

dumb—unable to speak
    The Dumb Soldier (APR) 88

dun—gloomy, dark colored
    Casey at the Bat (JULY) 143

ebb—to return like a wave returning back to the ocean
    Dover Beach (JULY) 131

efface—to remove a mark from the surface of something, to be worn out
    Our Australian Land (MAR) 63

effulgent—to emit a bright and shining flood of light like the sun
    Fashion (JAN) 27

embalmer—a person that preserved dead bodies
    To Sleep (OCT) 192

embower'd—sheltered or covered
    To Sleep (OCT) 192

enamelled—to be coated or covered
    In the Wood (JULY) 134

enshaded—to be kept in shade
    To Sleep (OCT) 192

ermine—a ferret like animal popular for its snow-white winter coat
    Autumn's Pall (NOV) 218

exultant—to feel or proclaim triumph
    The Australian Flag (JAN) 26

fain—to do something gladly or pleased, because you must
    June (JUNE) 108

fathom—a measurement of depth, deep thought
    Nessie (MAR) 61
    The Queen of Hearts (AUG) 155

feces—excrement, poop
    Elegant Grey (SEPT) 176

festoon—a garland or decoration that is hung with a sagging center, sometimes with its ends hanging down loose; it can also be a carved decoration representing a wreath that could include fruits, flowers, and leaves
    The Wound (MAR) 61

fetter—anything that restrains or prevents something from moving; like chains around a person's hands or feet or ropes tied around an animal's limbs
    I Broke the Spell that Held Me Long (JAN) 21

fickle—to be wishy washy, unable to make up one's mind
    Epitaph (JAN) 28

filament—a fine fiber
    A Noiseless Patient Spider (OCT) 188

foe—enemy
    Old Ironside (JULY) 130

foreworld—ancient time or world
    Forgotten (JULY) 127

forlorn—sad and lonely, deprived
    Nature (MAY) 95

fraught—loaded with or heavy laden
    A Blown Rose (MAY) 100

fretted—its surface being made rough
    My Cathedral (JUNE) 107

furze—another term for the gorse plant, a plant within the pea family with yellow flowers
    The Custard (NOV) 208

futile—when something is useless, pointless, unable to produce anything
    Faith (FEB) 48

gall—bitterness, anger
    As Created (AUG) 157

gambolling—to playfully run and jump about
    In Possum Land (JUNE) 110

garniture—a set or collection embellishment or decorations on something
    The Martyr Tree (MAR) 58

gaunt—thin and starved looking, appearing to have sunken in cheeks and starving
    A Song of the Navajo Weaver (NOV) 214

genial—merry, cheerfulness
    A Leaf (OCT) 183

genocidal—deliberately killing a large group
    A Skeeter Conversion (JUNE) 110

gentian—a specific genus of plant commonly found in the mountains of Germany
    September (SEPT) 175

gladioli—the flower gladiolus
    A Sunset Fantasy (JUNE) 117

glean—to collect what little is left
    Ruth (OCT) 189

glebe—land, soil, or earth
    A Good Husband (MAR) 55

gloam—sullen
    Lonely Airs (JULY) 137

goad—a pointed tool to encourage an animal to move
    If You were Coming in the Fall (SEPT) 166

gossamer—a substance that is fine like cobwebs
    A Noiseless Patient Spider (OCT) 188

grenadier—a foot soldier
    The Dumb Soldier (APR) 88

grot—can be short for grotesque, to be very ugly, disfigured
  The Kraken (OCT) 187

gyres (gyre)—gyrate, to move quickly in a circular motion like a spiral
  Jabberwocky (OCT) 194
  A Midsummers Day (JULY) 135

harpies—a winged figure that has the body of a vulture and the head of a woman with clawed feet and fingers
  Old Ironside (JULY) 130

haunches—on an animal or human it is referring to the area of the body including both the buttock and thigh as one
  Fog (SEPT) 179

Hebe—daughter of Zeus and goddess of youth
  Haste Thee, Nymph (JUNE) 116

heretics—a person who teaches beliefs contrary to any particular religion
  A Parable (MAY) 106

hewed—made smooth by cutting
  A Musical Instrument (APR) 80

hoar(y)—hair that is white and grey
  A Blown Rose (MAY) 100
  Winter is Good – his Hoar Delights (DEC) 223

hoodoo—bad luck
  Casey at the Bat (JULY) 143

idle—being inactive, doing nothing
  A Skeeter Conversion (JUNE) 110

ignorant—not knowing, uninformed
  Dover Beach (JULY) 131
  If You were Coming in the Fall (SEPT) 166

inebriate—to be intoxicated or drunk
  Winter is Good – his Hoar Delights (DEC) 223

inwrought—a fabric decoration that is embroidered with great detail
  Forgotten (JULY) 127

imperturbable—unable to be disrupted or excited, calm
  At a Lunar Eclipse (MAY) 99

impish—mischievous, doing naughty things for fun
    Alma Mater (APR) 82

implore—to ask or petition earnestly, beg
    The Raven (OCT) 200

impudent—acting boldly with little thought of others
    Alma Mater (APR) 82

ire—wrath or anger
    A Leaf (OCT)183

jest—to joke
    Haste Thee, Nymph (JUNE) 116

jollity—cheerful celebration
    Haste Thee, Nymph (JUNE) 116

knells—ringing in a solemn and sad way
    A Dirge (AUG) 149

knout—a punishment inflicted by a whip
    Sonnet To Liberty (JULY) 129

kirk—Scottish word for church
    Block City (JAN) 32

lading—large load or cargo of a ship
    My Voice (AUG) 150

lament—to cry out, to grieve or mourn about something
    Life (NOV) 206

lave—to wash (term most often used in poetry)
    A Sunbeam Stooped and Kissed a Wave (JULY) 133

leaden—heavy and unable to move, made of lead
    The Land of Counterpane (Feb) 47

levee—an embankment made to stop the overflow of river water
    The Banjo Player (SEPT) 177

lilt–to do something quickly with fine dexterity
    Sanctuary (JULY) 135

linnet—a small bird from the finch family; found all over Europe and many bordering
countries and continents; it is brown and grey with a red forehead and chest
    The Lake Isle of Innisfree (MAR) 62

lull—to be still or calm
    Lines on a Sleeping Infant (MAY) 96

martyr—a person who dies for his beliefs
    My Cathedral (JUNE) 107

mead—in Latin it means "to be wet;" it is also an alcoholic drink made from honey and water; in England there is also a geographical area north of Oxford, England called Sunnymead
    The Captive Dove (JAN) 24
    Nature (MAY) 95

melancholy—a mood that is gloomy and depressed
    Casey at the Bat (JULY) 143
    Dover Beach (JULY) 131
    The Raven (OCT) 200

mesa(s)—an isolated mountain or land mass with a flat top
    A Song of the Navajo Weaver (NOV) 214

midge—a tiny two-winged fly
    Symphony in Yellow (NOV) 211

mien—one's look or manner
    The Raven (OCT) 200

millennial—referring to a thousand years
    The Kraken (OCT) 187

mirth—social excitement, gayety, showing amusement with laughter and noise
    The Bubble (JULY) 142
    Haste Thee, Nymph (JUNE) 116

monochrome—emitting light in a single color or a photo printed in a single color
    At a Lunar Eclipse (MAY) 99
    Casey at the Bat (JULY) 143

moored—when a boat is anchored or roped in place; an English moor is an open area of land that is covered in plants like heather
    Block City (JAN) 32
    Symphony in Yellow (NOV) 211

mould—another spelling of mold, but the term "water mould" refers to a specific organism (Oomycetes) that looks like a fungi
    The Yellow Violet (APR) 74

mouldering—when something is decaying, crumbling, or turning to dust
    The Rainy Day (APR) 78

musing, muse—to think, contemplate, ponder or meditate in silence
    Hope (AUG) 145
    A Leaf (OCT) 183
    The Noiseless Patient Spider (OCT) 187

myriads—an extremely high number
    A Song of the Navajo Weaver (NOV) 214

nepenthe—a medication or drug that eliminates pain
    The Raven (OCT) 200

nigh—something is near, happening soon
    The Bubble (JULY) 142
    The Yellow Violet (APR) 74

nosegay—a small bundle of flowers
    Flower Solute (APR) 75

nymph—a magical spirit that dwells in nature like water and trees
    Haste Thee, Nymph (JUNE) 116

obeisance—to bow or curtsey
    The Raven (OCT) 200

obstinate—stubborn
    The Whippoorwill and I (JULY) 136

odorous—when something has a sweet fragrant scent
    In April (APR) 71

omnibus—another name for a bus
    Symphony in Yellow (NOV) 211

ominous—implying a future act or event
    The Raven (OCT) 200

opaline—like a pearl
    A Sunset Fantasy (JUNE) 117

orthodox—those who follow a religious doctrine strictly
    A Parable (MAY) 106

pall—a cloak, a cloth that is placed over a dead body or casket
    Autumn's Pall (NOV) 218

Pallas—a Greek Titan god
The Raven (OCT) 200

pallid—to be pale, lacking color
A Blown Rose (MAY) 100
The Snow-Blossom (JAN) 33

pangs—extreme bodily pains, spasms
Deadly Dreams (OCT) 193

parson—a priest who is in charge of a perish (a territory)
The Village Blacksmith (MAY) 101

pennon—a small banner or flag
A Sunset Fantasy (JUNE) 117

pensive—to be in deep thought
Spring Night (MAY) 98

pith—the soft inside of a plant or tree that is spongy
A Musical Instrument (APR) 80

plaintive—one who complains, expresses sorrow or sadness
The Captive Dove (JAN) 24

placid—tranquil, calm, little movement
At a Lunar Eclipse (MAY) 99

Plutonian—referring to or comparing to the underworld
The Raven (OCT) 200

poignant—pointed, sharp, can be referring to taste, smell, or feelings such as regret or sadness
The Snow-Blossom (JAN) 33

polypi (polyp)—a sea creature with a mouth at the center that is surrounded by tentacles, like a sea anemone
The Kraken (OCT) 187

pomp—a parade or procession of grand splendor; like the entrance of a king into a room or a graduation ceremony
Fashion (JAN) 27

prepence—thought of beforehand
The Queen of Hearts (AUG) 155

prithee—a contraction of pray thee
The Whippoorwill And I (JULY) 136

privy—private
Nature (MAY) 95

promontory—high elevated land that is jutting out into a large body of water like the Rock of Gibraltar
A Noiseless Patient Spider (OCT) 188

prow—the front pointed part of a ship, the bow
Greece (JUNE) 115

quaff—to swallow large amounts of liquid at a time, to gulp down
The Raven (OCT) 200

quarry—a place, potentially a large deep pit, where stone is dug up
Winter is Good – His Hoar Delights 223

quay— a wharf or structure onto which one secures a boat or ship
The Moon (JULY) 139
The Weekly Mail (APR) 87

queer—odd, whimsical
The Ballad of the Harp-Weaver (DEC) 226

quell—to make quiet, to crush, to create peace
Life (NOV) 206

quince—an yellow oblong fruit that grows abundantly in Cydonia, Crete
The Owl and the Pussy Cat (MAY) 105

quip—to taunt or scoff
Haste Thee, Nymph (JUNE) 116

quire—another spelling of choir
Nature (MAY) 95

rapt—transported, carried away, ravished
A Southern Girl (JULY) 141

recoiled—came back
Casey at the Bat (JULY) 143

refluent—to flow backwards
Carving a Name (DEC) 239

rent—to rip or tear
Carving a Name (DEC) 239

repining—not being content with oneself, complaining or fretting
The Rainy Day (APR) 78

repose—to lay down and rest
Lines on a Sleeping Infant (MAY) 96

resplendent—when something is highly appealing because it is very shiny, bright and/or rich in color
Fashion (JAN) 27

rift—when something is torn or split apart, a split in something
Apple Blossom (MAY) 94

rill—a small brook
The Two Streams (OCT) 186

robust—strong, sinewy
I Dream'd in a Dream (NOV) 204

roseate—a rose like color
A Sunbeam Stooped and Kissed a Wave (JULY) 133

runcible—a spoon with a fork on its end, a spork
The Owl and the Pussy Cat (MAY) 105

sanguinary (sanguin)—accompanied with much blood shed, cruel, murderous
Deadly Dreams (OCT) 193

sapphire—a precious stone that comes in multiple colors, but most often thought of as blue
Greece (JUNE) 115

sate—to be satisfied, to be full or stuffed
Lines Written in Early Spring (APR) 79
A Musical Instrument (APR) 80

scudding—moving quickly in a straight line
Lines Composed in a Wood on a Windy Day (SEPT) 169

scythe—a tool for cutting grass or grain
The Dumb Soldier (APR) 88

sedges—a tall grass plant
September (SEPT) 175

sepulchre—a stone monument where a dead body is put to rest
My Cathedral (JUNE) 107

sexton—a lower officer of the church that takes care of remedial tasks
The Village Blacksmith (MAY) 101

sheaf, sheaves—a bundle of straw, to be collected and bound
> Autumn Within (NOV) 212
> Late Autumn (OCT) 181
> Ruth (OCT) 189

shroud—shelter, covering
> An Evening (AUG) 146
> Evening Star (AUG) 147

scimitar—a curved short sword used in Prussia and Turkey
> Dusk in Autumn (OCT) 185

sinew—tendon, fibrous tissue that binds things together like muscles to a bone
> The Tyger (AUG) 148

sinewy—strong and firm
> The Village Blacksmith (MAY) 101

sledge—a heavy headed hammer with a long handle
> The Village Blacksmith (MAY) 101

solitary—to live alone or to be removed from all company
> The Captive Dove (JAN) 24

Sophocles—an ancient Greek playwright who wrote over 120 plays and one of three greats
who wrote tragedies; only seven complete plays survive; he died circa 406 BCE
> Dover Beach (JULY) 131

sovereign—someone who is a ruler or most powerful
> Nature (MAY) 95

spangle—to glisten or shine, to be decorated in with small, shiny details
> The First of May (MAY) 91
> A Leaf (OCT) 183

spray—a small shoot extending from a branch; small particles of water that leaves a wave
and floats around in the air
> A Sunbeam Stooped and Kissed a Wave (JULY) 133
> The Caterpillar (APR) 73
> Dover Beach (JULY) 131
> Late Autumn (OCT) 181
> Lines Composed in a Wood on a Windy Day (SEPT) 169
> Seaside ABC's (JUNE) 114

spurn—to push, brush, or kick away
> If You were Coming in the Fall (SEP) 166

squalling—crying or screeching out loud
> The Moon (JULY) 139

stately—majestic and dignified
> My Cathedral (JUNE) 107

stile—alternate spelling of the word style or can be referring to a set of stairs or steps
> A Day (MAR) 60

surcease—to stop
> The Raven (OCT) 200

swath—an area or row grass or grain cut by a scythe or lawn mower
> Field Path (APR) 75

sway—to influence and rule over through power
> June (JUNE) 108

swoon—to collapse into a fainting induced by extreme emotion
> The Mirror (SEPT) 176

tempest—a wild and dangerous storm
> A Leaf (OCT) 183
> The New Colossus (JULY) 125

Thames—a river that runs through London to the North Sea
> Symphony in Yellow (NOV) 211

thrall—a slave
> Bond and Free (FEB) 39

thresh—to beat grain from its shaft or corn from the cob
> The Village Blacksmith (MAY) 101

thrum—to strum an instrument, the end of a thread
> Willie Winkie (APR) 85

timorous—void of courage, scared of danger, nervousness
> In April (APR) 71

transient—not being in one place, not in a permanent place
> Life (NOV) 206

tread—to walk on or set foot on the ground
> Old Ironside (JULY) 130

tremulous—trembling with fear
> A Sunset Fantasy (JUNE) 117
> Dover Beach (JULY) 131

tresses—sections of hair that are in curls or ringlets
> Ruth (OCT) 189

trodden—to be walked upon
> The Answer (FEB) 51
> The Road Not Taken (SEPT) 182

troubadour—a French musical poem from the 11th to 13th centuries, love being a common musical theme
> The Banjo Player (SEPT) 177

trow—to think or ponder on something; if a person is to suppose, believe or trust something
> Marsh Hymn – Thou and I (JAN) 22

tumult—a ruckus, causing commotion and noise
> Casey at the Bat (JULY) 143
> Father (JUNE) 121

turbid—to stur, liquid that is opaque due to having some sort of particle in it
> Dover Beach (JULY) 131

turbidly—haughtily or proudly
> A Musical Instrument (APR) 80

twain—to be split in two
> A Sunset Fantasy (JUNE) 117

unapt—not ready or unprepared
> The Yellow Violet (APR) 74

unfurled—expanded or opened
> Opportunity (MAY) 103

unreproved—uncensored, not to be blamed or criticized
> Haste Thee, Nymph (JUNE) 116

upborne—to be supported or help up
> A Sunbeam Stooped and Kissed a Wave (JULY) 133

Van Diemen's land—the island of Tasmania, originally called this by most Europeans; its name was changed in 1856
> If You were Coming in the Fall (SEPT) 166

vanquished—to be defeated
> Old Ironside (JULY) 130

vermeila—a French term: a certain quality of jewelry that must meet very specific criteria
> Autumn's Pall (NOV) 218

vermilion—a bright shade of red
> My Voice (AUG) 150

vestibule—a space or room one enters before entering the main building
    June (JUNE) 108

vigor—with strength and enthusiasm
    Deadly Dreams (OCT) 193

visage—the way a person's face looks or their countenance
    Casey at the Bat (JULY) 143

votive—an item that is given to represent a vow fulfilled; this could be a medal, glass, or other object
    The Lady Who Offers Her Looking Glass to Venus (FEB) 51

waft—to be carried through water or air
    June (JUNE) 108
    Pilgrims (NOV) 215
    A Song of the Navajo Weaver (NOV) 214

wan—a sickly pale hue
    A Blown Rose (MAY) 100
    My Voice (AUG) 150

wanton—move or wander freely in a playful manner
    Haste Thee, Nymph (JUNE) 116

warbling—singing
    A Skeeter Conversion (JUNE) 110

wattle—in Latin it means shoot; it is a flexible stick or twig, a collection of sticks that are woven among each other; a stick used for supporting a thatched roof; to use twigs to bind something
    The Lake Isle of Innisfree (MAR) 62

weal—in Latin it means "to be strong;" republic or state; happiness or prosperity
    Frederick Douglas (FEB) 42
    Forgotten (JULY) 127

weft—an old way to say wave or to be cast away
    A Minuet of Mozart (JAN) 22

wend—to go or return when going someplace (used primarily in poetry)
    The Days When We Went Swimming (AUG) 152

whir—a continuous sound
    A Late Walk (SEPT) 174

wiles—manipulating and deceiving a person to convince them to do something
    Haste Thee, Nymph (JUNE) 116

winnow—to fan or beat about

writhing—to twist, contort, or squirm

wrought—worked; to work metal

yore—a long time past

zephyr—a breeze or light wind

Index
Search Poems by Subject

Miss Molly and the Little Fish (AUG) 157
My Sweet Little Sister (APR) 84
Ruth (OCT) 189
A Southern Girl (JULY) 141

God
Apple Blossom (MAY) 94
He Is Coming (APR) 78
I Love All Beauteous Things (SEPT) 173
A Little Bird I Am (JAN) 23
My Kingdom (MAR) 69
Now the Day is Over (DEC) 236
Oh, Smiling Moon (JUNE) 109
On Being Brought from Africa to America (FEB) 39
A Plea to the King (NOV) 203
Ruth (OCT) 189
A Scrawl (JAN) 20
The Stars (JULY) 137
A World Beyond (MAR) 67

Good Character
A Good Boy (MAR) 56
A Good Husband (MAR) 55
As Created (AUG) 157
Carving a Name (DEC) 239
I Dream'd in a Dream (NOV) 204
If (DEC) 240
Each Road (NOV) 204
Four Things Make Us Happy Here (NOV) 207
My Kingdom (MAR) 69
Only a Dad (JUNE) 123
The Respectable Folks (FEB) 38

Hope
Alchemy (NOV) 217
Chanukah Dreams (DEC) 220
Hope (AUG) 145
Life (NOV) 206
A Midsummers Day (JULY) 135
New Year Greeting (JAN) 19

Holiday
The Ballad of the Harp-Weaver (DEC) 226
Carol (DEC) 235
Chanukah Dreams (DEC) 220
A Christmas Dream (DEC) 230
Christmas in Australia (DEC) 234
The Feast of Lights (DEC) 221

Search by Poet

Search Poets by Country

Harper, Charles 127
Henley, William Earnest 196
Herrick, Robert 21, 41, 45, 55, 98, 207, 208
Hood, Thomas 31, 189
Hopkins, Gerard Manley 72
Jennings, Elizabeth 148
Jonson, Ben 50
Keats, John 192
Kingston, William Henry Giles 54
Kipling, Rudyard 240
Lear, Edward 85, 105, 142
Milne, A. A. 90, 111, 176
Milton, John 116
Prior, Mathew 51
Potter, Beatrix 83, 91
Rands, William Brightly 40
Rossetti, Christina 25, 62, 155
Service, Robert W. 154
Shakespeare, William 108, 199
Shelley, Percy Bysshe 40, 149
Squire, Sir John Collings 34
Taylor, Jane 237
Tennyson, Alfred Lord 49, 65, 139, 187
Wordsworth, William 66, 76, 79

Germany
von Goethe, Johann Wolfgang 28, 75, 168, 204

Ireland
Allingham, William 90, 142, 145, 181, 224
Swift, Jonathan 25
Wilde, Oscar 66, 115, 129, 150, 211
Yeats, W. B. 20, 62, 99, 167

Japan
Matsuo Basho 82, 159, 217

Malta
Adams, Francis William Lauderdale 26

Scotland
Burns, Robert 41, 65
Campbell, Thomas 145
Doyle, Sir Arthur Conan 47, 106, 165
Grahame, Kenneth 234
Miller, William 85
Stevenson, Robert Louis 32, 33, 47, 56, 88, 120, 139, 153, 173, 210

South Korea
Gagnon, Caden 84

USA
Alcott, Louisa May 23, 54, 69, 97, 119, 151, 159, 163, 232
Alger Jr., Horatio 94, 108, 136, 239
Amans-Lucas, Elaena 158
Bowditch, Nathaniel Ingersoll 67
Brown, Sarah Janisse 161
Bryant, William Cullen 21, 74
Cawein, Madison Julius 100, 137, 140, 141
Crowther, Melissa 34, 135
Cutler, Elena 203
Dickinson, Emily 60, 67, 166, 195, 205, 217, 223
Dregge, Reagan 48, 61
Dunbar, Paul Laurence 42
Emerson, Ralph Waldo 26
Field, Eugene 171, 198
Field, Thelma Arlene DeGroff 92
Frost, Robert 39, 56, 72, 150, 174, 182, 195, 205, 209, 224
Glassett, Cambry 114
Guest, Edgar 35, 121, 123, 216
Ish-Kishor, Judith 220
Henrie, Jordan 223
Hiller, Juliette 109
Holmes Sr, Oliver Wendell 130, 186
Jackson, Helen Hunt 175
Johnson, Fenton 177
Kwok, Grace 103
Lanier, Sidney 22
Law, Steven Wesley 140, 189
Lazarus, Emma 125, 221
Liu, Kylie 193
Longfellow, Henry Wadsworth 37, 78, 101, 107, 149, 170, 178, 207, 212, 225
Lybrand, Forrest 110
Martinez, Lily 58
Mellor, Kathy 163
Melville, Herman 113
Millay, Edna St. Vincent 159, 177, 197, 204, 220, 226
Moore, Clement Clarke 231
Moore, Marianne 113
Nielson, Kathryn 78
Owens, Christine 160, 176
Perrine, Niccole 82
Poe, Edgar Allen 46, 96, 104, 147
Posey, Alexander 213
Riley, James Whitcomb 20, 83, 109, 156, 157
Sandburg, Carl 163, 179, 188

Shepherd, Cayden 92
Shults, George Francis 233
Smith, Clark Ashton 33, 218
Soldano, Joseph B.72, 230
Sparkman, Nicholas C. A. 112
Teasdale, Sara 22, 30, 38, 48, 71, 98, 134, 167, 168, 169, 185, 217, 239
Thayer, Ernest L. 143
Thomas, Adison 178
Thoreau, Henry David 38, 95, 215, 219
Walker, Bertrand N.O. 214
Watson, Sarah Beth 238
Whitman, Walt 128, 176, 188, 204
Whittier, John Greenleaf 184

West Africa
Wheatley, Phillis 39

Zambia
Fairs-Billam, Isla 138

References

Bagert, Brod & Cobleigh, Carolynn. (1995). *Poetry for Young People: Edgar Allan Poe.* Sterling Children's Books.

Chang, Shao-Min, and Chung-Hey, Chen. (2016). Effects of an intervention with drinking chamomile tea on sleep quality and depression in sleep disturbed postnatal women: A randomized controlled trial. *Journal of Advanced Nursing, 72*(2), 306-315. Retrieved from: https://pubs.acs.org/doi/abs/10.1021/jf051513y.

Gunawardena, Dhanushka, et al. (2015). Anti-inflammatory activity of cinnamon (C. zeylanicum and C. cassia) extracts–identification of E-cinnamaldehyde and o-methoxy cinnamaldehyde as the most potent bioactive compounds. *Food & Function, 6*(3), 910-919. Retrieved from: https://pubmed.ncbi.nlm.nih.gov/25629927/.

Hale, Gloria. (Ed.) (1997). *Read Aloud Poems for Young People: An Introduction to the Magic and Excitement of Poetry.* Tess Press.

Hanson, William. (2018). *Bluffer's Guide To Etiquette: Instant Wit and Wisdom.* Haynes Publishing.

Law, Steven Wesley. (2015) *Polished: Poems.* Kindle Direct Publishing.

Milne, A.A. (1924). *When we were Very Young: A Yearling Book.* E.P. Dutton & Co.

Owens, Christine. (2019). *Relaxed Homeschooling: Books and Life's Hidden Curriculum.* Kindle Direct Publishing.

Post, Emily. (2017). *Etiquette: The Original Guide to Conduct in Society, Business, Home and More.* Skyhorse Publishing.

Shan, B., Cai, Y. Z., Sun, M., & Corke, H. (2005). Antioxidant capacity of 26 spice extracts and characterization of their phenolic constituents. *Journal of Agricultural and Food Chemistry*, *53*(20), 7749-7759. Retrieved from: https://pubmed.ncbi.nlm.nih.gov/16190627/.

Stevenson, Robert Louis. (1909) *A Child's Garden of Verses.* Current Literature Publishing Co.

Wheatley, Phillis. (1838). *Memoir and Poems of Phillis Wheatley.* Library of Congress.

Little Rabbit Trails
2021
International Homeschooling
Poetry Contest

Theme is
Patriotism

Learn more at
www.littlerabbittrails.com/poetry-contest

**Contest will open for entries
March 2021**
Any homeschooler or homeschooling
parent may enter the contest.
Cash prizes and 16 people will be
published in
A Year of Poetry Tea Time: Patriotism

Everywhere you find
stories of patriotism.

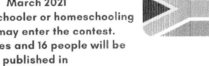

Made in the USA
Coppell, TX
30 July 2022

8058372BR00227